Examining Intelligence-Led Policing

Examining Intelligence-Led Policing

Developments in Research, Policy and Practice

Adrian James
Senior Lecturer in Criminal Investigation, University of Portsmouth, UK

First published 2013 by
PALGRAVE MACMILLAN

Palgrave Macmillan in the UK is an imprint of Macmillan Publishers Limited, registered in England, company number 785998, of Houndmills, Basingstoke, Hampshire RG21 6XS.

Palgrave Macmillan in the US is a division of St Martin's Press LLC, 175 Fifth Avenue, New York, NY 10010.

Palgrave Macmillan is the global academic imprint of the above companies and has companies and representatives throughout the world.

Palgrave® and Macmillan® are registered trademarks in the United States, the United Kingdom, Europe and other countries

ISBN: 978-1-137-30736-1

This book is printed on paper suitable for recycling and made from fully managed and sustained forest sources. Logging, pulping and manufacturing processes are expected to conform to the environmental regulations of the country of origin.

A catalogue record for this book is available from the British Library.

A catalog record for this book is available from the Library of Congress.

Contents

Foreword

Policing has always been imbued with a rich mythology, or rather competing mythologies. Its promoters, practitioners and supporters (the majority of the population for most of the last century, if opinion polls are to be believed) regard the police as the essential and largely successful guardians of the public against depredation by crime and disorder. Its critics (most people when modern police forces were first established in the early 19th century) saw the opposite: a force that protected the hierarchical social order against demands for justice, and used covert, underhand surveillance and other spy tactics to achieve their objectives.

What both sides had in common was a view of policing that focused on crime control, with the detective as the epitome of the police craft, and achieving a remarkable degree of effectiveness. Scotland Yard, it was said, always got its 'man' – and hence the public could sleep peacefully and go about their business securely and safely.

Just over half a century ago an alternative picture came to challenge popular and police folklore, whether supportive or suspicious. Empirical researchers, on both sides of the Atlantic, began to observe and analyse what police did in practice, and how well they did it. This research punctured many illusions. It turned out that the majority of calls for help made to the police were not about crime, at least not in a straightforward way. They were for a dizzying variety of emergencies and problems. Furthermore, none of the traditional police tactics for dealing with crime, uniform – supposedly preventive – patrol and after-the-event detection, seemed to have an impact on crime levels according to research evaluations.

Crime rates rocketed in the 1980s – a real rise confirmed by the new tool of crime surveys, not just an increase in recording, consolidating the already rampant politicization of law and order initiated by Margaret Thatcher in her bid for power. Detection rates plummeted, as the growth of crime hugely outstripped police resources. Both contributed to an increasing sense that the police were failing in what had popularly been seen as their prime job and skill. At the same time, the new consensus on neo-liberal economics, 'freeing' markets and cutting welfare, joined in the early 1990s by born-again 'New' Labour, accentuated the deep socio-economic causes of crime. A new consensus on tough law and order promoted policing and punishment as the key saviours (although Labour also spoke about getting tough on the causes of crime).

It was in this context that the police, here and in North America, began to explore and implement a variety of competing (although ultimately compatible) innovative strategies to rectify the limitations of traditional approaches. The main contenders were community policing (COP), problem-oriented policing (POP), and intelligence-led policing (ILP). When crime began a sustained fall in the mid-1990s, throughout the Western world, police leaders were not shy to claim credit. 'Crime is down; blame the cops', boasted (ex)-Chief Bill Bratton of the New York Police Department. Debate flourishes about how to explain the crime drop, although few would doubt that more effective policing played a part (mainly, according to the 'security hypothesis', because of tighter physical protection of property, especially cars and houses, the one tactic that is as universal as the crime fall).

The 'National Intelligence Model' (NIM) has been a key element of these attempts to develop innovative, more effective methods of policing that have been pursued in the last 20–30 years, not only in Britain but also in North America and throughout the world. This hugely informative and impressive book offers a detailed, critical account and analysis of the NIM's origins, implementation and impact.

It combines a number of research methods: original archival historical work, interviews with key players, a comprehensive synthesis of what is technically secondary literature but includes many hard-to-obtain items that are on the borderline with primary sources (memoirs, internal policy documents), and an observational and interview-based ethnography of two forces, one urban and one county force. The book provides a sophisticated and convincingly argued explanation of the 'rise and fall' of NIM in UK policing, built around a well researched historical and cultural context, combined with detailed analysis of contemporary police politics. It draws on interviews with key participants in both the creation and the implementation of the NIM, as well as a wide array of documentary material.

The argument is situated within a sound theoretical framework, drawing mainly on political science literature on policy change, and on previous studies of policing. The author has both a deep understanding of and strong views about the subject, derived from his own distinguished experience as a detective. But he bases his conclusions on well-marshalled evidence and maintains an appropriate level of objectivity and distance. The book is engagingly written, and is clear, readable and logically structured. It maintains a lively pace and is easy and enjoyable to read.

The book is the first comprehensive analysis of NIM, and as such makes a significant original contribution to knowledge and understanding of contemporary policing policy and the functioning and reform of police organizations. The book is also a mine of information and insight on detective work and policing more generally. The reviews and use of the academic and professional literature on policing are insightful and wide-ranging. They display a clear grasp of the debates about the role, cultures, management and impact of policing, and the combination of practical detective experience and academic knowledge makes for an exceptionally fascinating account of key issues in police investigation.

The historical chapters on the origins of NIM place it in a much longer context of the relations between detective branches and police overall, going back to the early 19th century development of modern forces. The emergence of NIM is analysed in a detailed account of the internal and external politics of policing in recent decades, and the increasing dissatisfaction with orthodox approaches. It is also shown as congruent with wider cultural and policy developments such as neoliberalism and the application of New Public Management principles.

The role of Sir David Phillips, former Chief Constable of Kent, as the key policy entrepreneur championing NIM is thoroughly probed. Despite Phillips' success in getting his colleagues in ACPO and the Home Office to support NIM, the book shows its impact was largely superficial. Lip service was paid to it, but it failed to transform organizational practice as intended, apart from limited impacts in some places and specialisms. The reasons are probed persuasively: the hold of orthodox cultural attitudes and ways of working; the role of 'fiefdoms' and vested interests; the competing demands of alternative policing programmes notably Neighbourhood Policing, which – whilst arguably compatible with NIM in principle – in practice operated as more of a competitor. Despite this, the book advocates NIM as of particular value in the current climate of austerity, offering a way of achieving more with less through intelligence-led analysis of priorities.

The book is a valuable addition to our understanding of a key aspect of current policing developments, and a must-read for all academics, policy-makers and practitioners in the area. Beyond that, it will be of interest to all who are concerned about policing. The author has drawn on both his distinguished career as a detective and manager of information, and his academic education. The product of these influences is a book that should be a long-lasting reference-point for debates about policing.

Robert Reiner
Emeritus Professor of Criminology
Law Department
London School of Economics

Preface and Acknowledgements

On one level, writing a coherent and credible narrative that explains police investigative practice and intelligence work in the contemporary era is a simple undertaking. Policing has never been more transparent than it is today and even the simplest of literature or Internet searches will return a (virtual) plethora of information on: investigative doctrine; operational tasking; police information management; and intelligence protocols. Explaining how and why that practice developed and using that analysis to say something meaningful about investigation and intelligence in modern times is a much more challenging task.

It may seem strange that an examination of intelligence-led policing (ILP) that aims to address developments in research, policy and practice revisits the earliest days of the new police but, arguably, it is only with the passage of time that policies, strategies and their outcomes may properly be evaluated and put into context. Conversely, seen through the increasingly long lens of history, events are shaped and reshaped in public consciousness; made clearer or more ambiguous, variously, by the scholarly dissection of old arguments; by the discovery of new facts, opinions and ideas; and by that routine process (speeded up exponentially in modern times by the tools, techniques, and technologies of modern science) by which over time, what once were widely accepted truths become no more than shibboleths.

The assertion that one cannot know the present if one does not know the past may have become something of a cliché, but it is true nonetheless. As the reader will see, the police service's understanding of its past, particularly in the areas of investigation and intelligence, is partial and inadequate. Lacking an institutional memory worthy of the name, the service has become locked into a pattern of behaviour in which putatively revolutionary approaches to investigation and the management of intelligence in reality represent little more than repeated efforts to reinvent the wheel. Each failure confirms the inability of the service to use its two greatest assets, its people and its information, in the most productive ways.

The objects of my investigation in the modern era were the innovative, putatively paradigm-shifting, strategies that have been introduced into mainstream policing since the Second World War. That includes strategies that have been the subject of research such as: Problem-oriented policing (POP), problem solving, and community-oriented policing strategies and others, less well researched such as: the Aberdeen Policing Scheme; Unit Beat Policing (UBP); and the Kent Policing Model (KPM).

The particular focus of my research into ILP in the contemporary era was its most recent iteration, the National Intelligence Model (NIM), which emerged in Britain at the end of the 1990s. Its authors wanted it to overhaul intelligence work, and revolutionize investigative practice in the mainstream. In terms of policy transfer alone, it may claim some success; it has been adopted by many institutions in Britain's public sector and seems to have inspired ILP strategies across the developed world. Overwhelmingly, almost unquestionably, ILP is seen as a 'good thing'. Certainly, it has emerged relatively unscathed from scholarly scrutiny.

In critically assessing ILP and the NIM, I have drawn upon scholarly research, archival materials, the biographies of notable figures in policing, and other documentary sources. My analysis of the contemporary landscape of investigation and intelligence in Britain is based on: my own fieldwork; the examination of police-generated intelligence assessments and other documents; interviews with key actors in central and local government, the police, and police and local authorities; and, not least, the experience gained over 30 years' police service.

I acknowledge the limitations of my research. I approached the data from the perspectives of researcher, detective, and intelligence officer. I have tried to balance subjective reflection with objective analysis throughout but I do not claim to be a value-free commentator. My own experiences in investigation and intelligence work unquestionably have shaped my values, attitudes and beliefs, and my perception of the policing milieu. Ultimately, I tried to use my 'insider' knowledge positively, to convey a better understanding of the police investigative and intelligence worlds, and to examine what the story of ILP tells us about policing and about the police organization in modern times.

I am grateful to the following who gave generously of their time and energy to assist my research:

Sir David Phillips, Director of NCPE, former President of ACPO and Chief Constable of Kent Police

John Grieve, former Deputy Assistant Commissioner and first Director of Intelligence in the Metropolitan Police in modern times

N01 – ACPO member, responsible for crime policy

N02 – Former Kent commander

N03 – ACPO member, key role in NIM implementation

N04 – Former ACPO member

N05 – APA official

N06 – ACPO member, responsible for intelligence

N08 – local authority analyst – County

N09 – crime reduction manager – County

N010 – local authority chief executive

N011 – chair of the local police authority – County

N013 – Home Office official

N015 – senior official, strategy unit – Urban

N016 – inspector, corporate tasking and coordination – Urban

N019 – BCU intelligence manager – County

N021 – BCU intelligence researcher – County

N022 – BCU senior analyst – County

N023 – BCU analyst – County

N024 – BCU analyst – County

N026 – principal analyst – County

N027 – BCU commander – County

N028 – BCU CSP chief inspector – County

N029 – BCU CSP chief inspector – County

N032 – County DOI

N030 – former constable and collator – Urban

N031 – member of senior command team – Urban

N033 – BCU commander – Urban

N035 – BCU detective chief inspector – Urban

N036 – BCU chief inspector partnerships – Urban

N038 – BCU detective inspector, intelligence manager

N039 – BCU senior analyst – Urban

N040 – BCU constable, intelligence researcher – Urban

N042 – BCU detective sergeant, focus desk supervisor – Urban

N044 – BCU analyst – Urban

N045 – BCU constable, FIO – Urban

N046 – former constable and collator – Urban

N049 – BCU constable (patrol officer) – Urban

N050 – senior intelligence official – Urban

N051- former detective superintendent in Kent

N052 – local police authority member – Urban

N053 – ACPO member – Urban

N054 – NCPE executive

N055 – former detective inspector and NCPE trainer

N058 – local authority crime reduction manager – Urban

N059 – former constable and collator – Urban

N063 – former detective chief inspector, and RCS commander
N065 – Home Office senior official
N066 – BCU constable (patrol officer) – Urban
N070 – BCU sergeant (criminal justice unit) – Urban
N074 – BCU police constable, school liaison – County
N075 – BCU constable (patrol officer) – County
N076 – BCU constable (patrol officer) – County
N077 – BCU constable (patrol officer) – County
N079 – specialist detective (inspector)
N084 – intelligence analyst
N098 – Urban DOI
N100 – former detective chief inspector
N101 – Police Federation representative
N102 – NCIS Senior Executive

List of Acronyms and Abbreviations

AC	Assistant Commissioner (Metropolitan Police)
ACC	Assistant Chief Constable
ACPO	Association of Chief Police Officers
AFP	Australian Federal Police
APA	Association of Police Authorities
ASB	Anti-Social Behaviour
BCU	Basic Command Unit
CCIM	Canadian Crime Intelligence Model
CDA	Crime and Disorder Act 1998
CDIIIU	Central Drugs and Illegal Immigration Intelligence Unit
CID	Criminal Investigation Department
CISC	Criminal Intelligence Service of Canada
CMM	Crime Management Model
COMPSTAT	Computerized Statistics
CPA	Crime Pattern Analysis
CRM	Crime Reduction Manager
CSP	Community Safety Partnership
DCI	Detective Chief Inspector
DI	Detective Inspector
DOI	Director of Intelligence
DS	Detective Sergeant
ECIM	The European Criminal Intelligence Model
FIB	Force Intelligence Bureau
FIO	Field Intelligence Officer
FIRT	Force Intelligence Review Team
GMAC	Greater Manchester Against Crime
GPMS	Government Protective Marking Scheme
HMIC	Her Majesty's Inspector of Constabulary
HQ	headquarters
ILP	Intelligence-Led Policing
JAG	Joint Action Group
KPM	Kent Policing Model
Met, The	Metropolitan Police Service
MIB	Metropolitan Intelligence Branch
MoPI	Management of Police Information
NCA	National Crime Agency

NCIS	National Criminal Intelligence Service
NCISP	National Criminal Intelligence Sharing Plan
NCPE	National Centre for Policing Excellence
NCRP	National Community Reassurance Plan
NCRS	National Crime Reporting Standard
NCS	National Crime Squad
NDIU	National Drugs Intelligence Unit
NIAT	National Intelligence Analysts Training
NIM	National Intelligence Model
NPIA	National Policing Improvement Agency
NPM	New Public Management
NPP	National Policing Plan
NSLEC	National Specialist Law Enforcement Centre
NYPD	New York Police Department
NZCAG	New Zealand's Controller and Auditor General
NZP	New Zealand Police
NZPPM	NZP Policing Model
OPS	Obscene Publications Squad
PACE	Police and Criminal Evidence Act
PAT	Problem Analysis Triangle
PBM	Partnership Business Model
PCC	Police and Crime Commissioner
PIP	Professionalizing Investigation Programme
PMCA	Police and Magistrates Courts Act 1994
POP	Problem-Oriented Policing
PSNI	Police Service of Northern Ireland
RCMP	Royal Canadian Mounted Police
RCS	Regional Crime Squad
RIO	Regional Intelligence Office
RIPA	Regulation of Investigatory Powers Act, 2000
RISC	Research and Intelligence Support Centre
SB	Special Branch
SDS	Special Duty Squad
SID	Systems for Investigation and Detection
SMT	Senior Management Team
SOCA	Serious Organised Crime Agency
SPI	Smart Policing Initiative
UBP	Unit Beat Policing
USDoJ	US Department of Justice

1
Setting the Contemporary Policing Scene

Introduction

Since its emergence in Britain as a discrete policing strategy, ILP has been advanced as a panacea for the most pressing of policing's ills; the police's seeming inability to meet the ordinary expectations of their staff, their communities *and* their political masters. ILP strategies have been adopted across the developed world. Wrapped in the rhetorics of crime-fighting, reflexivity, and capacity-building, they usually have been presented as innovative and cost-effective solutions to society's problems. Overwhelmingly and unapologetically realist in nature, they demonstrate that the police take crime seriously and are ready and willing to take decisive action when needed.

In Britain, ILP seems to have reached its apotheosis with the National Intelligence Model (NIM). The NIM's authors wanted it to revolutionize intelligence work in policing in England and Wales, and to underpin a new 'single service', intelligence-led approach in mainstream policing. In this book, I explain the emergence of the model and examine its real influence on policing. I also explore what the NIM narrative reveals about ILP and the police organization. In this opening chapter, I set the scene for that analysis by assessing material that readers need to know to appreciate the contribution that this book makes to the canon of ILP research. The subjects addressed include: police intelligence work; the police organization; oversight of the police, policing, public policymaking and of course ILP.

Intelligence-led policing

The true meaning of the term ILP has never really been settled. In Britain, it is confusingly applied to a variety of 'crime-fighting' processes that rely on the efforts of analysts and intelligence specialists engaged in crime mapping, crime pattern analysis, data analysis and other problem solving approaches. There is another dimension to ILP which also relies on analysts and other specialists but in that case the emphasis is on the targeting of groups or individuals using covert methods; with their arrest, or some other intervention to prevent further offending, the intended outcome. Beyond those approaches, other novel strategies also have come to the fore. They are worthy of examination because each has challenged the traditional reactive policing paradigm and each patently influenced the NIM.

ILP in the modern era

Arguably, it was the introduction of Unit Beat Policing (UBP) in 1967 that provided the foundation for ILP in the modern era.[1] The specialization of patrol that accompanied UBP, established the local intelligence system in mainstream policing on which the modern intelligence structure is based. The introduction of the collator, an individual tasked with collecting and evaluating information collected by patrol officers was a significant milestone in the development of ILP and the specialization of the police workforce.

Commonly, the development of ILP is linked to concerns about: organized crime; the search for 'best evidence': the discrediting of investigative strategies that relied on suspects' confessions; and the availability of increasingly sophisticated surveillance and information technologies. Chan's (2003) suggestion that ILP's appeal is that it promises new, problem solving ways of dealing with increasingly sophisticated and prolific offenders and Reiner's (2010) argument that it allows the police to claim solutions to the problems associated with reactive policing strategies, certainly accord with my experience.

The explicit support of Britain's Audit Commission (1993) for ILP signalled a significant shift in policing discourse. However, the reader will see that what the Commission lauded as ground-breaking, simply restated strategies used by police commanders at least 60 years earlier (many of which re-emerged at regular intervals thereafter). That highlights, at a very early stage, one of my key messages. That is, not only is there little that is truly new in policing but also that the police service lacks an institutional memory that is worthy of the name.

There is scepticism about whether ILP represents a fundamental transformation of policing or something simply bolted on to existing structures. Enthusiasm for it has been greater amongst academics and public than policymakers and police commanders for whom 'the political risks involved are considerable', particularly when efforts to change the police often 'fall far short or fail' (Skogan, 2008, p.23). Reiner argued that there are sufficient, well-researched examples of innovative policing strategies to suggest that targeted policing can succeed in having a 'significant, if modest' effect on crime and fear of crime (2000, p.217). However, the appeal of ILP to commanders has always been limited; the police elite's innate orthodoxy has meant that it has had much less impact in the mainstream than rhetoric suggests.

Problem-oriented policing (POP)

POP was another of the proactive approaches putatively embraced by the British police service in this period. Goldstein (1979) popularly is credited with originating the style known as POP in the USA and his ideas spread across the developed world. Nobody has influenced policing more in that context. POP examples can be found across the USA, in Canada, Australia, New Zealand, Britain, and in many other nations.

Goldstein (1979) argued that a continuing emphasis on improving the police organization (evident in policing across the Western world at that time) was unlikely to raise the standard of service delivered to communities. Instead, police should aim to reduce the volume of problems that came to their attention to a manageable level by embracing a commitment to more systematic processes of inquiry. That would mean defining problems more specifically, collecting information more widely and engaging in a broader search for solutions. Those ideas also were central to the NIM.

In Britain, POP has usually been enacted through a standardized toolset utilizing analysis and environmental scanning. British analysts have favoured the SARA method, a sequential process involving in turn: (environmental) Scanning, (intelligence) Analysis, Response and Assessment (evaluation of the appropriateness of the response). Although Tilley (2003) has suggested that in practice, the process is much less structured with a great deal more overlap than the construct suggests.

POP requires that police take the initiative in addressing and in forging robust partnerships with communities. Goldstein (1979) thought this would be welcomed by the police establishment. However, he underestimated the resistance of the police rank-and-file to challenge the prevailing value system. Cope (2003) found that POP was not universally welcomed. Cultural resistance often led to the misuse or exclusion of analysis from operational responses. In Britain, POP is seen as 'soft' policing and though almost every force purports to engage in it, it is not, and never has been, a popular career choice for action-oriented patrol officers and detectives.

Community policing

In Britain, the first authoritative call for a system of policing more finely tuned to citizens' needs was made in 1977 by John Alderson, chief of the Devon and Cornwall force (1973–82). Others such as Kenneth Newman, Commissioner of the Metropolitan Police (1982–87) (hereinafter, the Met) were keen to take up Alderson's challenge. Community policing strategies are now commonplace in Britain and many of the multi-agency problem solving approaches they have spawned are consistent with the proactive, preventative, policing that Newman (and others who succeeded him) championed. However in the 1970s, Alderson's views contrasted sharply with the majority, authoritarian, and orthodox, view in British policing expressed for example by James Anderton, chief of Greater Manchester Police (1976–91) who argued forcefully and consistently for the maintenance of the crime control *status quo*.

Community policing has been linked to crime reduction initiatives, often in partnership with communities. In Britain, the first formal partnerships emerged from the Scarman Inquiry into the Brixton riots (Scarman, 1981). Their further development was encouraged in a variety of Home Office circulars and consultation papers. There is widespread agreement that the most significant development in that context was the publication of the Morgan Report (Home Office, 1991). Morgan proposed that, with wide-ranging powers over education, housing and planning, local authorities should play a fuller part in crime prevention.

Partnership was boosted by the Crime and Disorder Act 1998 (CDA), which placed a statutory duty on chief officers and local authorities to work together to formulate crime reduction strategies. The identification by Innes (2004) of 'signal crimes'; incidents that act as warnings about threats to people's security, that may disproportionately impact the way they think, feel or act, added to that debate. Community-focused strategies evolved into the neighbourhood policing programme that operates across Britain today. Tilley (2008) has argued that the programme merges the key elements of POP and ILP. However, the introduction of two major change programmes contemporaneously has resulted in confusion and muddle. Certainly, attempts to integrate the two have not worked out as positively as some would have us believe.

Using intelligence

Compared to the subject of policing in general, investigative and intelligence policies and practices have received surprisingly little attention. Intelligence has always been core business for the armed forces and for the security services, and there is an extensive literature on intelligence and information work in those contexts. However, even though intelligence has been central to the activities of many specialist police units in Britain for 130 years, it is only relatively recently with the emergence of the NIM that meaningful efforts have been made to exploit intelligence opportunities in the mainstream.

Police intelligence

Until the last decade of the twentieth century, intelligence was rarely used to inform investigative strategy in mainstream policing. Important for its application to the discovery of evidence, criminal intelligence largely did not merit much attention as a discipline in its own right. Nor was it a subject that exercised commanders in the mainstream (Flood, 2003). Whilst an intelligence architecture supporting the higher policing function was well established at the end of the twentieth century, intelligence work of the kind needed to support ILP largely was ignored.

There are a number of reasons for that. Albeit, sections of the police service utilized intelligence, often to underpin the delivery of covert policing strategies, intelligence work as most people would understand it, was never really valued in the mainstream. In my experience, knowledge of intelligence gathering techniques (usually gathering only; few meaningful efforts were put into anything other than the most rudimentary of analysis of the collected data) was passed down from generation to generation within discrete units as a form of oral history. The tools and techniques used by those units were jealously guarded; often hidden behind the impenetrable curtain of 'need to know' which, historically, invariably outweighed the 'dare to share'.

The seeming inability of the police service to use its intelligence effectively enough to underpin its protective services (as revealed for example by the murders of Holly Wells and Jessica Chapman) or to properly direct its operational activities, has been highlighted both in the media and by scholarly research. Tragic events such as the Soham murders had the effect of bringing the failings of police intelligence work into public view. In the same period, the Labour Government's explicit commitment to human rights was given force by royal assent of the Human Rights Act, 1998 and then the Regulation of Investigatory Powers Act, 2000 (RIPA). The latter, in particular, obliged the police service to completely overhaul its intelligence-gathering processes in response to the new challenges of RIPA compliance; in the process, bringing much greater transparency and accountability to those activities.

Flood (a senior officer in Kent in the 1990s and a significant figure in the story of ILP) argued that the ILP that emerged in Kent in that period (and that ultimately led to the creation of the NIM), was expected to revolutionize operational policing in the mainstream (2003). In the same period, Grieve (formerly a senior member of the Met and a leading British authority on criminal intelligence) developed an enhanced intelligence system for the Met, a project known as Systems for Investigation and Detection (The SID project), with which the NIM shares many features. Grieve suggested those developments signalled a new way of thinking about police intelligence in Britain, which needed 'to be reclaimed from the secret world, made less threatening to communities and used in their service' (2004, p.26).

Intelligence work and the NIM

The NIM has been subject only to limited review. Tilley (2008), Savage (2007), and Oakensen et al (2002) investigated the model in the context of policing policy. The particular focus of Kleiven's research (2005) was the extent to which the NIM influenced intelligence gathering in communities (considered by some in the police to be an essential precursor to the creation of policing plans); she found that the model's impact was negligible.

Collier (2006) and John and Maguire (2004) carried out empirical research into the NIM. The former found that there was tension at the local level 'between the resources allocated to volume crime and serious crime, and between response-led, intelligence-led and reassurance-led strategies'. That is an issue that has come up again and again in modern times and it is one I will explore later.

Collier (2006, p.115) also found that NIM processes were implemented partially and ineffectively because of: technological problems; 'the bureaucratization of processes'; and 'cultural resistance'. He highlighted an 'absence of rigorous evidence linking actions, results and contextual issues' in the police areas he visited. John and Maguire (2004) uncovered those same failings in the forces they investigated. Ultimately, their research led them to conclude that significant improvements were needed if the model was to achieve its purpose.

Collier described the NIM's tasking process (by which scarce resources would be allocated to the most pressing problems), which was central to the model, as having the potential to be relevant and influential because it could provide a framework to counter the police's tendency to put a disproportional emphasis on 'acquiring rather than retaining and utilizing knowledge' (2006, p.115). However, the reader will see that potential has not been realized.

Institutional memory

More broadly, intelligence work is linked to issues of knowledge management and organizational memory. Earlier, I alluded to the fact that the need to 'rediscover' ILP in the 1990s, pointed to a defective and partial institutional memory but also to the over-zealous guarding of craft secrets by sections of the service. Whilst there are rather obvious reasons for limiting access to secrets, the net result has been to restrict the ability of officers outside those coteries to identify best practice or 'what works' or to use that knowledge productively to improve their professional practice.

Knowledge management has been described as 'the process of creating, capturing and using knowledge to enhance organizational performance' (Collier, 2006, p.109). Ratcliffe argued that knowledge 'given context and meaning by the addition of organizational wisdom', is immensely valuable to any organization (2008, p.98). He recommended that knowledge management should be an 'intensive activity' for policing in intelligence-led environments. My own experience as an intelligence manager taught me that few in mainstream policing followed that advice. In great part, that was because those being asked to implement ILP were ignorant of the intelligence craft.

The supporters of the NIM thought it would provide the foundation of 'doctrine; for policing in the new millennium' (Flood, 2003). However, the proliferation of doctrine it signalled has not been universally welcomed. In 2010, the inquest into the police shooting of the lawyer Mark Saunders, suggested that the 'can do' organization may have been overloaded with codes, guidance and advice. In a letter to the Home Secretary, then Westminster Coroner, Paul Knapman, expressed his exasperation over the length and complexity of police manuals and their contribution to the failure of the operation he had investigated. He argued that complex and conflicting advice 'could be amalgamated, simplified or dispensed with' and that what was left should be 'set out in simple and unsophisticated language, minimising jargon' (cited in Davies, 2010, p.1). Its impenetrability to many aside, the greatest failing of police doctrine is that it can be interpreted as a kind of 'one size fits all' that strips away all those situation-specific shades, tones and fine distinctions to be found in real life. Shorn of those essential elements, doctrine may translate into little more than pre-programmed responses to policing problems.

The police organization

The police service of England and Wales is made up of 43 separate police forces, under the command of a chief officer, each with their own distinctive organizational structures that have developed according to their individual historical, demographic and geographical differences, and the styles and philosophies of successive chief officers. The structure of policing in England and Wales in the modern era was established by the Police Act 1964 (and confirmed by the Local Government Act, 1972).

Structure of British policing

It is important to explain the distinction between forces' headquarters and Basic Command Unit (BCU) functions because understanding both are key to understanding the operation of British ILP. The reader will see that the NIM imposed a duty both on force HQs and on BCUs to complete intelligence assessments that would (but in practice do not) contribute to regional and national forums in support of that single service ideal.

Typically, the force HQ accommodates its elite, specialist units, and the support functions necessary for the operation of the force. It is responsible for delivering policing services at the national and regional levels and for overseeing BCUs, which are usually aligned to local authority boundaries. BCUs' activities usually include patrol, response, the investigation of volume crime, partnership working via local Community Safety Partnerships (CSPs) and a range of local policing services. BCUs should also collect local (often termed, community) intelligence but the reader will see that is rarely given the priority it deserves.

Most services are delivered by uniformed officers; the uniformed branch is by some distance the largest in the service. Though significantly smaller, the Criminal Investigation Department (CID) is the next largest in terms of staff and resources. Of course, there are a number of other specialist departments in the police but the CID (and its relationship with the uniformed branch) is uniquely significant in the context of ILP because of its explicit role in crime control and investigation, and its traditional monopoly of organized intelligence work.

Association of Chief Police Officers (ACPO)

ACPO played a key role in the introduction of the NIM. The Association's roots are in the borough and county chief constables' associations, founded respectively in 1858 and 1896. Initially, they provided useful forums for members to meet and share ideas. Their role was enhanced significantly in 1919 with the establishment of the Police Council, an advisory body to the Home Office, made up of representatives of the police authorities and police forces. Rhodes has argued that the establishment of the Council amounted to the creation of a 'policy community' through which the police manipulated policy to their own advantage and to the disadvantage of others (cited in Wall, 1998, p.60).

In 1948, the associations were merged to form ACPO, which (until recent times) has had a growing influence on police policymaking. In modern times, that largely has stemmed from central government's preference for a single police voice on relevant policies and practice. ACPO exploited its high profile position in the service to claim that prize. There is a consensus that since the 1980s, ACPO has exerted huge influence on police policymaking. Its success, in part, has been attributed to its ability to 'fly under the radar', which has allowed it to preserve its 'traditional arrangements' of independence and localism whilst achieving its aims of representation and influence (Savage et al, 2000, p.153).

In the 1990s, ACPO carried out an important internal reform that Savage et al (2000) termed 'the presumption in favour of compliance'. ACPO expected that chief officers would toe the Association's line unless they could convince colleagues that there was a very good reason not to do so. Once ACPO's Chief Constables' Council ratified a policy, individual chiefs would be bound by it, unless they explained in writing to the ACPO President their reasons for non-compliance. Savage and Charman argued that this was necessary to unite what had previously been a 'fragmented and disunited body unable to "get its act together"' (cited in Ryan et al, 2001, p.36).

The ACPO council's decision to adopt the NIM as the standard for operational policing in the mainstream across England and Wales was a key event in the story of ILP. However, as the reader will see, the NIM narrative demonstrates as clearly as anything in modern times, that decisions taken on the basis of a 'presumption in favour of compliance' have not made the ACPO membership anything like as cohesive as the Association or its supporters have claimed.

Recently, ACPO has fallen out of favour with central government and that has significantly reduced its power and influence over the service. The election of the Coalition Government in 2010 signalled a fundamental change in the relationship between ACPO and Westminster. The Association now finds itself under increasing scrutiny and challenge. That largely is because, unlike those that have preceded it, the Coalition Government identifies ACPO as part of the problem of policing rather than as part of any solution to its ills.

Police cultures

Research into police culture in the 1960s, inspired increasingly revealing analyses over the following decades, as researchers gained greater access to the police organization. Gradually, the existence of discrete cultures rather than a single monolithic culture was acknowledged.

Rethinking police cultures

Reiner's research identified various 'cop cultures' that emerged from the organizational division of labour. He labelled those: *Bobbies; new centurions; uniform carriers* or *professionals* to differentiate between their differing personalities, job orientations and career ambitions (Reiner, 2010). Manning argued that there were many 'rationalities' in policing (2008, p.23).[2] Those partly are the product of 'modern bureaucratic form, and in part a function of their traditional mandate. Patterns of conflict, loyalty, and submission are situational and reflect contesting rationalities' which are not necessarily mitigated by the development of the bureaucratic organization (Manning, Ibid.). Manning concluded that whilst police organizations 'strive to maintain a rational face, a professional face, in spite of deep fissures within them', rationalities change over time to provide the power within the organization (Manning, Ibid.). Despite that continuing state of flux, there is one constant – the value set that dominates policing, which at its core is still composed of 'mediaeval ideas of duty, honor, personal loyalty to superiors and obedience' (Manning, Ibid.).

Clearly, the police organization has undergone significant change. The patrol function has been reshaped by community policing initiatives, team policing, problem-oriented policing and a myriad of variations on those themes. However as King-Taylor found in her study of the Met, even in the 1990s many officers felt that the force was locked into a 'paramilitary approach to management' that did not allow individuals to be 'creative, to be entrepreneurial, to use creative thinking, or to take a risk in problem-solving' (1992, p.117).

Sklansky argued that at the end of the last century, neither attempts to reshape US policing nor the new theories of inclusive management that emerged, necessarily delivered greater democracy, inclusiveness or accountability in law enforcement agencies. Instead, policing clung stubbornly to 'authoritarian management practices long discredited in other, traditionally hierarchical sectors' (Sklansky, 2007, p.31). Despite the rhetoric, those practices also constrain British policing.

Suits and uniforms

Detectives traditionally have held the advantage over their colleagues. From the establishment of the new police until very recently, they have been better paid than their uniformed colleagues and have been able to supplement their income by claiming allowances (Metropolitan Police, 2008). Detectives exploited that advantage to the full and took every opportunity to distinguish between themselves and the uniform department, to assert their autonomy. In effect, the Met became a 'divided force, partitioned into two separate branches, each with rigidly defined functions' (Hobbs cited in Matassa and Newburn, 2007, p.44).

At the beginning of the twentieth century, technological and organizational changes contributed to the legitimacy of detective work and of policing generally. For example in 1901, Britain's Criminal Records Office was established and the first effective fingerprinting system was introduced. Those developments contributed to the professionalization of the investigative function. However, they also reinforced the CID and uniform divide, enabling the department 'to further consolidate its independent position and to consolidate its numbers' (Hobbs, 1988, p.44). A view commonly expressed in that period was that the CID tended 'to regard itself as a thing above and apart, to which the restrictions and limitations placed on the ordinary police do not, or should not apply' (Royal Commission on Police Powers, 1929 cited in Evans, 1974, p.108).

That view was not influenced by any special CID training. On taking up his appointment, Basil Thomson, Assistant Commissioner Crime (head of the Metropolitan Police CID, 1913–19) found the department to be 'well organized, though perhaps a little rusty in the hinges' (Thomson, 1921, p.3). Few attempts had been made to change a system that seemed to confirm former Commissioner Mayne's assertion (made as far back as 1842 on the creation of the first detective department) that the nature of crime did not merit 'any complicated architecture for the response'. Instead 'informal apprenticeship' continued to be the rule (cited in Morris, 2007, p.18). This lack of training was addressed to some extent at the beginning of the twentieth century. However even then, training was limited to an understanding of the criminal law and 'the practical side ... was neglected' (Thomson, 1921, p.5).[3] Most senior detectives were firmly against the idea of extending detective training, which perhaps confirms that they viewed criminal investigation, like intelligence work, as craft.

Basil Thomson held that view. He divided detectives into two classes, 'the detective' and 'the thief-catcher'. Both demonstrated the 'method, industry, and local knowledge ... strongly cultivated at New Scotland Yard' (1921, p.5). However, the thief-catcher belonged to a unique class of:

> honest, painstaking policeman without sufficient education to pass examinations for promotion, but who made up for this deficiency by his intimate knowledge of the rougher class of criminals, his habits and his haunts, and by personal acquaintance with the pickpockets themselves ...

The risk in over-educating the detective force was that by increments the police would eliminate the thief-catcher for whom there was 'a very definite place in the scheme' (Thomson, 1921, pp.5–6).

Thomson's words may appear patronizing and certainly are idealistic but they also reveal much about the attitude of senior officers in that period. Thief-catchers inhabited the criminal world but they could be trusted to 'play by the rules' – that is, by those informal, unwritten craft rules – and to get the job done. They earned the admiration and respect of the police elite and consequently they were afforded latitude (far more than any uniformed officer would ordinarily be allowed) in their methods of operation. It was no surprise that it was to those kinds of men, those highly-prized thief-catchers that commanders turned in times of trouble and it was they who formed the nucleus of each of the new specialist detective units that emerged.

Those attitudes and beliefs endured to such a degree that, throughout the twentieth century, whenever the police elite faced a significant policing problem it almost unquestioningly accepted that the solution to that problem was the establishment of another specialist detective unit. The increasing specialization of the detective force in the twentieth century is noteworthy in the context of the NIM, because it confirmed a class system in policing that operated against the single service approach that commanders in modern times have seen as crucial to success.

That class system persists. In my recent research into the police's Professionalizing Investigation Programme (PIP) (James and Mills, 2012, p.139), the culture of the detective force was still seen by officers as a barrier to that modern approach even if it had been diluted somewhat as younger people had joined the department. A detective constable said that many officers still were mentored through their initial crime investigation training by officers who retained the 'does your face fit' mentality (or the 'fit in or **** off' mentality of the traditional detective culture, as a detective chief superintendent colourfully put it) rather than focusing on whether somebody could develop the skills necessary for the job.

Professionalizing policing

In the recent history of British policing, a consistent theme has been the effort to professionalize what traditionally was craft. In modern times, debates about the modernization of the workforce began at around the time that New Public Management (NPM) principles were introduced in the 1980s and have continued up to the present day. Home Office inquiries in that context (most recently, Winsor, 2011) focused on achieving best value through the rationalization of policing services. Equally, attempts have been made to secure a more transparent and accountable service through legislation and through the establishment of new oversight bodies. In contrast, though there has been much talk about transformational leadership and the like, there have been fewer meaningful attempts to change the culture of policing.

Professionalizing the police

In 2010, Home Secretary Theresa May commissioned then head of the National Policing Improvement Agency (NPIA – now the College of Policing) Peter Neyroud to undertake a review of police leadership and training. Neyroud's report contained a number of proposals and recommendations including the creation of a chartered professional body for policing, a new delivery body for police leadership and training and a new qualifications framework (Neyroud, 2011). Neyroud recommended, effectively, a side-lining of ACPO from policy debate. In future, ACPO will advise but will no longer play a key role in determining policy.

Another dimension has been added to that debate by Home Office plans to open up chief officers' jobs to experienced overseas recruits and middle-ranking officer roles to outsiders with business and leadership skills (Home Office, 2013). Those plans have met with a predictable degree of resistance from police chiefs but the department seems determined to see its plans through. Clearly, interesting times lie ahead for Britain's police elite.

Professionalizing investigation

The increasing complexity and sophistication of crime in modern times coupled with the growing scepticism of juries and the judiciary have been drivers of a more professional framework for investigation. In September 2005, NPIA introduced the Professionalizing Investigation Programme (PIP), a scheme that was intended to 'enhance the crime investigation skills and ability of police officers and staff involved in the investigative process' and to drive through new standards of investigation at all levels (NCPE, 2005, p.1).

PIP was a joint ACPO, Home Office and Skills for Justice (the police skills and standards organization) project that was intended to establish standards of professional knowledge and competency for investigators. The PIP programme is complemented by a competency framework; the whole is underpinned by Core Investigative Doctrine (NCPE, 2005a). Given the importance of knowledge and information to effective policing, the reader may find it surprising that there is nothing similar for intelligence officers.

Ironically, the increasing professionalization of investigation in the contemporary era has not necessarily been to the benefit of the specialist detectives as a discrete body. Arguably, it will not be to the benefit of the wider service either. Throughout this book, I present evidence of the privileging of the specialist detective force over others. Despite the periodic corruption scandals, there was an unwritten, and usually unacknowledged, contract between the police elite and the specialist detectives. Whenever the elite faced a significant policing or social problem it was to the specialist detective force it turned to solve or at least ameliorate that problem.

In 2007, a survey carried out by the Police Federation of England and Wales (the staff association for the police rank-and-file) found that trainees were being used to prop up 'the squeezed middle', the over-stretched CID offices and that, nationally; there was a shortfall of 2,000 detectives (Doward, 2007, p.1). In 2009, the Met was forced to admit that 800 of its 3,000 strong detective force was untrained (Davenport, 2009). This prompted commanders to order a 'sweeping reform' of the department and to return to its 32 BCUs, some of the highly-trained officers that staffed its specialist squads. Henceforth, if a detective completed five years attached to a specialist unit such as the Flying Squad or the Task Force, they should expect to be transferred to a BCU post for at least two years before they were allowed to apply for a posting back to the specialist detective units. The situation in London at that time was summed up by Alan Gordon, vice-chairman of the Police Federation who said that:

> The lack of experience and properly trained detectives is of particular concern. As with uniformed colleagues, their attention is very often directed towards incidents that fulfil targets and there is frustration that they are unable to concentrate on investigative detective functions (cited in Davenport, 2009).

Its implementation has been far from smooth. Former detective chief inspector N100 said that he believed that the Met Commissioner had the scheme under continuous review because senior commanders feared that taking experienced detectives away from the specialist squads would leave the force vulnerable. However, Police Federation member N101 suggested that rather than being kept under consideration, the policy was being implemented in a 'chaotic and haphazard fashion' as efforts were made to ensure the force's continuing resilience to the challenges it faced. Whilst there are obvious differences in the two statements, they both support the argument I make throughout this book about the continuing reliance of commanders on their 'Praetorian Guard'.

In January 2013, in a highly-publicized announcement, the Met's assistant commissioner Simon Byrne said that 800 detectives spread among 107 specialist teams, would be moved back into BCUs as part of a fundamental reorganization of the Met, which seeks to meet budget cuts of £500m (cited in Laville, 2013). Clearly, this is a significant development both in terms of individual officers' careers and of the Met's future. However, it should be recognized that Byrne is not referring to the specialist detective units that I discuss throughout this book (such as the Flying Squad) but local units of, essentially, trainee detectives. Therefore, at least in the short term, the Met will still be able to call on its specialists when the next crisis arises.

However, there are some rather obvious problems inherent in that strategy. The Met may be sacrificing its future investigative capability; failing to train detectives today may well lead to greater difficulties tomorrow. That is not to say that the Met may not recognize that fact. There are of course other ways it can supplement its detective force. For example, following the London bombings of 2005, counter terrorism officers from across the country were recruited into Scotland Yard and in December 2012, the Met ran an external recruitment campaign for its Rape and Sexual Offences, Child Abuse, Surveillance, Specialist Economic Crime, Gang Crime and Counter Terrorism Commands. However, in each case, Scotland Yard's gain has been another force's loss, which some may feel is a classic case of robbing Peter to pay Paul with the attendant risk of unforeseen consequences.

Oversight of the police

From 1964 until November 2012, responsibility for the executive function of forces was divided between the Home Secretary, local police authorities and chief constables.[4] Together with the introduction of Unit Beat Policing (UBP) and the Regional Crime Squads (which were significant developments in police investigative practice), the Police Act, 1964 was a significant element in the 'transformation of the police organisation in the mid-1960s' (Reiner, 2010, p.79). The Act also was a significant element in the story of ILP in Britain.

This section assesses the impact on policing of NPM, which in its own way also transformed policing, and acknowledges the introduction of new accountability arrangements; Police and Crime Commissioners and the Government's Strategic Policing Requirement.

The tripartite system of governance

The 'complex and much-debated' history of police governance (Reiner, 2010, p.227), and the wider interrelationship between police chiefs, police authorities and the Home Office has already been well chronicled by commentators such as: Marshall (1965); Lustgarten (1986); Reiner (2010). Therefore, this section presents no more than a brief characterization to contextualize the freedom (or otherwise) of chief officers to deploy staff and to determine the distribution of resources during the period that ILP was being developed in Britain.

Oliver (1997) argued that the 1964 Act removed the tension between central government and police authorities and between local authorities and chief constables on the subject of control. After its implementation, there was absolutely no doubt that the ultimate power lay with the Home Secretary and the responsibility for 'operational' matters explicitly was limited to chief officers (Jefferson and Grimshaw, 1984 cited in Reiner, 2010). Although, the common interpretation of the distinction between 'operational' and 'policy' matters was 'arbitrary and tendentious' and had no legislative basis (Reiner, 2010, p.227).

Chief constables, individually and through ACPO, were always keen to assert their right to 'operational independence' even though there was no legislative authority for such a right. Indeed, Lustgarten argued the essential correctness of the view first put forward by Marshall (1965). That was to say; that the doctrine of constabulary independence was 'no part of the tradition of "English liberty"' and was undeserving of the status afforded it by the judiciary (Lustgarten, 1986, p.65). Marshall (1965) characterized the relationship between the police service and its political partners in this period as 'explanatory and cooperative'. He contrasted that with the 'subordinate and obedient' kind of accountability to local communities, demanded by radical critics.

A common criticism of police authorities in the period following the 1964 Act, was that they did not use even the limited powers they retained very effectively, often deferring instead to chief constables' 'professional expertise' (see for example Reiner, 1991). Subsequent restructuring of police governance by the Police and Magistrates Courts Act 1994 (PMCA), delivered what Reiner (2010) called a 'calculative and contractual' style of accountability that reflected Government's centralizing agenda and a new commitment within Government to 'best value'.

In practice, the new powers of 'direction and control' the 1994 Act conferred on police authorities benefited them only marginally because, despite Government rhetoric, the PMCA was inherently centrist. The business that the business-like police authorities were meant to be doing was the business of Government, rather than its own (Reiner, 2010). Even where opportunities to influence chief constables emerged, authorities demonstrated a reluctance to challenge chief officers who (freed from detailed financial control by the PMCA) in principle were at liberty to 'row' in any way they decided. Though as Reiner noted, the reality was that chief officers' were able to choose any course they wished, 'so long as it was in the direction "steered" by the Home Secretary' (2010, p.233).

New Public Management (NPM)

The PMCA was introduced during a period in which there was a wider search for approaches that would deliver economy, efficiency and effectiveness. In other words, better 'value for money' in the public sector. Such policies were underpinned by NPM. Reiner (2010, p.24) argued that the application of what essentially was a private sector model represented a 'neo-liberal belief that private enterprise and market models' worked best in the modern era. The first manifestation of NPM in public policy was the Conservative Government's 'Financial Management Initiative' of 1982 which was intended to encourage better financial control of the public sector and the more accurate measurement of the outputs of investment in public resources.

Just a year later, the Conservatives' aspirations for the public sector were translated into objectives by Home Office departmental circular 114/1983 which encouraged the application of NPM principles to policing (Burrows and Lewis, 1988). Home Office circulars do not carry the force of law but there is no doubting their significance. For ACPO, circular 114/1983 was 'a seminal text that influenced the thoughts and actions of police leaders for a decade or more' (2008, p.23). Brooks noted that it introduced into policing the three E's (efficiency, economy and effectiveness) and 'policing by objectives' but also, more importantly in the context of this research, the notion that 'what gets measured is what gets done' (2010, p.1). That idea skewed operational policing activity because it encouraged commanders to ignore objective intelligence assessments and to forego longer-term (and potentially more efficient, effective and economic) solutions to policing problems, in their pursuit of short-term performance-related gains in the context of standards imposed by central government.

The Conservatives' 'setting' of the Audit Commission on the service in 1993 was followed by the commissioning of the Sheehy (1993) and Posen (1995) inquiries. Together, those moves challenged the power of chief officers and sought to engineer radical reform in policing (which despite record levels of funding had failed to deliver the reduction in crime that was popularly expected). However, ultimately, ACPO was successful in watering-down many recommendations. Newburn argued that in the process, it demonstrated that it had become 'a highly organized and effective national coordinating body [and] a supremely effective lobbying organisation' (2003, p.93). The NIM provides further evidence of ACPO's effectiveness in that regard.

The new emphasis on efficient, effective and economic criminal catching was detrimental to the single service approach because it served to reinforce the pre-existing divide between the CID and the rest of the service; it confirmed the business of detectives, 'crime fighting' as 'real' policing, and many of the functions of the uniformed department as ancillary to the policing mission. Certainly, the impact of NPM was felt much less in the CID and arguably had no impact whatsoever on the specialist detective squads.

Loveday argued that NPM actually strengthened the CID because the bureaucracy that accompanied it was based on mistaken assumptions about policing. The most significant of which was that more specialist departments, utilizing better technologies, could make a real difference to crime levels. This siphoned off officers from mainstream duties so that 'more and more non-uniformed officers watched fewer uniformed officers do more work that should have been their own' (Loveday, 1998, p.3).

Political and policy change

After the election of the Coalition Government in 2010, it quickly moved to reform policing through the abolition of police authorities. Their replacements, locally elected Police and Crime Commissioners (PCCs), have assumed the police authorities' responsibility to oversee policing in their area. On the face of it, the Coalition has delivered on the Conservatives' pre-election promise to deliver greater local accountability. However, the Government has also introduced a Strategic Policing Requirement, which places an obligation on forces to address major crimes such as terrorism, and to recognize that local problems represent only part of a bigger policing picture.

The question of how that plays out in practice is yet to be answered but given the history of policing there is bound to be some tension between the local and the global imperatives. What is apparent is that a form of regionalization of some policing services (as adjoining forces merge some policing functions) that had begun under the Labour administration has only been given impetus by the public sector cost-cutting that followed the election of the Coalition.

The oversight bureaucracy

A new bureaucracy was needed to monitor the police's progress in implementing NPM reforms. The authorities' abolition and their replacement with PCCs have not diminished that need. Initially, rather than trying to achieve this by direct action, central government exercised its influence by proxy through its 'instruments': Her Majesty's Inspectorate of Constabulary (HMIC), ACPO and national specialist policing units (such as NCIS) (Reiner, 2010, p.229). The Audit Commission too, played a significant part in overhauling policing and investigation at the end of the last century and its role is examined here.

HMIC

Since the codification of the NIM on 12 January 2005, HMIC has primary responsibility for assessing NIM compliance but it has overseen British policing since 1856. From its establishment until 1993 (when the first lay inspectors were appointed), all HMICs were recruited from ACPO ranks (or equivalent). Usually, those appointed were at the end of their police careers. Not only did inspectors owe their continuing employment to government patronage but they also were steeped in the service's bureaucratic tradition. It was only to be expected that the resulting organization would be deeply conservative.

A recent study of the roles, values and attitudes of chief officers highlighted the 'unresolved ambiguity' at the heart of the relationship between the Home Office, its inspectors and the service (Caless, 2011, p. 149). In a survey carried out between 2009 and 2010, of 89 ACPO members surveyed, 71 expressed a negative opinion of HMIC (Caless, 2011, p.155). One said that HMIC was 'just a kind of comfort blanket for the Home Office ... quite inefficient and the quality of their work is very variable' (Caless, 2011, p.151).

In September 2012, Tom Winsor, a barrister and former rail regulator, was appointed as the first HM Inspector of Constabulary selected from outside of policing. This controversial appointment initially was challenged by Parliament's Home Affairs Select Committee and by senior police officers. Nevertheless, Winsor has taken up the post. Critics have questioned his ability to provide operational advice to chief constables and to the Home Secretary. It remains to be seen how the appointment will play out. Nevertheless, the Home Office's will to make his appointment work should not be underestimated.

Audit Commission

Though the Commission's influence has declined in the contemporary era, in the period that the NIM was formulated its remit was to scrutinize public sector spending. It played an important role in reshaping perceptions of criminal investigation and was a persuasive advocate of ILP. As much as anything, its introduction confirmed the shift towards the calculative and contractual model of governance described by Reiner (2010).

For a period at the end of the last century, the Commission and ACPO worked symbiotically so that the latter welcomed investigations as the means of providing impetus for reform (Savage et al, 2000). However, by the end of the century, the Commission had turned its attention to other areas of the criminal justice system. Even so, its influence on modern police history was considerable.

Public policymaking

There is a consensus that the sociology of organizations makes an important contribution to the study of the policy process because most policymaking takes place within institutions. Hill argued that sociology is particularly important in interpreting the translation of policies (like ILP) into action and 'exploring issues about the behaviour of workers within complex organisations (among which state bureaucracies loom large)' (2009, p.9). Though an understanding of mainstream political science literature is perhaps just as important.

In that context, a range of theories has been developed to explain the public policymaking and policy implementation processes. Some concern themselves with bureaucratic power and the domination of those within the institutions affected by the policy. For example the 'garbage can' model advanced by March and Olsen (1996, p.251) posits that actors 'act within definitions of alternatives, consequences, preferences (interests), and strategic options' that are strongly affected by their institutional contexts.

An institutional theory-linked approach which captures the environment, within which the NIM was conceived and developed, is Kingdon's 'Agenda Setting' approach. Kingdon conceives of an agenda as a 'list of subjects or problems to which governmental officials, and people outside of government closely associated with those officials, are paying serious attention to at any given time' (Kingdon, 2003, p.3). Rather than being comprehensive or rational, solutions are connected to problems and both are connected to 'favourable political forces' (Kingdon, 2003, p.20). The combination of these elements is most likely when policy entrepreneurs take advantage of policy windows opened by those problems or political imperatives. Therefore the prominence of an idea on an agenda relies not on its source nor even on the fact that there may be an entrepreneur encouraging policy change but rather it is the 'climate in government or the receptivity of ideas of a given type' that is key (Kingdon, 2003, p.72).

Kingdon's approach is limited in that it does not fully consider the implementation process, which in itself can be an ambiguous concept. Hill (2009) argues that once policy leaves the rarefied atmosphere in which it was created, it is influenced by the reality of the outside world so that it becomes much more complex as it is translated into action. Early implementation studies focused on examining the process of putting a policy into action. Later that top-down approach was challenged by those who argued for a 'bottom-up' perspective that recognized that 'implementation actors are forced to make choices between programmes which conflict or interact with each other' (Hill, 2009, p.203).

I relied on Sabatier's approach to public policy implementation to help me evaluate the extent to which the NIM was properly implemented. He suggested that researchers can synthesize top-down and bottom-up approaches when a 'dominant piece of legislation structuring the situation' is present (Sabatier cited in Hill, 2009, p.204). Such was the case with the NIM, which was codified by the Police Reform Act 2002. Sabatier (1986) also highlighted that public policies rarely achieve their aims without major revision and that policymakers and those tasked with implementation must be flexible, resourceful and willing to reach compromises to achieve their goals. The reader will see later just how flexible, resourceful and acquiescent were those charged with NIM implementation.

2
A Brief History of Investigative and Intelligence Practice in Britain

Introduction

Far from being a product of times, the roots of ILP are to be found in the earliest history of the new police. I examine the emergence of the police, and developments in criminal investigation, police patrol and intelligence work up to the introduction of the 1964 Police Act, which was a defining event in police history that fundamentally, altered both the structure and governance of policing. I explain that the orthodoxy that constrains policing today has its roots in the history of the police and, particularly, in the origins and development of the detective force.

The police mission

In the earliest days of Britain's police, its elite underplayed its crime fighting role so as to secure the future of what was for many, a highly contentious and unwelcome development. The organized, centrally controlled Metropolitan Police created by Home Secretary Robert Peel and placed under the control of two Justices of the Peace, Charles Rowan and Richard Mayne, was an anathema to many because it 'offended against a tradition which held that social control should be a private, local and voluntary matter' (Ignatieff, 1979, p.25). To those so offended, the police represented 'continental despotism' (Ignatieff, 1979, p.6).

Employing officers out of uniform 'smacked of spying and of the political intrusiveness ascribed to police institutions on continental Europe' (Emsley and Shpayer-Makov, 2006, p.7). Therefore, from the outset, the force's leaders went to great lengths to avoid any suggestion that officers were government spies and prioritized the prevention of crime. The importance of crime detection was downplayed to secure public consent for the new highly contentious policing arrangements.

The police elite emphasized that the routine business of policing was the uniformed patrol of London's streets. Those patrols would be identified instantly as police officers by their distinctive uniform. Patrol officers were instructed that their primary objective was to ensure the 'security of persons and property [and] the preservation of public tranquility' and that prevention of crime would achieve the force's objectives 'better than by the detection and punishment of the offender after he has succeeded in committing the crime' (Metropolitan Police, 1829, p.1).

Publicly, the Commissioners asserted that they had neither the capacity nor the inclination to take on crime investigation and they appeared content to leave it to the pre-existing magistracy and their agents, such as the Bow Street Runners (evidence to the 1833 and 1834 Parliamentary Select Committees cited in Roach, 2004, pp.75–6). Mayne took every opportunity to allay public fears of police spies, and Peel himself declared 'God forbid that [I] should countenance a system of espionage' (Smith, 1985 cited in Rawlings, 2002, p.168). However, as so often is the case, the rhetoric did not match the reality; officers were employed in plain clothes from the earliest days of the organization (*The Times*, 11 November 1830 cited in Rawlings, 2002).

However, it was only four years later that the Commissioners were forced to admit that in the investigation of robbery 'We have found it better done by persons in plain clothes, who were not thus known to the thieves, both in preventing them and in catching them when they have been going in' (Parliamentary Papers, 1833: vol. XII, page 407 Select Committee). That of course suggests that the police knew who they needed to watch in the first place.

Even then, sensitive to public opinion, they defended those deployments as exceptional and limited to detecting offenders when they were 'going in' (actually committing offences) when otherwise they might evade arrest. Clearly, from the earliest days of the police, its leaders were under pressure to produce results. However, they needed to achieve those results in ways that were acceptable to a critical and suspicious public. As history has shown, that is by no means a simple task.

Recent analyses suggest that in the earliest days of the police, the responsibility for performing what today would be understood as detective duties fell to the magistrates and their agents such as the

Runners, just as it had done before the creation of the new police. Though the Runners' achievements in recovering stolen property and making deals on behalf of victims rather than focusing on arresting offenders, commoditized policing in a way that, arguably, may once have been acceptable but was unwelcome in the Peelian era. Summarizing the policing arrangements that Peel oversaw in the earliest days of the new force, Clutterbuck argued that the Home Secretary headed a system that performed three discrete functions; 'preventative patrol and the control of public order via the Metropolitan Police, and the detection of offenders via the Bow Street Runners' (2002, p.125).

Plain clothes policing

Eventually, media and public concern over what was perceived as incompetence in criminal investigation, forced a change in Home Office and police policy. Reiner argued that the expansion of the detective force in this period was the product of a moral panic. The public blamed the police for failing to counter a crime wave, which undermined the latter's carefully constructed appearance of effectiveness in terms of its core mandate (a construction which perhaps is under just as much attack today). However, demands from the propertied classes for the police to be 'armed with preventative powers similar to those exercised by the Continental police' were exactly what the working class feared (Reiner, 2000, p.57).

The Metropolitan Police Courts Act of 1839 and the Metropolitan Police Act of the same year set the stage for the entrance of the detectives. The Acts ended the rights of magistrates and their agents (including the Runners) to undertake the specialist duties that the effective detection of crime demanded.[1] The combined effect was to remove agents and their informers from active roles in the criminal justice system. However, this left a dangerous vacuum that had to be filled. In 1842, the Home Office turned to the Metropolitan Police Commissioners who had no alternative other than to expand their force's investigative capacity to fill that void, even if initially that was by stealth.

The first detective department

The department assumed the role previously fulfilled by the magistrates' agents but it also inherited the agents' practice of consorting with thieves and informers. Mayne was concerned that the adoption of those practices would encourage what has become known in the contemporary era as 'noble cause' corruption. He argued that though the force might achieve 'detections that might not otherwise have taken place', the agents' methods were both immoral and in practice incapable of limiting crime in the longer term (Mayne, 1842 cited in Roach, 2004, p.193). As the reader will see later, the Turf Fraud Case (and for that matter, the 'noble cause' inspired corruption cases of the modern era) proved Mayne's instincts to be correct.

The adoption of the Runners' methods represented a covert transfer of the craft knowledge, attitudes and values of the old detective system to the new. That is hardly surprising because the new force lacked specialized training or even regular duties. In the circumstances, with their existence barely acknowledged by their superiors, it was almost inevitable that the new detectives would embrace practices that (even in that period) many considered to be morally repugnant but which seemed to deliver the results that both the public and their masters demanded.

The detectives eagerly, and quickly, constructed for public consumption, an image of themselves as successful crime-fighters. They were assisted greatly by the emerging mass media and by the fascination of contemporary writers with 'true crime' stories. For example, Charles Dickens and his contemporary Wilkie Collins (the author of the first British detective story, *The Moonstone*, published in 1868) based their fictional detective characters on real policemen. Certainly, detectives' tales of their own exploits contributed to the construction of their image as 'possessing the monopoly on expertise' in investigation (Maguire, 2008, p.365), and to detective work as 'heroic, distinctive and even glamorous' (Emsley and Shpayer-Makov, 2006, p.131).

In 1867, the detective force numbered just 15 officers working directly to Mayne at Whitehall Place (later to become known as Scotland Yard). However in 1869, the force was substantially enlarged by Edmund Henderson (Mayne's successor) so that it numbered approximately 200 men. Adolphus Williamson (later Chief Constable of the CID and a considerable figure in British policing in his own right), the chief inspector in charge of the 'old' force was promoted to superintendent on a salary of £300 per annum and given command of the new body, which for the first time saw detectives posted to the 21 police divisions that then made up the Met (Shpayer-Makov, 2004, p.253).

The new arrangements were accompanied by a division of detective labour. Scotland Yard central office detectives dealt with murder and other serious crime, divisional detectives investigated local crimes and criminals. Basil Thomson (1936) (head of the CID during the First World War), noted that almost immediately there was friction between Williamson and the uniformed, divisional superintendents who wanted to control the detectives. Thus, not only was the distinction between 'specialist' and 'generalist' detectives (that has had such an impact on the effectiveness of mainstream policing in the modern era) established from the earliest days of the detective force but so was the tension between the detectives and the uniformed branch. I later will argue that both have undermined efforts to deliver the kind of single service approach typified by ILP strategies and advocated by the police elite in modern times.

Within the detective force, there was disquiet over the course Henderson had set. For example in 1870, Williamson made a bid for greater control; proposing a reorganization of the force to bring all detectives (both central and divisional) under his control (MEPO 2/134a). According to his plan, the new 'Detective Division' would be responsible for the reactive investigation of any crime. Scotland Yard (in the person of Williamson) would oversee the detectives' work but they also would report the progress of investigations to the divisional superintendents. However, Henderson rejected Williamson's plan as unworkable and (though the precise reasons for the rejection are unknown), significantly, the distinction between the central and local branches of the detective department which has continued into modern times was reinforced.

In 1877, Scotland Yard was rocked by the Turf Fraud case which confirmed the persistence of some less desirable elements of the old detective craft in the new force. The subsequent 'Trial of the Detectives' resulted in the imprisonment of senior detective officers for assisting felons to evade justice. It undermined Williamson, calling into question his ability to control his subordinates, and led directly to the Home Office establishing a 'Departmental Commission' to enquire into the 'State, Discipline and Organisation of the Detective Force of the Metropolitan Police' (otherwise known as the Ibbetson Commission).

The significance of the Commission's decision *inter alia* to establish a structure that guaranteed a detective a career in plain clothes, solely under the command of other detectives (very much against Henderson's advice) should not be underestimated. It confirmed a system that endured, largely unchanged, for almost 100 years and to the long-standing separation of the detective force from mainstream policing; a situation that remained unchanged until the appointment of Robert Mark as Commissioner almost 100 years later. Roach argued that it also led to 'inward-looking isolation and lack of outsider supervision that opened the door to corruption' in the detective force (2004, p.143). However, as the reader has seen, corruption had been a feature of detective work from its very beginning. Perhaps, it is more accurate to say that the new arrangements reinforced the detective craft and did nothing to mitigate detectives' pre-existing predilection for corrupt practices.

To draw a line under the past, the Commission recommended a complete reorganization of the detective force and the replacement of Williamson. In the Home Office there was an appetite for change that only an outsider could be trusted to deliver. It strongly recommended that an Assistant Commissioner, who should be a lawyer having magisterial experience, should be placed at the head of the detective branch, ranking next to the Chief Commissioner and having charge of the whole force in his absence. The individual appointed to that post was Howard Vincent.

Howard Vincent CID

On 8 April 1878, Vincent, a barrister, former soldier and newspaper correspondent, was appointed first head of the new 'Criminal Investigation Department'. Jeyes (1912, p.60) recorded that Vincent was afforded the title 'Director' to remove any 'uncanny associations' with the word detective that had so recently been discredited during the Turf Fraud affair. However, Moylan (cited in Browne, 1956, p.190) argued that the title 'Director of Criminal Investigations' actually was a direct translation of the French *Directeur des Recherches Criminelles* which perhaps suggests that initially there was an idea that the CID would be an entirely separate organization like the Sûreté in France.

Some argued that Vincent was unfit for the post (for example, he was rather uncharitably described as a 'briefless barrister with ... little or no knowledge or experience in police matters' (*Reynolds' Newspaper*, 1880, 15 August). However, his nomination for the post was the product of assiduous planning. In 1877, he had enrolled in the Paris Faculty of Law to carry out his own investigation of the French detective police. Thereafter, he impressed the Home Secretary by presenting a thorough critique of that system to the Commission and was recommended for the job by the Attorney-General (who had prosecuted the Turf Fraud case).

Vincent also benefited from the abandonment of the principle that police recruits should be drawn only from the working class communities they served. Peel's determination to avoid a caste system in the police had meant that even though the armed forces potentially were rich sources of recruits, for many years ex-warrant officers and non-commissioned officers were favoured over 'gentlemen' officers. Wall argued that rather than representing 'policing of the people by the people' as Peel publicly had claimed, this was an attempt to 'ensure that the relationship between the police and the public remained close and that control over ... the "dangerous classes" was maximized while the potential for disorder was minimized' in a cost-effective way (1998, p.21). However, as the force developed, it was clear both to the police elite and the Home Office that better-educated recruits were needed. Therefore, recruitment was opened up to commissioned officers. Ultimately, Vincent was a shoo-in for the post.

Confirming the Home Secretary's control over the force, Henderson publicly announced Vincent's engagement but he played no part either in his selection or appointment. Those responsibilities instead fell on Home Secretary Cross who had commissioned the Ibbetson inquiry (Roach, 2004, p.164). Vincent reported directly to the Home Secretary over Henderson's head. In this period, it clearly was the politician rather than the police chief who was in control of the CID; a situation which Vincent used to his advantage even though he had neither statutory nor disciplinary power over the force.

The new CID soon attracted public comment. Mr Bridge, the Hammersmith Police Magistrate 'chafed unmercifully' a detective who appeared before him as 'crime investigator' rather than detective (*The Era*, 1878, 14 April). Another, who styled himself a 'criminal investigator' was told by a second Magistrate to 'Call yourself a constable, I suppose you are one' (*The Graphic*, 1880, 4 September). There certainly was enough work for the new department. For example in 1879, its detectives made 4,862 arrests, 65 percent of which resulted in convictions. In that year, officers conducted 2,066 inquiries that did not require any arrest and travelled throughout the United Kingdom and to Australia, Barbados, Belgium, Canada, France, Germany, Holland, Italy and Spain in pursuing their investigations (Vincent cited in *The Graphic*, 1880, 4 September).

Despite having no disciplinary power over his staff and being short of experienced lieutenants, Vincent reformed the department (a task made especially challenging by the Fenian outrages in London in the period), introducing new arrangements for supervision throughout the ranks. He appointed another 60 divisional detectives and 20 special patrols, further formalizing the distinction between Scotland Yard detectives and their divisional colleagues. His decision to continue the practice of appointing officers to the CID for the whole of their police careers signally reinforced the exclusive nature of the detective craft.

Vincent wrote extensively on legal and police matters. In 1882, he published *A Police Code and Manual of Criminal Law* which was used as a basic textbook for police forces in Britain and throughout the British Empire for many years after his death in 1908. Vincent's *Code* can be considered the first attempt by the British police to codify investigative practice. Mr Justice Hawkins provided the foreword for one of its early editions. His words provide a fascinating insight into the culture of police work in that era, elements of which can still be observed in the modern force. He exhorted constables to:

> Obey every order given to you by your superior officer without for a moment considering the propriety of it. You are not responsible for the order, but for obedience. In yielding obedience let the humblest member of the force feel that by good conduct and cheerful submission he may himself rise to be placed in authority to give the orders that he is now called upon to obey (cited in Vincent, 1886, p.5).

Vincent's advice to detectives was intended to encourage the single service approach pursued by other commanders in modern times. He noted that 'the detection of criminals ... can only be attained by cordial cooperation, the absence of craving for individual credit, free interchange of information, great activity, and the constant adoption of fresh and unexpected measures' (Vincent, 1886, p.53). The ability of detectives to unravel crime; depended upon 'the energy, the ability, the judgement, the zeal, and the integrity of the detective force' (Vincent, 1886, p.109).

From 1883 to 1884, Vincent edited the *Police Gazette*;[2] the first intelligence circular to transmit descriptions of wanted offenders, details of stolen property and the like. The Gazette has gone through many reviews and revisions but is still in circulation today. He was an innovator and unlike his predecessors did not disavow 'continental' methods. He favoured using informers and undercover operatives as *agents provocateurs*, though he was rightly wary of encouraging improper relationships between detectives and those from whom they sought information. He started a collection of photographs of convicted felons and was completely unconventional in his methods (arguably because he had not been conditioned by a lifetime in the police).

In 1883, Vincent established the Special Irish Branch (later renamed Special Branch) which became the first of the specialized squads 'spun off' from the CID. This was the first, but by no means the last, example of the police's predisposition to assemble a squad of officers, usually detectives, to combat 'crime waves' or to tackle new crimes. In this case, the event was the failure of the police to prevent an attack on Clerkenwell Prison by a group of Irish nationalists, despite having received accurate intelligence from the Irish Police warning of the attack (Emsley and Shpayer-Makov, 2006, p.83). The new unit brought 'added kudos and consolidated [the] CID's monopoly over investigative techniques' (Matassa and Newburn, 2007, p.44). It also signalled a significant split between the ordinary detective and those tasked with responding to events on the national stage.

Clutterbuck argued that the establishment of the squad represented a 'quantum leap' in the methodology of the detective force as it signalled a new, longer-term approach to intelligence work of the kind that has come to be associated with specialist detective units in modern times (2002, p.351). Table 2.1 is adapted from Clutterbuck's fascinating account of the emergence of the Special Branch at the end of the nineteenth century. It suggests that the tools and techniques now associated with 'high policing' (Brodeur, 1983), in fact have their roots in the nineteenth century.

Table 2.1 Police methodologies against 'political' crime

Methodologies Against 'Political' Crime and the Earliest Identified Year of Use

Method	Year
Use of covert officers to gather intelligence	1833
Covert monitoring of public meetings	1833
Covert monitoring of target organizations	1833
Surveillance of target individuals	1866
Operational use of information from active informants	1867
Use of detectives to gather intelligence from other UK Forces (by working in other force areas or by request for assistance)	1867
Use of detectives to gather intelligence from other countries (by working abroad or request for assistance)	1867
Co-operation with a UK 'Secret Service'	1867
Use of detectives to gather intelligence systematically at ports	1872
Intelligence gathering from convicts and their visitors/contacts	1888
Specific tasking of informants	1888
Lifestyle' payments to informants	1888
Gathering overt information from the media	1880
Interception of communications (postal and telegraphic)	1880
Systemized collection/collation/recording of intelligence	1880

The utility of the methods Clutterbuck describes were recognized by police commanders and adopted by the new specialist squads which, as the reader will see later, were introduced throughout the twentieth century and which have become such an influence in policing in modern times. The reader also will see that the squads' monopoly on their use ensured that they always had the best information available to any section of the service and that they exploited that knowledge in ways which reinforced their power and influence and which also elevated their status within the detective craft.

Cultural division

Vincent recognized that the divide between the CID and uniformed branches was detrimental to the development of the police and 'with much detriment to the public service' (MEPO 2/134d, 26 October 1880). He made many attempts to ameliorate those differences. For example, in his police code he cautioned detective officers to be 'watchful' about taking cases away from uniform constables and:

> Especially guarded against the arrogation of individual credit, and if they have any information which may secure the arrest of a criminal, they should communicate it to the officer who is placed in a position to work it out, instead of reserving it for themselves.

His identification of the corrosive effect of that cultural divide demonstrated his insight and his management skills but his influence on the craft of detective work was understandably limited. An unintended consequence of investigative reforms was that the CID became even more distanced from the uniform men as the latter resented the former's higher rates of pay and their general air of superiority and that divide was perpetuated into modern times.

Despite the detectives' opinion of themselves, Vincent believed that it was their inadequacies that were at the heart of the problem. He blamed the force's superintendents for selecting CID men who were 'far removed from the best quality' and by leaving them to their own devices to investigate cases so that 'there was neither control nor cooperation, neither intelligence nor thoroughness as a general rule' in their investigations (MEPO 2/134d, 26 October 1880). That suggests that some senior officers prioritized other functions over crime investigation (hardly surprising given the founding principles of the force).

In a memorandum that gives a fascinating insight into Vincent's opinion of detectives' abilities in the earliest days of the CID, he noted that their dealings with other constabularies often indicated incompetence in even the simplest of tasks (MEPO 2/134d, 26 October 1880). Sadly, there is no record of a response to his proposal that CID superintendents should all be trained 'in the same school of the Criminal Law' to improve a department that 'never had any stability' and which was 'defective in the time of Sir Richard Mayne' and 'defective during the period of the divisional detectives', or alternatively that they be replaced by existing chief inspectors or by local inspectors eligible for promotion who were of 'suitable calibre' (MEPO 2/134d, 26 October 1880).

However, it may be assumed that it was not until 1935 with the establishment of the detective training school in North London that such training was delivered. Even then, trainers focused on the criminal law rather than on delivering instruction in the practical everyday skills that detectives might need. It would be another 50 years before any meaningful steps were taken to remedy that situation (as a response to the introduction of PACE in 1984).

Much more a gifted administrator than a great detective, Vincent's influence on the development of investigative practice cannot be overstated. As Basil Thomson (1936, p.180) recorded, Vincent 'increased the strength of the Department ... greatly improved the filing of criminal records and took care that the various sub-branches of his department worked smoothly together'. There were those who resented some of Vincent's changes but Howe (1965) (another barrister who later would assume command of London's CID and would also go on to lead the force) argued that despite the many challenges Vincent faced, he had a lasting effect on the development of the CID.

New chief: Old problems

In 1884, on Vincent's departure, the idea of a separate detective department reporting directly to the Home Secretary was finally abandoned. The post was 'regularized' and his successor, James Monro, given the title of Assistant Commissioner, directly accountable to Henderson.

In 1892, differences between the Scotland Yard and divisional detectives came to the fore once again during the trial of the poisoner Thomas Cream, even though suggestions of jealousy between the two publicly were refuted.[3] Lock (1993, pp.141–2) has argued that the acrimony between divisional and Yard detectives 'cannot have been helped by the fact that while many of the former were still grubbing away in comparatively primitive surroundings, the latter were moving to quarters in the splendid New Scotland Yard' though by the time the building was completed it was already too small to house the force's headquarters staff.

Detectives did not have things all their own way. In the wake of the infamous 'Jack the Ripper' murders in London's East End there was a backlash against the CID. The *Pall Mall Gazette* ran a series of articles that were critical of Warren (who had assumed command of the Met in 1886) and the conduct of the investigation by his men. Warren stood accused of favouring uniformed men over the detectives with the result that the gap between the two sections of the force was widened further to the detriment of the investigative effort:

> [Warren] could not be got to see that the detectives were in any way more efficient than his ordinary constables. If he wanted any work done that could not be done by Z 324, with his helmet on his head and his blue coat on his back, he would simply put Z 324 in ordinary clothes and expect him to do the work of a detective (Stead, 1888, p.1).

Stead argued that as a result, 'detectives were discouraged, discredited, and sat upon, and the dormant feeling of jealousy and animosity between the two branches began to grow apace, to the no small disadvantage of the service' (1888, p.1). However, Fido and Skinner (1999) countered that criticism of Warren's treatment of the CID, was but one stick with which to beat an individual who had proven to be a most unpopular Commissioner. Warren, a former Royal Engineers officer brought from his command in Africa to take over the running of the force, saw the police's future as no more than an adjunct of the military and he objected to the control exercised by 'civilians' in the Home Office. Basil Thomson wrote that it was characteristic of Warren that his annual reports to the Home Secretary 'omitted all reference to crime in London, though space was given to the question of boots and saddles' (1936, p.188).

A defect that became obvious in the years following the establishment of the CID was that each division and even the Yard detectives, increasingly operated as discrete units. Certainly, little thought was given to the single service approach that has found such favour (at least at the level of rhetoric) in modern times. In 1919, Frederick Wensley, an enormously popular and respected CID Superintendent, suggested that command and control of the detective force would be improved by adding an extra layer of management.[4] His suggestion was taken up and the Met was split into four sectors; each covered by a

CID superintendent, the group immediately being dubbed by the press the 'Big Four'.[5] Wensley also recognized that the Met needed a mobile reserve. He recommended that a roving group of detectives should be established to counter the increasing mobility of law-breaker. Thus, the Flying Squad was born.

The Flying Squad

Given the social and political history of the Met, it is unsurprising that its detective force has always had a huge influence on investigative policy and that most of the early specialist squads emerged in London. For 36 years, Special Branch had stood as the lone example of a police force tailoring a bespoke solution to an emerging crime problem. However, in 1919, the Met established the Flying Squad (popularly known as the 'Sweeney' but more commonly known to detectives simply as 'The Squad').

Wensley argued that the CID needed to adopt a far more 'fluid' response to 'the development of methods of rapid transit – particularly the motor car – [that] was bringing about a state of things in which the detective was placed at a great disadvantage' (1968, p.195). The new squad was made up of detectives under officers of 'special capacity, who could move rapidly and operate in any division where there was an epidemic of crime' (1968, p.195). It has been suggested that the really significant advantages that the Flying Squad held over the divisional detective force were its mobility and flexibility. From the outset, the squad was provided with a number of 'fast cars', vans and tenders to carry out its duties. In 1931, it was equipped with 16 cars and three vans giving it a capability that was the envy of its divisional colleagues.

However, it is worth highlighting that the detectives themselves received no special training for their work. Wensley himself later argued that the reasons for the success of the squad had been misrepresented. In his view, 'the blood and bones of all practical detective work is information' (cited in Lock, 1993, pp.177–8). Rather than relying on 'fast cars, wireless, police boxes or any other mechanical device' the real value of the squad lay in the calibre of its detectives and the quality of the information that they were able to obtain. He said that 'the Flying Squad catches thieves because it knows thieves' (Wensley, 1968, p.196). In other words, it succeeded because it had the best 'thief-catchers', skilled in the detective craft, with access to the best information in the force. The reader will see later that Wensley's words continue to hold true in modern times. Despite many efforts to improve intelligence work in the mainstream, the specialist detectives continue to hold a near-monopoly on the best intelligence and are the most skilled and experienced exponents of the detective craft.

Howe has provided another perspective on the Flying Squad, noting that its officers were the 'storm troopers of the CID' and that they were detested by the criminal underworld to which they were known as 'the heavy mob or the heavies' (1961, p.82). Howe's words lend weight to my argument that the police elite have always been in awe of the specialist detective force to which it has turned whenever its legitimacy has been threatened. I return to that point later.

Yet, the squad did not always have things its own way. A Flying Squad detective is recorded as having complained that with 'smash and grab raids, housebreaking and larcenies in the street ... prevalent ... the need of the cars and vans is felt by the Squad' (MEPO 2/1880, 10 December 1931). Hence the officer's outrage that 'a regular fast car had to be used both night and day for three weeks' as the spare squad car had been taken without the squad's permission by Special Branch to ferry 'somebody called Gandhi' (MEPO 2/1880, 10 December 1931). The squad continues to operate today as 'SCD7, the Flying Squad'.

Before moving on to assess further developments in detective work, I examine the work of the Dixon Committee. There have been many inquiries into criminal investigation and the detective force but this inquiry was particularly significant because it established the pattern of detective work for the rest of the twentieth century. The committee's most significant deliberations were on the chasm that had opened up between the CID and the uniform branch (which had been an issue since 1842 and showed no sign of narrowing) and on the subject of intelligence management, which had become more of a problem as improvements in transport and communications had allowed offenders to extend their reach across divisional and force boundaries.

Home Office Committee on detective work, 1933–36

The committee was established on 12 May 1933 under A.L. Dixon, a senior Home Office official, to 'inquire and report upon the organisation and procedure of the police forces of England and Wales for the purpose of the detection of crime' (MEPO 2/4967, Section 1). It was made up of Home Office officials and chief constables. Again, as much as anything, the establishment of the Committee demonstrated the Home Office's continuing influence over the detective force.

To contextualize the Committee's deliberations, it recorded that in 1933 the aggregate number of police officers in England and Wales, across a total of 181 forces, was 60,000. The detective force numbered 2,600. Predictably, the Met was the largest force with 20,000 officers (1,000 detectives). The smallest force was maintained by the Borough of Tiverton with an establishment of 11 officers. Some forces had only 'one or two men' set aside for detective work whilst others had none at all (MEPO 2/4967, Section 1).

Intelligence work in the 1930s

It is indicative of the challenges faced by those seeking to develop police intelligence work over the last century, that many of the Committee's deliberations in this context still have currency today. There was huge concern over the collection and sharing of intelligence, variations in record-keeping practices, the unsystematic use of records, the inefficient use of those records by investigating officers and the infrequent use of them by uniformed officers. The Committee concluded that efficient detection depended upon the capacity of the police 'to obtain, sift and draw deductions from information'. Unless those problems were resolved there was little prospect of improving investigative practice (MEPO 2/4967).

Given the importance attached to 'hotspotting' and intelligence analysis in the modern era, the Committee's decision to reject an embryonic geographic information system is worthy of note. It was 'disposed to think that no very useful purpose would be served by the preparation of elaborate maps or statistics' but it was agreed that developments within forces (particularly the Met) would be monitored (MEPO 2/4967, Section 1). The reader can see that the Committee recognized the need for rudimentary analysis of the intelligence that police officers collected. However, it expressed no view on how this might be achieved.

Stimulating a debate over cross-border crime that has currency today, members argued that less importance should be given to force boundaries 'in the ordinary day-to-day work of crime detection' (MEPO 2/4967, p.28). However, arrangements needed to be made that would overcome the inherent disadvantages of the existing system so that police action could be 'applied to a common purpose over a wide area' whenever necessary (MEPO 2/4967, p.5).

Those arrangements should include local records for local criminals who did not 'habitually travel from place to place' and committed the bulk of crime (the forerunner of collators' records, which will be discussed later) and regional or national records for those who extended their operations over wider areas and were often responsible for the more serious crimes. The Committee highlighted that local police should know the criminals in their area but there also should be some mechanism by which detectives in adjoining forces should have access to local records (MEPO 2/4967).

The Committee's observation that an effective intelligence system was a fundamental requirement of efficient investigative practice may be a statement of the obvious but it is questionable whether any appreciable progress in this context was made until UBP was introduced some 30 years later. Even then, progress was extremely slow. The Committee's deliberations on intelligence work are significant because they go to the heart of ambitions for ILP in modern times. The report reveals the consistency of policing problems over more than half a century. It also shows that many of the proposals presented today as modern solutions to the challenges of modern policing, in reality are at least 60 years old.

CID and mainstream policing

The Committee established a definition of a 'detective' that extended beyond commonly accepted descriptions of the role in that era. A detective was a police officer who formed 'part of the detective organization of a force ... engaged in specialized crime work and not routine police duties other than crime'. A caveat later was added that 'specialized crime work' extended to 'inquiries and intelligence work' (MEPO 2/4967, Section 1). The precise nature of that work was not explained but clearly, as far back as the 1930s, detectives were engaged in intelligence work. Though it was to be another 20 years before a formal intelligence system was established.

Relations between the uniform and detective forces continued to be a significant issue. The Committee decried CID protectionism as undesirable and inefficient. It noted that the fractious and difficult relationship between the branches hindered the overall investigative effort (MEPO 2/4967). Even though the CID had a monopoly on criminal investigation in the Met and other large forces, the Committee was not prepared to endorse that as national policy. The minority argument that 'uniform officers should not be encouraged to concern themselves' with crime investigation because 'they may, by precipitate or ill-informed action, prejudice rather than assist the work of the detectives' was rejected (MEPO 2/4967, draft final report, p.39). However, that such fears were raised at all is worthy of note.

Particularly significant in the wider context of this discussion was an observation by Chief Constable Wilson of Cardiff City Constabulary that the scope of detective work should be increased by 'working from the criminal to the crime rather than from the crime to the criminal'. Wilson suggested that in the event of an 'epidemic of crime' of the same type, the police should 'keep a careful watch on likely suspects'. He cautioned however, that this type of work 'called for a considerable expenditure of manpower' and that detective strengths should take this into account (MEPO 2/4967, minutes, Section 217). This is evidence that ILP, the targeting of suspect individuals or populations, featured in policing discourse many years before it was endorsed by the Audit Commission. There really is little that is truly new in policing today.

Policing after the Second World War

Many have written about the challenges facing the police service after the Second World War (see for example Emsley, 2011). The important issue in the context of this study is that police numbers were well below what the Home Office considered necessary for the effective delivery of policing services. The problem was particularly acute in the metropolitan forces. Whilst recruitment was a concern, the greater problem was the retention of relatively young but experienced officers on whose 'physical and mental alertness, the efficiency of the force must depend' (Home Office, 1949, p.2). That challenged the efficiency, effectiveness and very legitimacy of the police and had to be confronted.

The Aberdeen Policing Scheme

Perhaps the most innovative attempt to meet that challenge was the Aberdeen Policing Scheme. Thus far, the scheme has merited little more than a by-line in police narratives. However, it was a novel and bold experiment that deserves much more scholarly attention than it has been afforded to date. Overall, the scheme was extremely well received within the force. Yet, it failed to find favour in the wider service. Here, I explain the scheme's influence on British policing and advance an explanation for its rejection by the police elite. The sources of my information are: records held at the National Archive; notes of a lecture delivered at the Port Edgar, Police Training School on 9 March 1951, by Chief Superintendent A.J. Matheson of the Aberdeen force (from the Grampian Police Archive); and the testimony of former Inspector Douglas Smith (an accomplished shorthand writer who contemporaneously recorded the Matheson lecture), at 93 years of age, the last surviving member of the Aberdeen City Police from that era.

Chief Constable James McConnach introduced the revolutionary scheme on 4 April 1948. His aim simply was to improve his officers' lot. Working a beat properly was hard work. Many potential recruits were put off by the mundane nature of the work; 'the trying of doors and shaking padlocks and so on' (Matheson, 1951, p.3), whilst, many serving officers found the work too arduous and morale in the force (and across the whole service) was very low. McConnach was determined to reduce the monotony of the constable's job by eliminating the routine examination of property and by giving his men more variety in, and responsibility for, their work. McConnach's instructions to his men were clear:

> [They] were responsible for a certain area in the city. Each team had to keep its area free of crimes, complaints and accidents ... they could do it as unorthodox as they wished as long as they were not offensive to the public and outwith the law; they had to keep the police end up and do the job whichever way they cared.

Matheson, the scheme's designer, noted that the 'men took to it ... like ducks take to water' (1951, p.4). Though some officers expressed concern that the benefits of rapid response brought about by the scheme might be outweighed by the impact on police/community relations, Matheson argued that in fact the contact with the public was improved by the new scheme.

The scheme was piloted in the north of the city. Beats were abolished and officers were posted to car patrols in teams of four. Sixteen patrol cars were fitted with radios, which allowed them to contact each other and the force control room.[6] Each car also carried a camera which was of 'immense value at accidents ... for observation on betting houses [and] for photographing the "street bookie" ... on the job' (Matheson, 1951, p.13). In January 1949, the scheme was extended to the rest of the city. That extension also signalled a development of the system; some foot beats and patrols were retained and mobile patrols were superimposed on them, rather than replacing them.

As the reader will see later, the major difference between the Aberdeen scheme and the UBP experiment that followed 20 years later was the overt investment in intelligence work in the latter. However, it may be argued that the Aberdeen scheme was in fact the first formal attempt to deliver ILP because it is clear that the number of officers deputed to police the different sectors of the force varied according to the time of day, the day of the week and the policing requirements of the area (Brook, 1948). That suggests that the force was carrying out at least a rudimentary analysis of policing problems.

The success of the scheme attracted interest from elsewhere in the UK and from as far away as Australia. Representatives of the West Riding of Yorkshire, Birkenhead, Eastbourne, and Hull forces visited Aberdeen to study the scheme with a view to adopting something similar in their own force areas. Significantly, the scheme also brought itself to the attention of Lord Oaksey, commissioned by Parliament to enquire into police pay and conditions of service.

The Oaksey Inquiry and the Aberdeen Scheme

In the aftermath of the Second World War, the Home Office was concerned enough about police morale and numbers to commission an inquiry. That inquiry was chaired by Lord Oaksey. Oaksey was tasked *inter alia* to consider: recruitment and retention problems; police pay; pensions; and working conditions.[7] On 2 December 1948, he appointed a working group of 12 members of the police elite, to assess the Aberdeen scheme as a model for British policing. That group was led by Sir Frank Brook, HMIC and included James McConnach and the Scottish HMIC, S.A. Kinnear.

Remarkably, the working group visited Aberdeen and with surprising rapidity, completed its report by 21 December 1948. Broadly, most members of the group rejected the scheme. However, that bland statement hides a tension that is revealed when two versions of the group's report are compared. The first, (MEPO 10/16), includes a section headed 'Discipline' that contains a thinly-veiled indictment of McConnach's control of his force that is absent from the second, which was submitted to Oaksey (MEPO 2/8487). That first section notes:

> The Aberdeen system allows very wide discretion and freedom to the individual constable. The Chief Constable has relaxed the more formal aspects of discipline within his force to a degree which many of us consider would not be desirable throughout the police service (MEPO 10/16, p.21).

The first version (one assumes, a draft) also notes that the whole group was of the opinion that the beat system 'must be retained to a certain degree'. However, in the submitted version, perhaps unsurprisingly, that McConnach and Kinnear dissented from that view. There seems to have been some 'horse-trading' between the group members. Whereas, in the draft report, the scheme is described as 'no rival to the beat system but a variant and development of it (MEPO 10/16, p.21), in the submitted version that note is elaborated upon to explain that 'the system differs from the beat system in the fundamental respect that it abolishes the individual responsibility of a constable for a definite area and substitutes the team responsibility of a group for a larger area' (MEPO 2/8487, p.10). Despite the benefits claimed for the scheme (which are acknowledged by the working group in both versions), providing officers with freedom of thought and action was (in the view of the majority) a threat to discipline that simply could not be countenanced.

Oaksey's response to the report displays a mastery of civil service understatement. Couched in terms that appear entirely reasonable to those unfamiliar with British political discourse, Oaksey wrote:

> This experiment in Aberdeen is the outstanding example of attempts to improve the working conditions of the men ... without a sacrifice in the efficiency of the force ... The working party were not convinced that the scheme was suitable for general adoption and we do not wish to dissent from them ... But we are strongly of the opinion that the Aberdeen experiment provides a challenge for every other chief constable in the country to study the problem for himself. The efficiency of the force and the service it renders to the public must naturally take first place, but the amelioration of the men's working conditions is of great importance and the Aberdeen experiment has shown that improvement in the two spheres is not always mutually exclusive (Home Office, 1949, pp.6–7).

Despite Oaksey's appeal to the police elite to find ways to improve the lot of the constable without sacrificing the efficiency of their forces, the working group's report was to signal a hiatus in meaningful attempts to reform police patrol for another 20 years.

The rise of the specialist detectives

Having seemingly rejected the notion of improving police effectiveness through the reform of mainstream policing, the police elite thereafter looked elsewhere for solutions to the extraordinary challenges that emerged. The increasing specialization of the detective force in the twentieth century should be viewed in that light. The expansion of the specialist detective force also is noteworthy because it extended the reach and influence of the CID and the detective craft and confirmed the class system in policing, which undermined the notion of a single service approach to crime control in modern times.[8]

Rawlings (2002, p.21) noted that increasing the number and remit of specialist detective squads was a key strategy for dealing with 'crime epidemics' in the modern era. The regular depiction of the CID as the saviours of the service also confirmed the idea of the department as an elite and perpetuated the divide between the CID and the uniformed branch. In at least one case, that of the Special Duty Squad, it fostered the idea that detectives were not bound by the same rules as their uniformed counterparts.

The Special Duty Squad (SDS) or 'Ghost Squad'

The squad was the brainchild of Percy Worth, Chief Constable of the CID (MEPO 3/2033). It was a response to the huge rise in crime that followed the Second World War. The SDS was a small squad of 'selected CID officers' recruited from the Flying Squad for the 'sole purpose of acquiring information concerning the activities of criminals' (MEPO 3/2033, 18 May 1945). Worth recruited the SDS from the Flying Squad because his experience had taught him that 'the more valuable information about persistent and dangerous criminals invariably emanated from squad officers'. Worth considered that those officers possessed a greater ability to 'contact and control informants' than their divisional colleagues and that their informants were 'well controlled' and 'more productive'. To Worth, these men represented the 'best of the best'. In other words, they were the thief-catchers above all other thief-catchers – the greatest exponents of the detective craft.

Worth seemed to have accepted without challenge, that detectives concealed the identity of their informers and that they rewarded them without the knowledge of their senior officers; this was purely a matter of trust. Worth wrote that the key issue was to obtain information and act upon it quickly. Money was available to be spent on informers and spent it should be (MEPO 3/2033, 18 May 1945). Gosling, a founding member of the SDS, records that the squad's head, Howe's, assessment of the situation was that things were 'getting out of hand'; there was both too much crime and too few arrests. Clearly, desperate times called for desperate measures. The squad's express purpose was to acquire information 'concerning the activities of persistently clever and dangerous criminals' (Worth cited in Gosling, 1959, p.11).

This signalled a remarkable development in detective work as the squad were given powers 'previously unheard of in the CID' (Worth cited in Gosling, 1959, p.11). Worth and Howe were operating in a very different policing environment from detectives in modern times. The latitude afforded to the four detectives who made up the new squad was surprising, perhaps shocking to modern sensibilities. Their sole purpose was to 'infiltrate into the underworld and establish and maintain contacts with anyone who can give information which will lead to the arrest of criminals' (Gosling, 1959, p.14). According to Gosling the squad was 'virtually given *carte blanche* and told to produce results'. Crime control explicitly was afforded precedence over due process as detectives were given licence to operate as they wished. Tellingly, they were assured by Howe that 'You will not be asked any questions about the source of any information you discover' (cited in Gosling, 1959, p.15).[9] Clearly, a blind eye would be turned to unethical practice as long as it was in a noble cause.

Gosling's (1959) fascinating account of his SDS career details many interactions with informers. In those post-war years, the police were faced with a new kind of criminal; 'cruel, ruthless and well informed'; operating in the 'thieves market' that was post-conflict London. In his view, the SDS was an attempt to 'wrest the initiative from the criminals' (Gosling, 1959, p.20). Gosling's view was that:

> If every policeman 'worked to rule' – and a great many of them do – I reckon that more than 90 percent of the crimes committed in Great Britain would remain unsolved. That's the dilemma ... We must use informers – and that means we have to play fair with them. You mustn't give them away either to other criminals or to other policemen (Gosling, 1959, p.19).

In that crime control-dominated milieu, detectives could be investigator, judge and jury. Gosling recalled circumstances in which he 'may have to let a man go free after he has committed a crime' because he could then 'put the squeeze' on him afterwards' (1959, p.19). Clearly, these methods were perceived to be legitimate and effective as the squad's tenure was extended three times. Over the three years and nine months it operated, it solved 1,506 cases, made 789 arrests and recovered stolen property valued at £253,896. Scotland Yard paid out almost £25,000 in rewards to the squad's informers in that period (Gosling, 1959), representing a considerable increase on the £3,695 spent in the previous five years (MEPO 3/2033).

Criminal Intelligence Squad 9 (C9)

Criminal intelligence as a discipline within the police service (as opposed to intelligence work linked to extremism or subversion, probably commenced in the early 1950s with the formation of another specialist squad, the Metropolitan Police's 'C9' branch.[10] The branch provided a central point of contact for provincial officers investigating country house burglaries committed by London-based criminals. Known as the 'Home and Colonial' by its members, it was staffed exclusively by detective officers who were specially selected from the Met for their abilities as 'thief-catchers' and officers from the other English forces who had undergone a similar selection process.

The unit concerned itself only with intelligence about serious and organized crime and provided only a very limited service to mainstream policing. The collection methods routinely employed by the unit utilized the most sensitive covert policing techniques available to the police. Though in those times, the principle of 'need to know' was strictly applied and those methods and the information that they generated were protected not only from public view but also from divisional detectives and the uniformed branch.

CID culture also was an important factor in that protectionism. In that regard, little had changed since the 1930s. Moreover, there was competition within the CID with some detectives guilty of hoarding intelligence for personal gain (officers used it to earn overtime payments or to bring themselves to the attention of senior officers and thus secure advancement in the force). Tangentially, Grieve (2004) noted that intelligence could not easily be shared in any event because there was no local intelligence structure worthy of the name to receive it, in any force in the country.

Essentially, C9 represented the embryonic intelligence system for the UK. It worked closely with another Scotland Yard unit (CB6), which was staffed by Home Counties officers, whose staff were responsible for checking the Yard's criminal records for details of the criminal history of offenders arrested in their home force areas. The unit represented the single point of contact in the Met for other police forces and law enforcement agencies but it was soon swamped with work and it was quickly realized that there was a need for a larger unit that had a greater capacity to use the intelligence it collected more productively.

Criminal Intelligence Squad 11 (C11)

In 1960, the Criminal Intelligence Branch 'C11' was established. The department became the regional criminal intelligence branch for the south-east of England. Based at New Scotland Yard, its remit was to 'collect, evaluate, and disseminate information about organized crime and prominent criminals' (ACPO, 1975, p.1). Kelland, Assistant Commissioner of the Met in this period, noted that 'London was the natural centre for the densely populated south east region and it was important that the Met should take a lead' in the field of criminal intelligence. As a unit with a regional responsibility, C11's Met officers also were joined by officers seconded from other forces in the south-east (Kelland, 1986, pp.233–4).

C11 collected information about the activities of career criminals thought to pose the greatest threat to the social order in London and the South-East. In the 1970s, it became the first intelligence unit with a national responsibility. Echoing the words of Wilson, the chief constable of Cardiff in 1936, Grieve (2004, p.28) has noted that the motto of the new unit was 'the criminal not the crime'. To enable the branch to focus on its central aim, C11 was allowed to exercise a high degree of selectivity in the choice of subjects worthy of its interest (and to ignore most of the more than three million individuals recorded in the records of the National Criminal Intelligence Office) as to do otherwise 'would completely destroy the objects for which the branch was formed' (ACPO, 1975, p.1).

Criminals of interest to the squad were known as 'C11 nominals'. Once so labelled, individuals remained of interest to the police for the rest of their lives.[11] C11 began rather modestly in 1960, on the first floor of the 'old' Scotland Yard on London's Victoria Embankment. In 1963, further regional intelligence offices (RIOs) based on the C11 model, were established in Birmingham, Cardiff, Durham, Glasgow, Liverpool and Manchester. In addition to gathering information about serious and organized crime for the Met, the units acted as regional clearing houses and also provided the national lead on intelligence for certain types of crimes designated by the Home Office (usually associated with national or international crime). Just like C9, the new units provided only a very limited service to mainstream policing.

It was intended that C11 should seamlessly link in with the new local intelligence system (see section on UBP). However, its officers quickly found that although some information they wanted could be obtained from local records, most information of real value was held in the Criminal Records Office (then known as C4) or the Metropolitan Police Registry (which archived a wide variety of official records). C11 officers also trawled through intelligence files held by the other specialist squads to find information that they could add to C11's records.

Anecdotally, C11 is said to have obtained its most useful information from the Flying Squad, which is not really surprising given that the squad contained those most skilled in the detective craft.

In 1971, C11 adopted an experimental criminal intelligence computer system (MEPO 3/2033). However, it was beset by technical and staff difficulties. It broke down frequently and inputting work proved unpopular with staff. In 1973, having collected together all the intelligence available to it, the branch held 130 dockets on individuals 'about whom so much data is held that it cannot conveniently be held on cards' (that is, those of the greatest interest to detectives), intelligence on 2,500 individuals of 'major interest' and 50,000 nominal records containing particulars of individuals and companies. At that time, the branch was made up of 82 staff (71 police officers and 11 civilians) under the command of an officer of the rank of Commander. As an indication of the growth of the branch, by 1983, having successfully computerized its data, it held a total of 152,186 records (HL Deb 1983 col.969–70).

The criminal intelligence branch is now known by the title Metropolitan Intelligence Branch (MIB). Staffed by a large number of detectives and intelligence specialists, it represents not just the oldest but the largest and most influential force intelligence department in Britain.

Regional Crime Squads (RCS)

The next significant addition to the specialist detective force was the Regional Crime Squads (RCS). Section 13 of the 1964 Police Act included a voluntary collaborative agreement between constituent police forces to establish the squads which came into formal existence on 1 April 1965. Once again, detectives were specially selected from their constituent forces for their 'thief-catching' and craft abilities. The squads' aim was to counter what was perceived to be a growing threat from organized crime, particularly in relation to offenders who crossed force boundaries. Essentially, the nine regional squads were intended to be the operational arm of the pre-existing regional criminal intelligence offices.

The arrangements for the new squads were made in the course of a series of regional conferences overseen by officials from the Home Office Police Research and Planning Branch, representatives of Her Majesty's Inspectorate of Constabulary (HMIC) and force elites (HO 287/665). Each region was headed by a regional coordinator (of detective chief superintendent rank) who was responsible to a chief constables' management committee made up of the chiefs of the participating forces, and an HMIC representative. Regional coordinators reported to the national Executive Coordinator based at the Home Office (which was evidence of the Home Office's continuing influence over policing policy).

Although there largely was agreement on the need for a regional response to the growing problem of organized crime, a personal communication from the HMIC representative for Wales to J. Haughton, Head of the Police Research and Planning Branch indicates that the squads may have been resisted in some corners. He commented, 'I am glad that we can make a start on this venture which I have been campaigning for since 1960 and I can only hope that the results will convert such unbelievers as we have.' (HO 287/665a, 4 December 1964). The same communication indicates that Home Office planning for the squad's new branch offices was not as thorough as it might have been. The (unidentified) HMIC member observed that he was:

> Not very impressed by the need for squads at Hereford, Newtown or Abergavenny. Hereford ... comes under No. 4 District [that is, in England rather than in Wales]. Newtown is in the centre of one of the largest expanses of nothing in the country and indeed such crime as does occur is worried to death by the existing CID and uniform personnel who are fairly numerous. Abergavenny is not a centre for crime purposes and has the County Police headquarters there by historical accident only.

In interview, former RCS branch commander N063 said that the squads collected intelligence about suspect individuals or populations and that their officers made extensive use of informers, telephone 'tapping' and the other covert policing techniques that were not routinely available in mainstream policing. This served to sharpen the distinction between mainstream policing and the specialist detectives even further.

3
Intelligence-Led Investigation

Introduction

This chapter continues the narrative up to the rediscovery of ILP strategies at the beginning of the 1990s. Specifically, it assesses the extent to which that iteration of ILP which emerged in the modern era, largely concentrated expertise and resources in the specialist detective squads. It examines the further development of a kind of class structure in policing that has undermined the single service vision for policing that has been advocated by many police leaders in modern times. Moreover, it examines the policing and policy contexts of criminal investigation and detective work in the modern era because their influence on ILP in the contemporary era is considerable.

UBP, intelligence work and the CID

This section is largely informed by previously unpublished primary research carried out between 1967 and 1969 across England; the research was completed by officers attending the Bramshill 'Special Course' and was part of their formal summative assessment.[1] I discovered the data in the archive of the National Police Library. This, essentially forgotten, material may be in the police archive but it is not part of the police organizational memory; certainly, it has had little discernible impact on subsequent practice.

The architects of ILP in the contemporary era could have learnt much from the implementation failure associated with this policy. The UBP experiment provides a good example of the kinds of challenges that public sector change programmes face. It is also relevant to the analysis of ILP because the roots of Britain's modern local intelligence system can be found in that programme. On one level, it simply represented another attempt to revolutionize patrol. However, others such as Reiner (2010) have argued that 'revolutionary' policing tactics like UBP are hugely symbolic; they are as much about legitimating the role of the public police as they are about reducing or preventing crime. They are a response to government and public identification of the limits of policing and are meant to re-establish the role of the public police as the primary agency of social control. Certainly, UBP introduced only relatively modest changes 'dressed up' in the scientific and technological values of the period.

UBP's influence on patrol

Rand noted that by the 1960s, the old 'Shorncliffe' system of beats and patrols that had been introduced by Mayne (and which, as the reader has seen, was perpetuated by the commitment to the *status quo* of the Aberdeen scheme working group) 'had little to commend it other than tradition' and that changes were needed (1970, p.14). However, he highlighted that the selection of a model that favoured mobile over foot patrol was odd, given the success of schemes elsewhere that recently had been introduced, particularly those in the Netherlands, which indicated exactly the opposite.

Following experiments by the Home Office Police Research and Development Branch into the preventive capacity of foot patrol in Manchester, Sheffield, Newcastle and Cardiff a small-scale UBP scheme was piloted in Kirkby, Lancashire in the spring of 1967. Rand noted that the Kirkby experiment produced fast response times to calls for assistance but that 'communication with the public was diminished and therefore information did not flow' (1970, p.14). Consequently when the UBP experiment was extended to Accrington Lancashire, an attempt was made to learn from those mistakes. The best features of the Kirkby scheme were adopted, with the four new mobile patrols being supplemented with eight area officers.

Rand argued that as a result of the claimed success of the Accrington pilot, on 3 July 1967 UBP was introduced throughout the city of Birmingham (1970, p.15). Therefore in just one year, UBP went 'from a small experimental scheme to total adoption in an entire police force' despite the fact that:

> There had not been time to ascertain if there was any significant difference in crime figures, nor had there really been time to allow operational problems to show themselves properly. Even in 1970, it

is arguable that there has been an insufficient time interval to satisfactorily review the trends in the matter.

Williamson noted that the introduction of area policing in Newcastle in March 1967 (as a precursor to UBP) resulted in an 8.3 percent fall in recorded crime and an increase in the detection rate from 40.8 percent to 45.1 percent and as a result, UBP was introduced in the force almost a year later. Williamson clearly was not persuaded by the police data that emerged, commenting that the figures probably were 'spurious'. However, they were taken as evidence of the success of the area system by senior officers and men (1971, p.5). In his view, UBP was introduced in an environment characterized by obfuscation and uncertainty but the police pressed on regardless (Williamson, 1971).

Home Office encouragement to implement UBP often meant tangible rewards for police commanders (the 'carrot and stick' approach, which will be familiar to police officers in the modern era). For example, in Newcastle upon Tyne, the decision to accept the change from beat patrol to UBP meant that 'more equipment – cars and radios' was made available to local commanders (Williamson, 1971, p.6). Enthusiasm for additional resources overrode issues such as the need to consult staff over the changes. Two-thirds of all constables affected were not given any choice in their new duties, and the lack of prior discussion with staff associations led the Newcastle upon Tyne Police Federation to make a formal complaint to the chief constable (Williamson, 1971). According to Williamson, the discrepancy between the elite's conception of UBP and its interpretation by operational officers was a significant factor in its failure.

Given the history of public policymaking and the challenges routinely faced by those seeking to effect change, it can be no surprise that difficulties were experienced during the implementation process. After all, few public policies are implemented in the way that their creators intended and determining whether a policy is a success is no easy feat. In some places there was open hostility to the idea of the abolition of the beat system. For example, in Durham many complaints were received about the low visibility of police officers, particularly in town and city centres (Gearon et al, 1969). In rural areas of Bedfordshire it was found that due to the low levels of crime and other technical problems (for example, poor radio coverage), the system was 'adapted' to meet local conditions (Evans et al, 1968). A major issue across England and Wales was the shortage of patrol officers. The police elite attributed these difficulties to the formula applied by the Home Office to calculate force strengths, rather than to any problems with UBP itself (Coe et al, 1969).

Though it was expected to improve police/public relations, UBP since has been criticized for damaging police community relations by introducing an overly-reactive 'fire brigade' policing style that alienated officers from the communities that they served (Mawby, 2008; Reiner, 1992). The redeployment of 'street police' to motor vehicles to create 'car police', did not achieve the development of strategy and tactics in the ways envisaged by Gregory (1967) and other advocates of the system. Recently, Reiner (2011) has argued that the primary function of the police is peacekeeping. Therefore, police performance should not be judged in terms of the crime rate on which they can have only a marginal impact. Being good at 'fire-fighting' may be as much as the police should aspire to.

UBP and local intelligence

An important feature of UBP was the 'collator', an individual tasked with establishing a local intelligence system that would both inform local officers and act as a conduit for intelligence that needed to be passed elsewhere in the police organization. This was a significant development of the criminal intelligence process in mainstream policing because previously there was almost a complete absence of 'timely information' available to the beat officer or the crime investigator (Rogers, 2004, p.3).

In interview, former detective sergeant N070 said that before collators there were no formal arrangements for collecting information from beat constables. Officers were issued with a 'beat book' which described their beats and patrols and which gave them hints on how to work those beats. He said that the 'women police' (then a distinct entity) 'had some good files on women and children' though the assimilation of that department into the main body of the service in 1973 meant that 'all that was thrown away' (rather than being added to the organizational memory – arguably, because no such memory pre-existed).

Gospel et al noted that the appointment of collators represented 'the start of an entirely new era in police records' because prior to introduction of the new system (1969, p.11); information held by individual constables (about the areas that they policed and the communities and individuals that they came into contact with) was lost whenever an officer transferred, resigned from or retired from the force. N070 said that before the advent of collators, information was held in 'old experienced officers' heads' and nowhere else.

Collators collected information from a wide variety of sources (although a large proportion of it came from patrol officers, from whom the collator would proactively seek out the latest 'word on the street'). They then forwarded that information to others who had requested it or were thought to need it. They maintained a daily record sheet containing information they had collected, distilled and evaluated; a main index of offenders or suspects living on (or who were known to frequent) the division; a suspect vehicle index; an index of serious or unusual crimes; a prostitutes index; and a street index (which included various types of premises of interest to the police such as licensed premises).

This placed a significant and largely unacknowledged burden on collators. After all, they had no previous experience or 'best practice' to rely on and they rarely were given any training for their work. Several respondents, who worked as collators in that period, said that selection criteria for the new posts were applied arbitrarily. Former south-east London collator N046 said that when the system was implemented in his division, the job was given to 'the laziest man at the station'. While former central London collator N059 said that he was offered the post when it was quickly recognized by supervisors that the original appointee 'was not up to the job'. In some cases, those appointed to the role were out of favour with their supervisors. For some, the collator's job was almost a 'punishment posting'.

Many other factors served to undermine the effectiveness of the new arrangements. Two former collators (N030 and N059) said that they worked with little assistance and without any of the technological aids available to intelligence staff today. In the course of their research in the south-east, Coe et al (1969) found that in some forces, collators were regularly given ancillary tasks that took them away from their intelligence duties. In the north-east, collators often worked in cramped and inappropriate conditions (Gearon et al, 1969) and even the strongest advocates of the system admitted that it could be inefficient.

An early Home Office evaluation of UBP found that a large amount of the information that was passed to the collator was never used (Gregory, 1967). The system did not address the lack of interconnectedness in the national intelligence system as it was essentially intended to be a repository of information for local officers. Though collators were instructed to forward information on offenders to the clearing houses at headquarters level, this was an inefficient process and local police received little intelligence in return; a point made repeatedly by my respondents.

UBP's impact was intended to be felt far beyond intelligence work. Gregory argued that it would change the role of supervisors so that leadership would become more important than supervision (1967, p.8). Inspectors would become 'strategists' keeping themselves up to date with crime trends and directing the daily work of sergeants. Rather than spending their time checking up on constables, sergeants would utilize 'modern [*sic*] communications and mobility' to become 'leaders and tacticians' so that supervisors would be able to mobilize forces very quickly (Gregory, 1967, p.8). Gregory imagined 'a sergeant in the early hours ... marshalling his units and carrying out a sweep through the area, checking persons and property' (1967, p.8). He argued that:

> With this method of rapid, unexpected action, the police are on the offensive, using modern and sophisticated equipment to catch offenders when they are off their guard, and to harass them by the necessity of being more on guard than before.

In a sense, what Gregory was proposing was nothing new. That was exactly how the Aberdeen scheme operated. However, the research evidence available suggests that his vision of proactive UBP was wildly optimistic. Certainly no accounts of such events were uncovered in this research. In the absence of such evidence, it can only be surmised that the reactive paradigm continued to dominate throughout the life of the experiment.

UBP and the CID

The popular perception of the changes brought about by UBP, reinforced by the image of the panda car popularized by contemporary British police dramas such as *Z Cars*, is that it was focused almost exclusively on the uniform department. The CID was meant to play a crucial role, with divisional detectives being part of the new 'area' units so that the car beats would be supplemented by 'area' uniformed officers and detectives but in practice the latter's involvement was minimal (Rogers, 2004). It was entirely predictable that as early as 1975, a Home Office study would report 'inadequate implementation' of the scheme (Mawby, 2008, p.280).

In principle, under UBP some CID officers would be supervised by local police commanders rather than by their detective chief superintendent. This, explicitly, was a measure that was intended to break down the divide between the uniform branch and detectives that had always existed. However, just one year into the experiment, Gregory observed that UBP demanded 'a certain basic structure for the CID which was not the same as that in use in many forces' (Gregory, 1968, p.46). It also was clear that the new commitment to joint working was restricted to the divisional CID with no attempt at all made to bridge the continuing divide between the divisional CID and specialist squads.[2]

Unsurprisingly, the commitment of detectives to UBP teams varied from force to force. For example, in Kent and Durham, divisional CID officers were not allocated to the new teams (Coe et al, 1969; Gearon et al, 1969). In Bedfordshire, CID officers were attached to the teams. However, they were overwhelmed by the volume of crime they were expected to investigate (Evans et al, 1968). In Manchester, Salford and Birmingham, it was claimed to be impractical to attach CID officers to the new teams because of differential crime rates. In some areas, detectives carried an enormous caseload while colleagues in other areas were under-employed (Watson et al, 1969; Gospel et al, 1969; Bennison et al, 1968). In Kent, divisional detectives undertook all crime investigation, freeing up the area teams to concentrate on patrol. Though in an attempt to comply with the spirit of the system a liaison system was established between beat constables and detectives (Coe et al, 1969). In Birmingham, it was decided that many of the beats (which continued to exist) 'did not lend themselves to be used as a basis for the organisation of the CID' (Gospel et al, 1969, p.9).

Rawlings (2006) argued that though UBP provided new opportunities for improved cooperation between the uniformed and detective branches, the cultural divide was never overcome because the policy was presented by police managers without any real conviction. A significant factor was that managers always were reluctant to undermine CID's carefully constructed image of detection as 'complex and skilled' (Rawlings 2006, p.65). UBP was intended to revolutionize patrol but its success depended *inter alia* on the cooperation of the detective force. As the reader has seen, this was rarely forthcoming in practice.

Three years after UBP was introduced, the police still could not determine if the scheme had made a difference to levels of crime (Rand, 1970). However, by the 1970s, UBP was the standard method of delivering local policing. Clearly, implementation was something of a leap of faith, there was no formal evaluation before it was implemented nationally and in fact 'scant evaluation research' to assess and support its continuation (Weatheritt cited in Mawby, 2008, p.280). I will later argue a similar leap of faith has been taken by investors in ILP in the contemporary era.

Rather than collaborating with the uniformed branch to deliver area policing, the CID was able to sidestep some pretty substantial changes in mainstream policing by citing local difficulties caused by differential crime rates or caseloads. From this distance, it may be too much of a stretch to say with any certitude that behaviour amounted to the kind of avoidance strategies often employed by elite police units (Skogan, 2008). However, the result was that the CID retained its separate identity and kept its distance from the uniformed branch, and continued to operate according to its craft values and traditions.

Today, there is almost universal agreement that UBP was a failure. Commentators have described it as at best 'misconceived' (Newburn, 2003, p.59) and at worst 'a disaster' (Mainwaring-White in Newburn, 2003, p.60). That should be no surprise. Fundamental flaws were apparent as far back as 1971. Williamson argued that the experiment was always 'unlikely to achieve some of its major goals' and that any gains made in terms of mobility and response times were far outweighed by the deterioration in the relationship between police and public (1971, p.13).

In the case of UBP, seen through the lens of history, it now seems clear that the scheme was understood inconsistently by those who were expected to implement it. Consequently, different people interpreted it in different ways. A significant factor in that misinterpretation was the failure of commanders to harness the experience and expertise of the detective force (particularly the specialist detective force) in crime-fighting in the mainstream. The reader will see that recognizing that fact, those who sponsored or developed ILP models in modern times sought to overcome that division by harnessing a single service approach to a proactive paradigm. However, in those endeavours, they were only partly successful. Given the history of policing, its cultural divisions and the continuing dominance of the reactive paradigm that should come as no surprise.

Commanders in the contemporary era still pursue the single service dream. Commissioner Bernard Hogan-Howe's 'Total Policing' is the latest iteration. Hogan-Howe first popularized the idea of Total Policing in his previous post as chief constable of Merseyside Police and it was common currency in policing by the time he left the force in 2009. In Merseyside, it was claimed that Total Policing recognized the value of an approach in which all the component parts of the force worked together to deliver its strategic aims; the force was, in effect, one team contributing to 'Total War on Crime, Total Care for Victims and Total Professionalism' (Merseyside Police, 2009, p.9). It was only to be expected that his message would be welcomed by a Coalition Home Secretary committed to the idea of policing as crime control and that Hogan-Howe would continue to pursue those goals in his new post.

The Met has been quick to publicize the successes of the new initiative. The raw data, in terms of arrests, vehicles seized, etc. makes interesting reading but perhaps Total Policing should not be judged solely on its headline results. Hogan-Howe's scheme is meant to demonstrate a unity of purpose that the riots of 2011 suggested was sorely lacking in his force. Total Policing, just as UBP before it, should be seen as an attempt to regain legitimacy for the Met in the face of stinging criticism from the public, its political masters and even from some senior police officers (see for example, Pilkington, 2011), over its inability to quickly bring order back to London. Such schemes also are hugely symbolic. In a phrase much loved, and oft repeated, by police commanders in modern times, they 'send a message' to criminals that the police are back in business with both the will and the capability to fight crime in all its forms.

Scrutiny of the CID

At the beginning of the 1970s, the Home Office made a concerted effort to address what it saw as the CID's abuse of its powers. In 1969, Home Secretary James Callaghan appointed Frank Williamson of HMIC to oversee an investigation into corruption involving three Metropolitan Police detectives. Hobbs has noted that Williamson's investigation was completely undermined by the fact that 'information was leaked to officers under investigation, crucial documents disappeared, and senior detectives conducted a campaign of lies against him' (1999, p.1). This meant that Williamson's inquiry was short-lived and ultimately did not lead to any prosecutions; Williamson resigned in disgust. However, the particular concerns about corruption amongst Met detectives raised by that inquiry stimulated the Home Office to redouble its efforts to reform the Met's detective force.

Commissioner Robert Mark

In 1972, Robert Mark, formerly chief officer of the Leicester City Police and latterly an Assistant Commissioner (AC) in the Met, was appointed out of 'left-field' to the post of Met Commissioner with a mandate to deal with detectives' corruption. Mark was an outsider but he attempted to exploit the inside knowledge he had gained in the post of AC to attack the CID's working practices in an effort to erode their power.

As much of an outsider as Vincent had been almost 100 years earlier, Mark found, just as Vincent had before him, that the relationship between the detective and uniformed departments was problematic. He noted that the uniformed officer continued to bear 'the brunt of violence ... and he has long resented the airs and graces of the CID [which continued to regard] ... itself as an elite body, higher paid by way of allowances and factually, fictionally and journalistically more glamorous' (cited in Hobbs, 1988, pp.72–3). With the aim of eradicating CID corruption, Mark overhauled the department, removing CID commanders, replacing them with senior officers from the uniformed branch, and bringing in a system of 'interchange' between the branches so that detectives no longer would serve in the CID for the whole of their professional lives.

Systematic CID corruption practised by the 'firm within a firm' of London detectives was the major focus of Mark's time in office (Cox et al, 1977, p.5). Cox et al argued that Mark was aware that CID corruption was a significant problem but that he did not appreciate its scale or extent until he assumed the leadership of the force. Early in his tenure, fresh allegations of corruption were made against the Drugs Squad and the Flying Squad. By this time, confidence in the detective force was so low that *The Times* newspaper published 'serious allegations' against the detectives of the Obscene Publications Squad 'because the editor and his legal advisers did not believe that if the allegations against the detectives were disclosed properly to the Met they would be properly investigated' (Mark, 1978, p.107). Mark argued that a Home Office investigation of *The Times* was characterized by 'ineptitude' but he was satisfied that the newspaper's revelations had 'disclosed to the world that there was a widespread and ... justified lack of confidence in the way in which allegations of crime by Metropolitan detectives were investigated' (1978, p.108).

Unlike their provincial counterparts, the Met's CID 'enjoyed an immunity from external supervision and investigation' which facilitated a variety of wrong-doing (Mark, 1978, p.122). This fell into three categories. Firstly, there was a comparatively minor form of institutional corruption which included suppressing charges or failing to bring previous convictions to notice. Often (echoing the efforts of the post-war Ghost Squad) this kind of corruption was done under the cover of recruiting informers. Secondly, more 'spectacular corruption' affecting senior officers or the specialist squads and thirdly, a 'widespread general acceptance; of noble cause corruption that was "necessary" to bend the rules' (Mark, 1978, p.122). Mark considered that he owed it to the honest detectives to root out the bad. He was moved to comment that in his view, the CID at that time was 'the most routinely corrupt organisation in London' (Mark cited in Hobbs, 1988, pp.72–3).

As part of a wider programme of anti-corruption measures, Mark established 'A10' Scotland Yard's first internal affairs department to take over the investigation of crime committed by members of the CID. The area detective commanders (the modern day equivalent of the 'Big Four') were relieved of their operational duties and instead assumed 'advisory and supervisory' roles (Mark, 1978, pp.128–9). He appointed a new CID commander to take charge of the specialist squads and directed that all detectives serving outside those squads were put under the command of local uniformed commanders. In the longer-term, plans were made for the routine 'interchange' of CID and uniformed officers (Mark, 1978, pp.128–9). Rawlings has argued that Mark's efforts in this regard (which very much mirrored Vincent's efforts almost 100 years earlier) were an attempt to stimulate the moral re-education of detectives through enforced transfers into the uniform (2006, p.65).

Mark's reforms brought some success in the fight against corruption. Within a year, two officers a week were leaving the force 'prematurely' and bank robbery, 'a crime particularly associated with police corruption' had fallen from the 65 offences recorded in the previous year to 26 offences in 1973 (Hobbs, 1999, p.1). In April 1973, Mark appointed Deputy Assistant Commissioner Gilbert Kelland to investigate charges of corruption against Scotland Yard's Obscene Publications Squad (OPS). Working on information provided by jailed Soho pornographer Jimmy Humphreys, Kelland and his hand-picked team of detectives exposed a long-standing criminal conspiracy between pornographers and those charged with policing them (Tomes, 2004). The exposure led to the conviction of a dozen detectives, including a commander and a chief superintendent. Kelland's reward was to be promoted to the post of Assistant Commissioner 'A' department with responsibility for uniformed policing and in August 1977, following Mark's resignation, he was transferred to the post of Assistant Commissioner (Crime) (as the post of Director or Chief Constable of the CID had been redesignated) by Mark's successor David McNee (Tomes, 2004).

Hobbs' account of the interaction of detectives and criminal entrepreneurs in the East End of London in that period, offers a fascinating insight into the reflexive occupational culture of the CID in the 'urban milieu' (1988, p.2). The working personality of detectives was marked out by 'deceit, evasiveness, duplicity, lying, innuendo, secrecy, double talk and triple talk' (Hobbs, 1988, p.197). Once CID status was achieved, new detectives 'quickly meld[ed] into the department's style, pursuing its rituals to form a new link in the tradition of the CID (Young, 1991, p.81).

These traditions required recruits to adopt the dominant culture and priorities of the department which included distancing themselves as far as possible from the 'formal administrative restraints' of uniformed policing to allow themselves to deal with 'real' crime (Hobbs, 1999, p.1); that was certainly my experience as a young detective in North-West London. The elevation of mainstream uniformed officers to the CID enhanced their power and reach, signalling a switch from the ordinary to the extraordinary 'from the maintenance of order to thief-taking' (Hobbs, 1988, p.210).

Mark (1978) believed that his changes fundamentally altered the balance of power between the CID and the uniformed branch in London. Cox et al have argued that though Mark may have been perceived as the 'reformers' champion ... some of the people who ought to have been punished were so well entrenched that only time, and the formal process of respectable retirement, could dislodge them' (1977, p.218). Hobbs (1988) too has argued that despite his best intentions, Mark left the elitist detective culture fundamentally intact. Given the sequence of events that culminated in Mark's appointment, it is incongruous that the reforms that brought the Met's divisional detectives under the control of local uniformed commanders should leave specialist squads (perceived to offer the greatest scope for corruption) relatively untouched.

It is ironic that in 1976, Mark resigned his post over plans for a new police complaints system. McBarnet (1981) has argued that Mark was not against further control of the police; on the contrary he argued for the machinery and procedures that could combat police malpractice and corruption. However, he was against a system that, in his view, would undermine internal accountability and reduce his control over his force and resigned rather than be forced to work within such a system (McBarnet, 1981, p.116).

Incidentally, Mark has claimed to be the first Commissioner to implement ILP strategies (though they were not known by that name in that period), arguing that he was forced into that action by 'the refusal of successive governments ... to allow the police adequate resources to fulfil their primary function of prevention' (Mark, 1978, p.293). The police 'long had a shrewd idea of the patterns of major crime and of those involved' which justified Mark's concentration of 'comparatively small numbers of hand-picked men and women to specialise in intelligence gathering and surveillance' in specialist squads. However, as he attested, the numbers involved in such work were small and the vast majority of the force continued to operate in orthodox ways.

Operation Countryman

As if to underline Mark's failure, the resilience of corruption amongst specialist detectives at Scotland Yard and the inadequacy of CID governance arrangements were demonstrated again in 1978 when accounts emerged of the involvement of Flying Squad detectives in armed robberies. The 'Operation Countryman' team of provincial detectives (at one time numbering more than 90 officers) was tasked to investigate London's detectives.

The Countryman inquiry lasted four years, and ended in what is commonly perceived to be failure. However, even though it secured only two convictions, the inquiry cast huge doubt on the idea that 'endemic corruption in the Yard detective squads had been eliminated' (Reiner, 2010, p.82). Perhaps of equal if not greater concern was that the CID, in particular the specialist squads, remained unreconstructed, unreformed and continued to practice what Reiner has termed, the 'standard method of plain clothes criminal investigation' and the development of close, sometimes intimate, relationships with career criminals as informers in ways that 'operated perennially on the borderline of legality' (2010, p.82).

The relationship between detectives and informers, a key element of the detective craft, has always presented a conundrum for police managers. On the one hand, only those with intimate knowledge of a criminal act make useful and productive informers; on the other, those with that level of knowledge are probably involved in the act in some way (perhaps as prospective purchasers of illicit goods or as aiders or abettors of the principal offender). Too often, managers have shown themselves unable or unwilling to solve that problem. Arguably, what the failure of Operation Countryman also shows is that the detective craft was as resilient in the modern era as it ever had been.

Specialist detective work 1970–90

The enthusiasm for the specialist squad system that I described earlier, continued unabated into the modern era. The last quarter of the twentieth century saw the development of new detective departments that had an explicitly national (and increasingly, international) focus. In this section, I continue by examining the national detective bodies, the differential treatment of divisional and specialist detectives and the continuing resilience of the squad system.

National detective bodies

In 1972, the Metropolitan Police established the Central Drugs Intelligence and Illegal Immigration Unit (CDIIIU), the first detective unit with an explicitly national remit. Former RCS branch commander N063 said that the unit was staffed with specially selected Met CID officers and detectives from other Home Counties forces. At the beginning of the 1980s, the Home Office appointed a National Coordinator for Drugs Intelligence to oversee the creation of a National Drugs Intelligence Unit (NDIU) and in 1985 the NDIU took over the functions of the CDIIIU and took up occupation of the same suite of offices at New Scotland Yard. The metamorphosis of the CDIIIU into the NDIU largely reflected a desire on the part of the Home Office to develop a national strategy to combat the growing problem of drug trafficking. Met detectives were soon joined by others from across the UK and by HM Customs and Excise drugs investigators on lengthy secondments to the unit.

Neither the CDIIIU nor the NDIU possessed an operational capability. Their role solely was to collect, evaluate and disseminate intelligence 'packages' to operational teams within the police or HM Customs. Though the scope of their work was limited by this lack of operational capacity, the units provided a single point of contact for UK and foreign police departments, for Customs and border agencies and for others, such as representatives of the pharmaceutical industry. Though it was located at New Scotland Yard, the NDIU reported directly to the Home Office-appointed National Coordinator. N063 said that the NDIU was the first truly multi-agency intelligence unit established in the UK in the modern era and that apart from its intelligence function, the unit played an important role in informing Government policy in this period.

Matassa and Newburn observed that at the end of the 1980s there was increasing support within the police and the Home Office for further development of the '*de facto* policing establishment' and the appointment of a national body headed by an individual with the status that would allow them to speak for UK law enforcement and with the executive authority commensurate with the role (2007, p.59). Hebenton and Thomas (1995) noted that there was broad agreement on the need for such a development. Much of the debate surrounding the establishment of the new body focused on whether it should have an executive operational capacity beside its intelligence gathering function. The head of the NDIU and the executive coordinator of the RCS were in favour of such a change, whilst others such as the chair of the Police Federation were strongly against it.

Ultimately, the Home Office made the decision to limit the function of the new body to intelligence gathering and to charge the existing RCSs with the operational response. In 1992, the Home Office established the National Criminal Intelligence Service (NCIS) and appointed at its head, a Director-General with the status and authority that the police service had sought. The NDIU and the National Football Intelligence Unit (established in 1989) were merged into the new agency, as were various HM Customs intelligence units. The new body took on the responsibility for managing intelligence on national and international crime and also for producing an annual UK threat assessment.

The assessment considered the various threats to the nation from serious and organized crime, attempted to forecast developments in those areas and was intended to inform policing policy. However, N063 said that the assessment very much represented NCIS's view of the world because it was not informed by any intelligence analyses from forces. Intelligence analyst N084 said that in the early days of the NIM, there was a notion (part of David Phillips' original 'Big Idea' for the model) that intelligence assessments generated in forces would be used to inform the threat assessment. However, she said that those aspirations seemed, 'very quietly' to have been abandoned during the implementation process.

Soon after NCIS was established, further plans were announced for a national detective agency. The Police Act 1997 created the National Crime Squad (NCS) from the existing RCSs and placed NCIS on a statutory footing. The expectation was that the NCIS would manage the intelligence and the crime squads would provide the operational capability and expertise that the CDIIIU and the NDIU had lacked. In interview, N063 said that divisional detectives had little contact with the NDIU but that NCIS' facilities were used increasingly by RCSs and forces' HQ detectives unit as the NCIS matured.

N063 said that detectives' perception of the national policing arrangements was that the NCS was first amongst equals. Though on the surface NCS and NCIS enjoyed a symbiotic relationship, in practice the NCS generated most of its operations itself and would happily have ignored the NCIS except for the latter's monopoly control of telephone interception by the police. Serious Crime Squad detective N079 said that the popular perception of NCIS within police circles was that with no operational capability of its own, it was no more than a talking shop which occupied 'the ivory towers of Spring Gardens (its HQ in Vauxhall, London) without much real purpose'.

NCIS' lack of credibility was commented upon by many respondents in this study. Given the status of specialist detectives in policing, it is perhaps surprising that it was thought of in that way. One reason was the relative invisibility of NCIS' work but other factors such as the high proportion of civilian support staff employed in the agency (who could not be expected to understand, nor easily assimilate, the detective craft) and the attitude of the modern police service to intelligence work were also significant.

NCIS played a key role in developing the NIM (incidentally, the NCS played no meaningful part in its development) and promulgating it across the police service. However, the organization's 'distance' from the mainstream (both in terms of its national and international remits and the secrecy with which it generally operated) meant that NCIS' message that the NIM could revolutionize intelligence work and investigative practice never carried the weight that an objective observer might expect.

Controlling the detectives

At the organizational level, the accountability of the detective force is established through a hierarchical rank structure that provides a level of supervision aimed at producing a disciplined and responsible force. Just like their uniformed colleagues, detectives are subject to a police disciplinary code that may punish inappropriate conduct. Maguire and Norris argued that understanding the supervision of detectives and criminal investigations was the key to understanding CID inefficiencies and malpractice. In their view, the continuing 'frequent, informal contact' with criminals was but one factor in what they perceived to be the wider problem of 'supervision' (1992, pp.23–4).

Maguire and Norris felt that supervision in the CID was problematic because even though the supervisory ratio was higher than in the uniform department, there was much less actual supervision of detectives' work and CID officers of all ranks saw supervision as 'of necessity different to that in the uniform branch ... Supervision had to be based on trust rather than "checking up on people'" (1992, p.24). The final element of 'the problem' was the tendency of supervisors to carry their own individual caseload and to engage in activities similar to those undertaken by their juniors so that supervision was pushed into second place 'behind the job of clearing up crime'.

Divisional CID work largely was more transparent and accountable to uniform commanders than specialist detective work. The dual chain of command, under which divisional detectives worked, pulled staff in different directions. As divisional personnel, they were responsible to the local uniformed commander but they also had answered to the head of the CID at force headquarters. Maguire and Norris argued that the system reinforced the idea of the CID as a 'firm within a firm' because it 'generated periodic controversy and argument exacerbated by traditional rivalries ... and resentment ... of the tendency of CID officers to by-pass local uniform branch structures' (1992, p.26).

Research into specialist detective squads, revealed much about their ability to operate 'in the shadows', to distance themselves from internal supervision and scrutiny (Morgan et al, 1996).[3] Most squads professed to support force objectives. However, in practice those rarely translated into measurable operational standards and there was little use of performance indicators to monitor their work (Morgan et al, 1996). Maguire and Norris (1992) found that there was rigorous managerial control over activity and personnel in the squads they visited. However, this was not replicated across all forces.

Morgan et al (1996) were critical of the way in which force executives failed to scrutinize squad work. Squads accumulated only a very limited amount of management information so that their total running costs were rarely calculated (Morgan et al, 1996). Moreover, day-to-day operations were conducted independently of BCUs, and little information was available (either to the researchers or the BCUs) about how they generated work. Formal agreements to provide assistance to BCUs existed only in respect of surveillance. This severely limited BCUs' ability to obtain assistance for policing problems in the mainstream (Morgan et al, 1996). The reader will see in the case study chapters that this continued to be a significant issue in policing.

The relationship between the specialist detectives and the other sections of the service was an uneasy one. This was partly attributable to organizational history and partly to mutual suspicion over each other's motivations and aims. As the foregoing analysis has shown, suspicion hindered effective information sharing between the two. In interview,

NCIS executive N102 pointed to a further divide between the CID and the uniformed branch. He said that there was never a culture of intelligence, or of intelligence work, in mainstream policing. Detectives were reluctant to share information freely for fear of compromising investigations or revealing that they were interested in particular individuals or groups and, in the NCIS executive's view, there was never enough of a drive to get information out of people's heads into some kind of organizational memory. It might also be considered that the sharing of information was against the detective craft rules.

Often, the best sources of intelligence were kept from local officers. Information from informers, described by former detective inspector N055 as the life blood of the specialist squads, was never entered into the local intelligence system. Clearly, there were issues that today would be included under the heading of 'duty of care' (particularly in relation to the well-being and safety of the person providing the information). However, in the view of former South London collator N046, this was because informers were 'in the main down to CID staff' with whom collators had a 'bad' relationship. He said that as a local collator in the 1970s, he had never once received information from the CID. He remained convinced that even when appropriate safeguards were put in place, CID officers' belief in the dictum 'knowledge is power' was central to the detective craft and that 'need to know' always took precedence over the 'need to share'.

In the same vein, former West London collator N030 said that officers from specialist squads refused to share intelligence with their uniformed colleagues. They routinely carried out 'night raids' on the collator's office so that local officers could not identify those subjects of interest to the squads. Former south London collator N046 said that when officers from specialist squads visited his office during the day, they would go straight to the intelligence records without any invitation and often had to be asked to introduce themselves and to explain the purpose of their visit. It was the experience of ACPO member N03, that the CID made a contribution to local intelligence in this period but 'it was on their terms' and usually 'historical rather than current' and therefore in practice rather less valuable. There was little recognition by the CID of the benefits of a single service approach in this era because their craft conventions just would not allow it.

The resilience of the specialist squads

As I argued earlier, the Home Office and the police elite recognized the advantages of reforming the CID by bringing it under the control and influence of the traditionally more disciplined and better supervised, uniformed branch. However, attempts in the 1960s (through the UBP experiment) and in the 1970s and 1980s (as a response to the uncovering of CID corruption and malpractice) were only partially successful. Given the foregoing analysis and the sequence of events that led to Mark's appointment as Commissioner, and the subsequent reforms that brought divisional detectives under the control of local uniformed commanders, the squad system has proved, and continues to prove, to be extremely resilient.

Morgan et al (1996, p.3) argued that there was a need for a wide-ranging review of the very existence of specialist squads. In their view, the case for the squads was not made because of the lack of information about what they actually produced and too little attention was paid to weighing up the balance between the 'classic alternatives – squad or BCU'. Waddington criticized specialist squads in this period for exacerbating problems in mainstream policing by allowing the more capable officers to escape from the 'drudgery' of uniform patrol thereby 'deskilling' mainstream policing which was left to deal with the 'rump' of tasks for which no one else in the police organization wanted responsibility (1999, p.232). Whilst Reiner argued that the uniformed branch was treated as merely a reserve from which 'high-flying potential specialists could be drawn' (2010, p.92).

Squad managers emphasized their compliance with the administrative aspects of guidance from central authorities but in practice they focused on complying with those guidelines rather than attempting to achieve intended outcomes (in other words, squads were well practised at achieving what Goldstein (1979) has called 'administrative competence') (Morgan et al, 1996). This seemed to satisfy force executives who, despite the fact that their forces fell short of meeting centrally-imposed targets, continued to view specialist units as permanent and did not periodically review whether the arguments for setting up, continuing or disbanding the squads remained relevant. It has been noted that one supposed advantage of specialist units is that they can be 'dissolved when conditions and priorities change' (Waddington, 1999, p.233). However, Morgan et al (1996) found that alternatives to the squad system (such as providing a central source of expertise and guidance which could be accessed by investigating officers from BCUs) received little or no consideration.

At the end of the twentieth century, commentators acknowledged that the divide between the CID and the uniform branches was as wide as it ever had been. Though some researchers highlighted the differential treatment of the specialist detective force, little attention was given to why the police elite continued to afford it that latitude and that is a question that is worth some attention here. In the first half of the twentieth century, the elite saw the detective force and, increasingly, the specialist detective force, as the means by which many of their most challenging policing problems would be resolved. The analyses of the formation of the Flying Squad and the SDS in particular, provided compelling evidence to support that contention.

The establishment of the SDS also demonstrated that in response to political pressure, the police elite was not averse to turning a blind eye to ethically questionable means to secure what it perceived to be morally good ends. Its reluctance to challenge the CID, to bring it into line, was based on self-interest. According to that thesis, the continuing divide between the branches was a price worth paying. Senior commanders continued to defer to an unreconstructed specialist detective force in the second half of the century.

That is not to suggest that the specialist detective force always had things its own way. From time to time, the elite was forced to take, very public, action against particular squads (such as the Obscene Publications Squad in London – see Cox et al, 1977) or the Serious Crime Squad in the West Midlands (Hansard, HC Deb 25 January 1989) but otherwise, in the modern era, commanders rarely asked questions about the methods squads used. Where reform was considered, usually that was only in the context of the dissolution or reorganization of individual squads rather than the reform of a system which despite its successes reinforced divisions and challenged the single service ambition.

Policing with intelligence

Good intelligence might be considered to be essential for policing but as the foregoing analysis has shown, even though it was core business for specialist detective units, it was not considered important in the mainstream. Partly, this was a consequence of the policing styles that were adopted (or that evolved) in the mainstream, so that routine policing was essentially reactive in nature whilst specialist detective work largely was proactive. Reactive approaches represent the traditional 'fire brigade' style of policing that gives priority to responding to day-to-day demands. Proactive approaches often prioritize 'longer-term planning and agendas set by the police' (Maguire, 2008, p.437). Employed by the specialist detective force those approaches invariably involve the targeting of suspect individuals or groups. However, it must be highlighted that specialist detectives represent only a very small proportion of the detective force and that most detective work follows the reactive tradition.

Flood (2003) argued that a factor in the neglect of intelligence work was that traditionally most forces were too preoccupied with investigating reported crime even though they accepted the possibility that good intelligence systems might eventually help to reduce the overall level of crime. Therefore the mainstream reactive policing tradition meant that too great an act of faith was required to invest more widely in the intelligence function as there was no history of intelligence gathering in any formal sense outside the Special Branch and other specialist detective units.

The Baumber Inquiry

It was not until ten years after the introduction of the collator system that any serious attempt was made to raise the status of intelligence work in the mainstream. In 1974, ACPO established a sub-committee on 'Criminal Intelligence' chaired by G.H. Baumber, ACC of West Midlands Police. Between August 1974 and May 1975, the Baumber committee set to its task by visiting a number of police forces in England, Wales and Scotland and an RCS headquarters.[4] Baumber also commissioned a survey of the chief constables of England and Wales. He identified the absence of a common vision or strategic aim for intelligence and identified that in the 1970s there was not even a commonly accepted definition of the term in mainstream policing (ACPO, 1975).

Baumber found that the training offered to intelligence staff, where it was offered at all, was extremely limited. The selection and training of staff involved in intelligence work has always been an issue. Many have questioned the adequacy of intelligence training in mainstream policing in this period. In summary, local intelligence officers received little instruction for the duties they were expected to undertake with many posts being filled by officers who were unfit for (or otherwise unable to carry out) operational duties. This was in stark contrast to British military intelligence and the security services where intelligence work was always considered the preserve of the sharpest and most able minds (see for example Herman, 2001).

In an attempt to remedy what he had called a 'haphazard and controversial subject', Baumber recommended minimum standards for the collection and management of intelligence and a process for the development of intelligence, known as the intelligence cycle, that remains fundamentally unchanged today (ACPO, 1975, p.26). Baumber recommended improvements in the police intelligence structure (for example, by establishing new intelligence units at force, regional and national levels to provide an 'accountable chain of responsibility' for intelligence work) and in the training of intelligence staff (highlighting, for example, that it should be a 'countrywide requirement for every police officer to be 'educated as to the criminal intelligence process') (ACPO, 1975, p.27). However, this was long before ACPO had agreed its policy of 'presumption in favour of compliance' and Baumber seems to have been well aware that there was no guarantee that his recommendations would be accepted. Sensitive to those considerations, Baumber favoured the fudge of 'general principles' for intelligence work which could be adapted to local conditions (ACPO, 1975).

Interestingly, in terms of the subsequent development of intelligence work, Baumber and other committee members visited Thames Valley Police headquarters to view an experiment in 'computerized criminal intelligence'. He concluded that work was not sufficiently advanced to allow the committee to come to a decision on the potential of the end product (ACPO, 1975, p.27).[5] The result was that the possibilities offered by computerization of intelligence records in mainstream policing, were largely ignored for a generation.

The Ratcliffe Inquiry

In 1986, frustrated with its lack of progress in implementing a national intelligence system worthy of the name, ACPO commissioned a further study under A.B. Ratcliffe, ACC of Cambridgeshire Constabulary. Ratcliffe credited Baumber with being the first in the service to acknowledge that intelligence was more than the information obtained from informers. However, he found that few of Baumber's recommendations had been implemented (ACPO, 1986). Intelligence staff remained untrained and intelligence units were ill-equipped to meet the challenges they faced. Few chief officers had established force intelligence bureaux and even where such units were introduced, there was wide variation in their staffing and capability, and the proposed national intelligence office received little further consideration. Just as Baumber had done before him, Ratcliffe emphasized the need to coordinate intelligence gathering activities, to police in a more intelligent way by making better use of information to direct operational activity and to guide resource allocation. However, he was no more successful than Baumber in effecting meaningful change.

Flood (2003) and Grieve (2004) separately have argued that the service ignored the ACPO reports because it did not value intelligence. Skogan too has noted that intelligence is an important organizational function that often is 'short changed' (2008, p.29). Moreover, in interview, former RCS branch commander N063, reflecting on his experiences of police intelligence work, said that 'I always thought that we were the worst at what we should have been best at'. Now, one can only speculate why established models such as those used by the armed forces, the security services, and others highlighted by scholarly research in the USA appear to have been ignored. However, it may be that a different analytical framework is required. Sharing intelligence means sharing knowledge which can mean relinquishing power and control and breaching those unspoken craft rules. Conversely, it may be argued that establishing new knowledge systems can mean gaining power and control. Perhaps, it is that gain (or loss) of power and control that chief officers have resisted. As the reader will see that certainly was a factor in my Urban case study.

HMIC thematic inspection of intelligence

Unresolved, the debate about intelligence raged on and in 1997 yet another inquiry was commissioned; in this case by HMIC rather than by ACPO. The inquiry took the form of a thematic inspection of the intelligence capacity of the police forces of England and Wales. The inspectors made a number of recommendations to improve intelligence work in the UK (HMIC, 1997, pp.34–5). Most relevant in the context of this study were: that forces should appoint a senior officer, a 'director of intelligence' (DOI), to take ownership of the intelligence assets held by the force; that forces should publish an intelligence strategy with clearly defined aims, communicated to all. That they should establish a properly integrated intelligence structure from BCU through to force level and, that forces should adopt 'formal tasking criteria' for the deployment of its specialist units and introduce costing and evaluation of completed operations (all of which in due course became key elements of the NIM). HMIC's instructions signal that these structures and processes, which the reader might consider essential for effective, efficient and economic investigative strategies, largely were lacking in most forces in this period.

Stevens (2001) (a former Met Commissioner) described an intelligence ideal. He likened the police intelligence system to a pyramid. At its base were the basic command units, going up through force headquarters to upper levels populated by national and international agencies (such as NCIS and then SOCA). Stevens said that for the model to work effectively, it had to have structures that allowed intelligence to flow freely at and between every level and between agencies. The most important structures were at the local or BCU level because it was there that most officers operated and that most intelligence was collected. However, the intelligence process was just as important. It had to be understood by everyone.

As the reader can see, in setting out his ideal, Stevens glossed over many of the problems in intelligence work. Though a more objective commentator may question whether the evidence revealed by the inspection justified the optimism expressed in its report, HMIC (1997) professed itself impressed with the progress that many forces were making in developing their intelligence capability according to Stevens' ideal. However, its description of the different directions that forces across the UK were taking (praised by the inspectors as 'indicating an increasing focus on intelligence-led policing styles') also illustrated the lack of coordination of intelligence work in this era. Notably, one of the forces singled out for approval was Kent Police. Kent was commended for having restructured its 'policing philosophy around an intelligence led, proactive approach' particularly in its piloting of a new crime management model (HMIC, 1997, p.39). I will go on to examine those developments later. What was obvious was that a real commitment to intelligence work in the mainstream could open up the policing habitus to a variety of new approaches and it is to those novel approaches that I next turn.

4
ILP in the Contemporary Era

Introduction

This chapter traces the emergence and development of modern day ILP models in Britain. The first of those, the Kent Policing Model (KPM), is acknowledged as the template for intelligence-led strategies across the developed world. The second, the National Intelligence Model (NIM) (an elaboration and extension of the KPM), represents the apotheosis of ILP in the UK in modern times. In critically examining those models, I draw on secondary data and on primary research in the form of interviews I conducted with senior police officers and other officials who either were directly involved in commissioning, designing, or implementing one or both of the models.

Policing Kent

Tilley has argued that ILP, as we understand it in modern times, began with the development of the 'extensive and influential' KPM in the early 1990s (2008, p.313). The driving force behind both the KPM and the NIM that succeeded it, Sir David Phillips, the Kent force's chief officer, sought alternatives to the reactive policing styles that had dominated mainstream policing in modern times. His aim was to break what the Audit Commission (1993, p.40) had described as the 'vicious circle of reactive policing'.

An ACPO member who later was to play a key role in development of the NIM (N03) said that at the beginning of the 1990s, at Phillips' prompting, the ACPO council agreed to move the police organization from its entrenched reactive position. He said that the challenge was to manoeuvre the service 'into a position where it started to focus its efforts ... on those people who were causing the most problems' in a smarter, more proactive way. Some considered that shift to be revolutionary but, as the reader has seen; in reality it simply mirrored debates within the Dixon Committee some 60 years earlier.

Those matters do not necessarily inspire great philosophical debate. The police invariably need to do, and to be seen to be doing, more to combat crime. Policing largely is task-focused because it must be. A shift to a proactive paradigm seemed to offer the prospect of success and also was likely to meet with the approval of the service's political masters. However, the shift from the traditional reactive to a proactive paradigm risked changing the police/public relationship in ways that may threaten police legitimacy (Waddington, 1993).

That is because reactive policing largely relies upon members of the public deciding when a situation has become so intolerable that it requires police involvement. When a situation unfolds so that something is happening 'which ought not to be happening and about which something ought to be done NOW!' (Bittner, 1974, p.30). By that analysis, it is not the police's definition of order but the public's that holds sway. In complete contrast, ILP often entails the imposition of a police conception of order on the public and potentially, the reconstruction of the social world). That is a hugely significant shift that hitherto has received relatively little attention; it is a subject to which I return later.

The KPM did signal an important development in policing at the end of the twentieth century. Its influence on policing discourse in England and Wales was immense. It put Kent on the map as a progressive, dynamic and future-oriented force and gave its leaders a platform from which to proselytize the methods they had, putatively, inculcated in their force. Although many other forces in England and Wales went on to preach the same ILP mantra and to adopt some of the tools and tactics that could have underpinned real ILP strategies, very few carried through the structural changes that were necessary to produce the genuinely integrated system that the mainstreaming of ILP required (Maguire, 2008).

Kent's Crime Management Model

The first stage of the plan was to find a way to manage demand. In 1993, Kent established a 'Force Intelligence Review Team' (FIRT) with a brief to formulate an ILP strategy for the force. The team first produced the 'Force Intelligence Review', which established the framework for the KPM, which would be underpinned by a new crime management model. Kent commander N02 became a significant figure in that process. He and other senior commanders shared Phillips' vision. Though it was the latter's policy entrepreneurship that was key to changing the culture of the force.

Despite the explicit focus on proactivity, the architects of the KPM acknowledged that response (or reactive) policing would continue to feature heavily in the mainstream. However, they hoped the new strategies would lead to a new management system that might reflect the reduction in demand for its services. In turn, that would break the force out of the response mode, which took up all of its operational resources, and prevented the development of longer-term intelligence-led responses. This would provide its leaders with the capacity to resource the longer-term problem solving measures that FIRT members had identified. The first stage in this process was the introduction of a new Crime Management Model (CMM).

Launching the CMM, the force introduced new crime and incident desks. Their purpose was to screen incoming enquiries from the public and to identify those which required police attendance. In principle, calls that did not require attendance would be dealt with quickly and efficiently by telephone so that the force's scarce operational resources could be directed to those that really required attendance. That would establish 'tactical capability' that hitherto had been lacking. In practice the system allowed the force to manage demand but the Kent commander was concerned that those efforts focused on finding ever more sophisticated reasons for not dealing with crime.

N02's major concern was that the force's CID, which had become 'hidebound' and were locked into 'old reactive investigative concepts', controlled the crime management units. The solution was to take the units away from the CID. At the same time Kent supplemented the management units with the analytical capability that previously was lacking. That such measures were required provides more evidence of the division between the CID and the uniformed branch (to which I refer throughout this book). They also demonstrate that divide existed into modern times and was likely to be a major obstacle to the single service vision of ILP.

Kent Police Model

The CMM soon evolved into the KPM. Kent commander N02 suggested (albeit with a degree of levity) that in Kent in that period, crisis management was the norm. He said 'We just used to sit around and wait for the wheels to fall off and then [when they fell off] hid all the bits of paper that talked about wheels falling off'. He said that he and his senior colleagues realized the force was 'running faster and working longer hours to achieve less'. The collective view was that a complete overhaul of the way in which the force conducted its business was required.

Policy transfer is a broad concept, which I discuss later, but it usually refers to the process by which knowledge, policies, or other arrangements shift from one nation or policy domain to another. Some have argued that the case for policy transfer is overblown and that in many cases rather than policy being transferred from one domain to another, the outcome is nothing more than would reasonably be expected in a rational policymaking milieu (see for example James and Lodge, 2002). However, one can see the influence on the KPM planners of investigative techniques that already were in use in continental Europe. The influence of crime mapping and the science of crime analysis that recently had emerged in the Netherlands was particularly obvious.

The FIRT's work presaged need to produce an alternative to the reactive paradigm. The team accepted the finding of the Audit Commission (1993), that most offences were committed by a very few, usually known, offenders (FIRT, 1998, p.3). N02 said that he previously had tried, and failed, to move the force away from its traditional reactive mode of operation but his plans foundered. In part, because of the kinds of orthodoxy and resistance to change in the CID that I explored earlier and partly because of the competition from other sections of the force for the scarce tactical resources he needed to respond to the emerging threats his early attempts at intelligence analysis identified. He said:

> I was threatened with death by the CID for trying to change things ... It was a frightful period. They absolutely hated me because I'd been one of them and was seen as a renegade and a traitor ... I'd just got sick of the fact that we couldn't deal with serious crime.

N02 said that the police needed to become more proactive in their approach. The problems were rooted in the service's history and culture and essentially were of their own making. In his view, the tradition was 'all about opportunity ... the next call, or the next incident. All their effort and careful consideration and planning, is about how you manage events better once the event has occurred'. The FIRT identified that Kent's intelligence systems and structures of the period were equally reactive and passive. The review team therefore set itself the task of creating a model based upon 'cyclical and analytical approaches' that might manage the demand for services and also enable the force to switch 'more effort into planned operations' (FIRT, 1998, pp.1–2).

In a clear example of policy transfer in the public sector, the FIRT's starting point was the British military intelligence model. According to N02, the challenge for policing was to embrace a new set of disciplines that would standardize responses to policing problems, something akin to the British Defence Doctrine.[1] In that, the FIRT seemed to achieve a measure of success. Certainly, writing from a military/security perspective, Herman noted that the new coordinating structure for intelligence work advocated by 'professional policemen' in this period was 'an almost exact replica of the JIC model as it evolved in the Second World War and after' (1996, p.350).[2]

N02 said that the FIRT's aim was to establish 'what worked'. The team found that different methods were successful in different areas. However, the effect of each of them was short-lived. Former detective superintendent N051, who also was a member of the FIRT, said that it proved difficult to persuade frontline officers of the utility of these approaches because it was 'not the sexy side of the business'. Albeit that the underpinning philosophy of the new arrangements explicitly was crime control, which should have proved more popular to action-oriented street cops.

Arrangements were made to train specialists for the new roles they would assume. Indeed, the success of the KPM depended on the increasing specialization of the force. New 'Crime Scene Units' staff received forensic training to enable them to link crime scenes and to gather evidence to identify offenders. New, 'Area Crime Units' dealt with less serious crimes with promising lines of enquiry while 'Tactical CID Teams' replaced the specialist detective units, working on serious cases where greater investigative expertise was required. 'Case Investigation Teams' continued the investigation once an arrested person arrived at the police station.

The foundation of this new structure was the new 'Intelligence Unit'. Headed by an inspector as intelligence coordinator, it provided local commanders with short-, medium- and long-term intelligence forecasts. To accomplish this purpose, units were made up of source coordinators (informant handlers), technical officers (to carry out covert observations etc.) and field intelligence officers whose key function was to develop intelligence packages for tactical officers and, following the Dutch example, crime analysts.

Going forward, intelligence staff would use the tools and techniques of intelligence work that previously were not routinely available in the mainstream.[3] Given that the lack of sufficient or appropriate training for intelligence unit staff has been a feature of most analyses of intelligence work in the last 20 years, the development of the force's staff in that way was perhaps the most ground breaking of the force's plans. What is obvious from those plans is that the CID, essentially, was excluded from intelligence work and only a small minority of its officers worked in the new units, which reported directly to BCU commanders (via the intelligence manager) rather than to CID managers. This was a major factor in overcoming CID resistance to the new arrangements. However, the marginalization of the CID meant that the new units largely were not able to draw upon detectives' skills and experience in investigation and intelligence work.

The architects of the KPM claimed to recognize the fundamental importance of community intelligence in policing. The FIRT (1998) argued that the KPM would contribute to improved intelligence flows from the community. In interview, N02 said 'Actually, you do not build intelligence from the top down; you build it from the bottom up. You've got to have those flows from the bottom or you're not in business'. Formalized police/community partnerships were still some years away so perhaps it is unsurprising that the emphasis in the KPM was on finding local people who could help the police achieve their aims. However, the executive's words highlight just how little progress the service had made in this context in the 17 years since John Alderson wrote his seminal work on community policing, *Policing Freedom*.

The KPM posited a two-pronged approach. Local officers would be in regular contact with 'as many local institutions as is possible, in particular, town and parish councils', while uniformed officers would patrol particular localities (these have come to be known as crime 'hotspots') to provide a visible presence, to sustain local contacts and to support local volunteers (such as special constables and business or neighbourhood watch schemes). Kent's commanders recognized that there was a need to establish a process to coordinate the work of these different groups and thus the phrase 'tasking and coordinating' entered the policing lexicon.

The KPM was piloted in the Thanet BCU. Thanet (which includes the towns of Margate, Broadstairs and Ramsgate) is a holiday centre. Its population of about 123,000 greatly increases in the summer months and both public disorder and crime increase as a consequence. In 1993, the police recorded 15,108 crimes. The range of offences recorded was typical of many towns with the figures dominated by burglary offences though drugs and credit card fraud also were problems (Amey et al, 1996). ACPO member (NIM implementation) N03 said that the BCU was completely restructured. Over a 12-month period, 'key roles of intelligence management, tasking and coordination, operational review and analysis were created'.

The reorganization was intended to produce a tactical capability that would enable intelligence to be worked through effectively. N051 said that CID resistance to the plans continued but that was easily over-come by appointing one of the FIRT members as intelligence manager. N03 said that because Phillips' passion was intelligence he recruited into the intelligence world only officers 'who were the brightest of the bunch'. This was consistent with practice in military intelligence and in the security services and it is a policy that should be pursued much more rigorously in mainstream policing.

Promotion beyond the rank of chief inspector post depended upon the individual filling the post of intelligence manager for at least 15 months. Even though that gave rise to some succession planning and stability issues it made command teams particularly aware of intelligence issues. An intelligence career path, something that is still largely absent in policing, was created so that officers could progress through the ranks to the director of intelligence role. Intelligence posts also attracted additional competency-related payments.

Amey et al (1996) noted that the Thanet BCU's resources were realigned exactly according to the KPM ideal. This was a significant commitment by the force. However, N051 said that little was left to chance. The Thanet BCU was 'self-contained' with few notable policing problems and a supportive community. Thus, it was a safe choice for the experiment. In the former detective superintendent's view, 'if the KPM could not succeed there it could not succeed anywhere'.

N03 said that following implementation there was a significant reduc-tion in crime in Thanet. 'The figures were dramatic for reductions in those four key areas [of robbery, auto crime, burglary and drugs]. Dramatic, you're talking in certainly some areas of reductions of crime of 50 percent and it was very impressive'. However, he conceded that it proved difficult to relate that success to the new model alone as the FIRT made no attempt to separate out and evaluate its discrete elements.

This lack of meaningful evaluation of projects such as the KPM is a feature of policing. My own experience taught me that police officers are 'can do' kind of people, ready to rise to any challenge. Unfortunately, we rarely reflected effectively enough on our work.

Whether a task was completed in the most efficient or cost-effective way or even whether it should have been undertaken at all, were matters that were seldom considered. As the reader will see, mine was not a unique experience.

KPM roll-out

Amey et al (1996) attempted to evaluate the success of the CMM in four areas: the extent to which it delivered a reduction in reported crime; whether it was capable of ensuring the efficient and effective deployment of available resources; levels of victim satisfaction; and police job satisfaction. In terms of crime reduction alone, the results were equivocal. Significantly, their research highlighted that the CMM was designed to reduce priority crime (robbery, auto crime, burglary and drugs) and not to reduce crime in general as some would have us believe. Those tensions between the policing of priority crime and of second order criminality still manifest themselves today (certainly, they were a key concern for BCU commanders operating in the NIM environment).

The force could take some clear positives from the experiment. The scheme increased victim satisfaction with police actions and also provided greater job satisfaction for officers and staff (Amey et al, 1996). Neither of those achievements should be overlooked. Perceptions of police effectiveness are important indicators of police legitimacy. Whilst job satisfaction is a key indicator of morale and an important factor in staff retention.

Kent commander N02 said crime levels in BCUs fell as the KPM was rolled out across the county. However, he could not explain the reasons for that success. He conducted his own research, visiting each BCU in turn to assess the results for himself. He attributed the success of the model to more effective intelligence-led responses by officers, though the tactics employed in each BCU varied dramatically ranging from the targeting of offenders who were disproportionately responsible for high volumes of crime, to connecting up crime series, to hotspot management.

Former detective superintendent N051 said that the new tactics had success but that each was short-lived. He tried to link those discrete measures into longer-term plans, a task he found very difficult. Nevertheless, the official view was that the KPM was a success and that it should be rolled out across the force. County-wide implementation, accompanied by a programme of investment in information technology systems, took place in 1995 (Anderson, 1997).

However, beyond the Kent force, some had reservations about the extension of the scheme. There were 'inherent problems' in using the pilot sites as justification for a force-wide roll out of the model (HMIC, 1995, p.5). The Thanet experiment also was 'unscientific' in the sense that there was no control site against which to measure developments, and it proved impossible to prevent other Kent Police areas from adopting their own versions of the model (HMIC, 1995, p.5). HMIC also considered that the timescale for the evaluation was too short to be conclusive 'given the scale of the change' (1995, p.5).

Nevertheless, HMIC fully supported the decision to introduce the model across the force. In its view, the risks involved were 'understood properly' and were 'being managed effectively' (1995, p.5). Those are the messages that might have come across in meetings between HMIC and the force elite. However, the decision to roll out the KPM was not evidence-based. In a statement reminiscent of Weatheritt's comments on the implementation of UBP, N03 said that there was no objective evaluation of the KPM or consideration of any other external driver.

The implementation of UBP and the KPM are just two events in the long history of policing. Nevertheless, they are noteworthy in the context of this study because they reveal a willingness on the part of police commanders to commit significant resources on the basis of scant information. Subsequently, HMIC commended chief constable Phillips for providing 'a clear sense of direction to the force through the KPM' and commented that the work being carried out in Kent was 'deserving of success ... timely and has a significance which extends well beyond Kent to the police service nationally' (1995, p.7). However, it also conceded that there 'was an element of calculated risk' in reaching that decision (HMIC, 1995, p.7). The reader can judge for themselves whether it was right to take that risk.

The NIM

HMIC's (1997) thematic inspection on good practice in ILP was critical of the police national intelligence structure and called for an improved intelligence effort but, it was complimentary about the changes that Phillips was effecting in Kent. It was clear that HMIC and ACPO shared a common vision of integrating an intelligence-led approach within the culture of all forces. The putative success of the KPM persuaded ACPO that it could be a template for ILP across Britain. ACPO member (N03) said that Phillips persuaded his peers to develop the KPM to be 'a national model that everybody would buy into' and in 1998, ACPO and NCIS agreed the development of a new national model.

Mindful of the need to make the model acceptable to all, one of ACPO's first steps was to rebrand the KPM and thus the NIM was born. In 1999, the first version was announced to the service (NCIS, 1999). In interview, ACPO member N01 said that Phillips used his position as ACPO crime business area chair and then as President of the Association, to market the NIM. N01 became an advocate of the model because he wanted his force to be one of the leaders in intelligence management. He persuaded his police authority to spend £2.3 million 'to put in resources and change the way we did our business' to accomplish that aim.

N01 was completely committed to the NIM. He surmounted the resistance of others in his force by confronting those who had little enthusiasm for the model and by asserting his authority in much the same way as Phillips had done in Kent. He appointed a NIM 'champion' and forcefully instructed his senior commanders to support him. The reader will see later that this was just the kind of action that was necessary to overcome the orthodoxy and tradition associated with police organizational culture. However, this was a course that few other ACPO members were willing to follow.

In September 2000, ACPO met with the Home Secretary Jack Straw at Lancaster House in London to discuss police reform. Interviewed in 2005, NCIS executive N102 who played a leading role in drafting the NIM recalled that at that meeting, Phillips put forward the NIM as a police response to the Government's Police Reform agenda. However, two ACPO members (N03 and N06) said that Phillips was not speaking for the Association as a whole, which was divided over the utility of the model. There was a significant section of ACPO that believed the NIM belonged to NCIS; that it was suitable for dealing with international or organized crime but not something that the wider police service wanted or needed. N01 said that even amongst those who were implementing NIM there was wide variation in practice.

N06 who was responsible for intelligence policy said that despite the resistance of some members, Phillips succeeded in 'selling' the model to the Home Office. Despite members' reservations, Ministers wanted the NIM for British policing. N01 said that in early 2001, he assumed a key policy role in ACPO. He used that role to encourage other members setting about the task with enthusiasm; 'convincing, explaining, and persuading people that they should buy into' the NIM. He agreed an implementation timetable with officials at the Home Office's

Police Reform Unit who, like Phillips, were frustrated at the slow take-up of the model.

Home Office official N013 said that the department's view of implementation in that period was that 'the picture was mixed'. However, it was satisfied that the top-down approach that had been adopted by ACPO (targeting ACPO leads and champions) was 'bearing fruit' and it was content that the policy should be continued. N03 said that the police perception of the period was somewhat different. Though some forces were implementing the model, the police service was 'missing a trick' because ACPO was not driving it, 'it was under-resourced [and] there were no standards'. He said (rather presciently) that his opinion was that implementation was 'doomed to fail' unless more support was forthcoming from chief officers.

ACPO member (intelligence) N06 said that Phillips 'was getting a bit concerned about the rather flaky implementation' and he expressed those concerns in the ACPO council. He said there was an obvious need to 'grip it a bit more' and sensing that, Phillips pushed ACPO hard to accept his plans. Assuming the presidency of the Association in 2001 allowed him to redouble his efforts and at a council meeting in 2002, a resolution to support the implementation of the model was approved without meaningful challenge (N03).

N06 said that this was a key period in the development of the NIM. NCIS received £7–8 million which enabled it to maintain the NIM team on a full-time basis. The team's focus was on proactively contacting individual chiefs 'knocking on a few doors' to drive home the key messages of ILP to the forces. To assess progress, ACPO commissioned a baseline assessment of implementation to be carried out by the NIM team. It visited every force in England and Wales to inspect progress towards 'compliance'.

I have already questioned the notion of aiming for mere compliance. In this context, it is a goal to which organizations aspire in their efforts to ensure that staff acknowledge and comply with relevant rules. Referring to the seeming inability of police organizations to move beyond such limited aims, Goldstein argued that even when the police achieve what they consider to be a sufficiently high level of 'operating efficiency' they seem unable to shift their focus to 'the end results' of their efforts. He noted:

> The police seem to have reached a plateau at which the highest objective to which they aspire is administrative competence. And, with some scattered exceptions, they seem reluctant to move

beyond this plateau – toward creating a more systematic concern for the end product of their efforts (1979, p.393).

Goldstein was writing about US police agencies more than a decade before the NIM was introduced in Britain. However, that argument is just as relevant in the context of British policing in the twenty-first century. Senior intelligence official N050 also was disdainful of the police service's lack of ambition in this regard. In her view, NIM compliance was 'farcical'; policing should be measured against the desired outcomes of a process not according to the degree of compliance with that process. In my view, to date, the efforts of the NIM's supporters to claim any successes for the model have foundered on the absence of any meaningful evaluation of outcomes. Even where it can be claimed that NIM compliance has been achieved it has proved impossible to link that compliance to positive outcomes.

ACPO member N01 said that the baseline assessment showed that the gap between the six forces that he had previously assessed as having embraced the model and the 18 'hardest to reach' forces, had not closed. In other words, even that limited aim of administrative compliance was not being achieved. The Home Office was disappointed with the assessment but against a promise from N01 that the Association would put its house in order, the Home Secretary (David Blunkett) agreed that he would 'pull back a bit' from forcing ACPO to accept the model, which perhaps suggests that he and Phillips had established an alliance to see the NIM through. Former ACPO member N04 said that Phillips' success should be attributed to the 'disproportionate power and influence' the ACPO Presidency gave him and to his having the ear of a receptive David Blunkett and New Labour 'who were so desperate for answers – that they would drive through in a "kick ass" fashion – on what they saw as a recalcitrant and underperforming police service'.

N01 said that he committed the Association to full implementation by 1 April 2004. He persuaded Phillips to write to chief officers individually – 'it wasn't difficult!' demanding they describe the progress they had made in their force. He said:

> I got David Phillips to sign these letters – Dear, (personalised) your force has been visited by the baseline assessment team and we find the following. You will need to do ... if you are going to be ready by the 1ˢᵗ of April. There were ... two chiefs when they got the letters they were straight on the phone ... Various colleagues went out,

talked to them and talked to their teams and they squirreled around and started getting things done ... Everyone then started to move towards April.

ACPO member N06 said that the key was finding common ground between members who supported Phillips' crime control agenda and those committed to what I have called a 'preventative' proactive approach. He said that ACPO wanted 'to avoid the argument between the David Phillips' extreme enforcement position and the community policing people'. One way in which this was achieved was by emphasizing shared interests and common values and maintaining focus 'on the 75 percent that both sides had in common and not worrying too much about the wings'. ACPO's own research suggested that the NIM team's 'diplomacy' in not issuing prescriptive guidelines to forces was problematic. Members needed greater clarity about what ACPO required of them. Therefore, a decision was made to issue members a set of minimum standards so that they could see what full compliance looked like.

N01 said that together, the publication of the baseline assessment, the new NIM minimum standards and the ACPO President's letter resulted in a new synergy in the efforts of ACPO, forces and the Home Office to deliver on the implementation plan. He said:

> I think that's why it caught the imagination of a lot of us. I mean cops and Home Office and others because for the first time there was something really practical that we could implement that would demonstrably make a difference. We could actually say that if we gather intelligence, set out the priorities, we then [could] put our resources behind those priorities.

It was in this period that John and Maguire (2004) carried out their evaluation of the model. Commissioned by the Home Office, the researchers visited a total of 25 BCUs across three forces (Lancashire, Surrey and the West Midlands). They observed NIM meetings, examined intelligence assessments and interviewed intelligence analysts. The researchers also interviewed members of the NIM team and used its assessments of the implementation process to contextualize their own findings. They found that forces were making progress towards implementation of the model but there remained significant failings which were yet to be addressed. Those were: that the commitment of local commanders was inadequate; there was limited input from partners; consultative meetings were dominated by conflicts over competing priorities and concerns about performance; there was a lack of appropriate training; there were large 'knowledge gaps' amongst all ranks, and resistance to the NIM based on ignorance and on dislike of its overly 'academic' structure and language.

These were significant issues that the researchers hoped would be resolved as the model matured. However, the number and seriousness of the problems they identified should have persuaded the NIM team to pause and reconsider the plan it was pursuing. It appears that it did not and, as the reader will see later, unresolved at this stage of the implementation process, many of these problems proved to be intractable.

The philosophical roots of the model

It is worth questioning the model's philosophical roots and examining exactly what its supporters wanted it to achieve. Beyond his interest in and commitment to intelligence work, Phillips (and those who developed the NIM under his leadership) drew on the pre-existing intelligence cycle, intelligence structures and systems developed in the first half of the twentieth century by British military intelligence and the security services, and each of the new approaches to crime control that emerged in the 1980s that I described earlier. ILP strategies highlighted the importance of intelligence work. Community policing and POP strategies pointed to the limitations of public policing and emphasized the key role of partners in solving policing problems. POP also emphasized the importance of intelligence analysis. Just like COMPSTAT in New York City, the NIM sought to empower police commanders to deal more effectively with policing problems.

Moreover, the NIM ideal was supported by a commitment to best value that was emblematic of NPM, a feature of government policy in this period. It could be argued that the NIM represented little more than an eclectic 'pick'n'mix' of those pre-existing intelligence models and innovative policing strategies that emerged in the last quarter of the twentieth century. However, a business process that at its core is underpinned by a real commitment to collecting, analysing and evaluating the best available intelligence to produce meaningful outcomes has a compelling logic that would be appealing on both common-sense and business levels at any time. The NIM was a product of the *zeitgeist*. It is easy to see how in a period in which government was proclaiming that policymaking must be based on evidence of 'what works' (Cabinet Office, 1999), that the NIM would be particularly attractive to policymakers and professionals keen to demonstrate their commitment to that 'evidence-based' policy.

'Smart' policing initiatives like the NIM acknowledge that targeting scarce resources efficiently and effectively is key to preventing crime, improving detection rates and protecting victims more effectively. However, they cannot magically solve the problem of crime; the extent to which the demand for policing services can be managed is questionable. Police work goes far beyond dealing with crime; the police also fulfil the public's demand for a range of services under the broad headings of order maintenance, social service and service delivery.

Despite the NPM-inspired reforms of the 1990s, as a proportion of the overall requirement for policing services, there is little prospect of that demand being reduced. In interview, ACPO member (NIM implementation) N03 said that whilst the model was simply about 'intelligently understanding the threat that you face and policing it accordingly', the NIM can only influence *'proactive planned activity'* (emphasis added). In other words, the NIM could never be a factor in the greater proportion of routine police activity. In his view, the NIM's aim therefore was to answer the question, 'How can we police out problems effectively and resource them accordingly in terms of ... drugs, burglary, and auto crime'?

This is an extremely important point that merits further examination. N03's comments make it clear that despite the public claims that were made for the model's ability to reduce the overall level of crime, the NIM team recognized from the very beginning that the model could provide only a framework for pre-planned policing interventions against those crimes that have come to be described collectively as 'street crime'. That only lends weight to my argument that despite the language in which the model was couched, the NIM was inspired by a crime control rather than a public reassurance agenda.

There is another dimension to that debate which is about police legitimacy. As Waddington (1993, p.150) has noted, traditional reactive policing relies upon members of the public deciding when a situation has become sufficiently intolerable to involve the police. It is not the police's definition of order that is operative but that of the public. Proactive policing, whether that is ILP or even in some circumstances community policing, entails the imposition, by the police, of their conception of order on communities.

The NIM 'ideal'

Before going on to examine the Home Office's interest in the NIM, I want to explain the basic structures and processes that the service promised to sign up to. The reader will see that at the heart of the NIM lies, what appear to be, a simple set of arrangements that ACPO envisaged would underpin operational policing.

Intelligence collection

Force intelligence bureau (FIB) and local intelligence units should oversee intelligence collection. FIBs usually are controlled by the force's director of intelligence (DOI) and are staffed by intelligence officers and analysts. Offices have varied in size, according to the size of the force and the demands made upon it by regional and national bodies. In response to HMIC's (1997) criticism of intelligence work, local intelligence units based on the Kent model replaced the collator offices. Typically, they were headed by an intelligence manager of the rank of Detective Inspector (DI) and were staffed by intelligence officers, field intelligence officers, analysts, researchers and briefing officers. The intelligence manager is meant to play a pivotal role in developing the capabilities of the intelligence unit and in delivering accurate and relevant intelligence assessments. They should mediate between the operational and intelligence worlds, between the action-oriented and more thoughtful reflective milieus, to 'add value' and operational credibility to what otherwise might be evidence-based but operationally-naïve analyses.

Collation, analysis and evaluation

The key to the NIM's aim to manage and make sense of the large amounts of information collected by the police is intelligence analysis. Although there is an extensive literature on the subject, a brief description of 'analysis' and a synopsis of analytical techniques used by analysts working with the model are included here to explain their role in the NIM.

Analysts collect, review and interpret a range of quantitative and qualitative data 'to develop and support recommendations for tactical and/or strategic police activity'. Most are police support staff who attend a variety of training courses that teach them the basic tools of their trade. The NIM codified existing practice around nine standardized products and techniques. However, not all techniques are equal; the techniques predominantly used by police analysts are: subject profiling, Crime Pattern Analysis (CPA) and Network Analysis. Manning argued that the real utility of crime mapping and crime analysis has not been proved. He noted that they owe their popularity to 'those aspects of policing most appealing to the police themselves – their capacity to intervene and reduce officially recorded crime' (2008, p.21).

Subject profiling is the gathering of all available intelligence on a particular individual. CPA is the spatial analysis of crime patterns. The CPA-type analysis most commonly used is 'hotspot' analysis which identifies clusters of crimes or incidents. Its ultimate aim is to identify the nature and scale of crime trends and patterns, or linked crimes or incidents.

Network Analysis assesses links between offenders to identify criminal networks. At the preliminary stage of an operation, the aim often is to persuade commanders that a criminal network exists and/or that some intervention is necessary. However, intelligence analyst N084 said that where the investigation has been taken further forward, the aim usually is to identify intervention opportunities. All such analyses are of course constructs; analysts' representation of the social milieu. The techniques described here are a feature of investigation in the modern era.

However, both Manning and Gill have questioned the 'rationality' that these maps and charts purport to deliver. Manning criticizes the attempt at 'ritualized control' that crime maps may represent (2008, p.244). Whilst, Gill warns that network analyses can be 'over-invested with explanatory power' (2000, p.10). Ultimately, as Waddington (1999) has observed, they can amount to the imposition of a police view of the world; a police conception of order, and a police view of what needs to be done to return that social world to equilibrium.

Presentation of evidence/intelligence assessments

Analyses and other data should be presented in an intelligence assessment. The NIM process begins with a Strategic Assessment, an overview of the policing problems that commanders may face in the following 12 months. They should be prepared by each FIB and BCU. The FIB's assessment should inform the chief constable; the BCU's, the BCU commander. Force assessments should aggregate the BCU assessments. Completed every three months, subsequent assessments simply update the original unless the environment changes. The assessments should be discussed at the Strategic Meeting.

Tactical Assessments should be completed periodically thereafter (either weekly or bi-weekly). They should address only the priorities identified at the strategic meeting thereby ensuring that commanders remain focused on those problems that have been identified for action. These documented intelligence assessments should enable communities to assess the ability of the police to tackle policing problems in their areas. That is to say, if the intelligence picture remains unchanged then the quality of the assessments and/or the police commander's decision-making might reasonably be questioned.

Consultation

Strategic meetings should be attended by: the force executive or BCU command team (depending on whether it is a force or BCU meeting); together with resource owners such as the finance director; middle managers; the intelligence manager, the senior analyst and policing partners (particularly those involved in Community Safety Partnerships (CSPs)). The purpose of the meeting is to discuss the strategic assessment with partners and to decide on priorities, adding them to the Control Strategy (the 'what will be dealt with' list) or the Intelligence Requirement (the 'deferred but monitored' list). The purpose of the tactical meeting is to ensure that the plans made at the strategic meeting are carried through. The meeting should always be chaired by a senior manager. At force level this should be an ACPO member; at BCU level, the BCU commander.

Monitoring identified problems

Prioritization should be the norm – not that the police organization has ever been particularly good at that. Problems selected for the control strategy are allocated to middle managers who take personal responsibility for them. These Plan Holders should be of inspector or chief inspector rank. Partners should nominate a manager with sufficient control over the resources necessary to see plans through (NCPE, 2006b).

The responsibility for monitoring problems lies with the intelligence unit. In the final act of the strategic meeting the commander should issue a set of instructions to that unit requiring it to collect information in support of the control strategy priorities and those other problems included in the intelligence requirement. This action completes the NIM cycle.

Home Office, Policing Policy and the NIM

Home Office official N013 said that the NIM first came to his attention in 2000. He described the early treatment of the model by the Home Office as 'a bit schizophrenic'. Officials were unsure about the most appropriate section of the department to handle the model and at one time it was being administered by two directorates. First, the NIM was part of a project in the Organized Crime portfolio then for a period of six months or so it moved over to the Crime Reduction portfolio. N013 represented the Home Office in a number of discussions with ACPO over the future of the NIM. As a result of those talks he believed that the model would 'sit better' in the Policing Policy Unit. His recommendation to move the NIM for a second time (to Policing Policy), was agreed in the spring of 2002.

He said that the transfer of the project from Organized Crime to Policing Policy signalled a change in the department's attitude to it or at least 'that certainly was the perception at the time'. In the department, the NIM was seen as something that 'was a pretty fundamental overhaul away from reactive policing towards intelligence led policing'. Commenting on Home Office enthusiasm for the NIM, ACPO member (intelligence) N06 said that the NIM was an attractive proposition because it was seen as a rational model that offered the accountability and transparency that previously had been lacking. He said that though Phillips made some ambitious claims for the model, its principles were generally sound, noting 'I think some of his [Phillips'] people over-egged its claims but they said to Government if you have this you will reduce crime because that is what it's done in Kent. That was definitely a selling point'.

Prior to the attachment of the ACPO member (N03) to the implementation team, NCIS executive N102 oversaw the implementation programme from NCIS headquarters. He described an extraordinary meeting there in 2000, with an official from the Policing Policy directorate of the Home Office. This took place soon after Phillips had pitched the NIM to Jack Straw at the Lancaster House conference. He recounted with some amusement:

> They were looking for some new initiative ... I was talking to her [the Home Office official] about the NIM and she said 'If everybody did it what would the effect be'? I said 'I reckon if everybody did it we would get a 10 percent reduction in crime within 2 years probably'

... Of course, her eyes lit up – you know, 'We can tell the Minister we can get a 10 percent reduction in crime'. So, she said 'How much would it cost'? I said 'A rough estimate – looking at what it cost Kent to put intelligence units in place. You'd probably want about £12 million'. She said 'You can have it'. I fell off the chair!

Consequently, in a move that echoed the introduction of UBP in the 1960s, and against the background of New Labour's public commitment to 'evidence-led policy',[4] with little discussion and with no meaningful evaluation of Phillips' plans, policing policy was made.

N102 recalled that the offer of funding was not followed up immediately. However, it eventually was approved by Charles Clarke who was Minister of State at the Home Office (1999–2001). By the end of 2001, the £12 million was provided and was soon spent. This initial allocation of funds was dispersed through the ACPO Crime Committee to forces around England and Wales to fund 'NIM-compliant' processes.[5] N102 said that despite the funding, progress in implementation was 'erratic'. However, the Home Office was sufficiently persuaded of the contribution that the NIM could make to tackling crime that it included it in a 2001 White Paper the instruction that:

> All forces will be required to adopt the core elements of the NIM, which sets out a focused approach to gathering and using intelligence. The model has been validated, and it is approved by HMIC as representing best practice in the use of intelligence to fight crime (Home Office, 2001: Ch. 3 sec.9).[6]

ACPO member N01 said that police executives and Home Office officials that he spoke to, demonstrated real enthusiasm for the model. ACPO member N06 said that the Home Office liked the NIM because it was a rational model for policing. In that context, Phillips was pushing at an open door and just happened to be in the right place at the right time. The NIM had the twin merits of promising crime reduction and of being relatively inexpensive so it was no surprise that it would be welcomed by the Home Office. However, the extent to which he was the right man in the right place at the right time should not be underestimated.

In that context, Phillips should be considered a 'policy entrepreneur'. The defining characteristics of policy entrepreneurs are their 'willingness to invest their resources, time, energy, reputation and sometimes money, in the hope of a future return' (Kingdon, 2003, p.122). They are people who seek to initiate 'dynamic policy change ... through attempting to win support for ideas for policy innovation' (Mintrom, 1997 cited in Savage, 2007, p.129). Invariably, they have a particular expertise, political connections or negotiating skills and they are persistent. In combination with the other qualities described, persistence is 'disarmingly important' (Kingdon, 2003, p.181). Phillips certainly fitted that bill.

Mintrom (1997) argued that policy entrepreneurs promote their ideas by identifying problems, networking with other influential actors in relevant sectors to influence policy debates and by building coalitions of support that advance their causes. Examples can be found in every public policy sector. In the recent history of policing, chief officers such as John Alderson, Kenneth Newman and Peter Imbert are recognized as policy entrepreneurs (and also 'police entrepreneurs') who made a significant contribution to the refocusing of policing, reworking the implied contract between police and communities in ways that emphasized partnership working and preventative activity. However, the influence of policy entrepreneurs in the development of investigative practice has received relatively little attention. In Phillips' case, he networked with other significant actors to build a coalition of support for ILP and the NIM.

Policy entrepreneurship is an important factor in the formulation of public policy. The organizational environment is another. Cohen et al (1972) advanced the 'Garbage Can' model as a means of understanding the policy process in organizations. They argue that in those organizations, people often fail to define their preferences sufficiently clearly, they tend to have only a partial or fragmentary understanding of the organization's vision and aims, and they tend to drift in and out of the decision-making process.

Kingdon has offered a revised 'garbage can' model. In this case, the 'garbage' consists of three process streams: problem recognition, the formation and refining of policy proposals, and politics (2003, p.87). The three streams operate independently of each other but they come together in the policy 'garbage can' to create the policy agenda and to determine the character and extent of policy change. Policy is produced when 'a problem is recognised, a solution for change is available, the political climate makes the time right for change and the constraints do not prohibit action' (Kingdon, 2003, p.88). The policy entrepreneur is often the catalyst for policy change, bringing together the different streams to deliver solutions for 'receptive' audiences who often are neither logical nor rational.

By this analysis, decision-makers in organizations more often seek problems to which they can apply identified solutions and decision-making bodies function as 'a collection of choices looking for problems. Issues and feelings looking for decision situations in which they might be aired, solutions looking for issues to which they might be the answer, and decision-makers looking for work', each 'choice-opportunity' is a 'garbage can into which various kinds of problems and solutions are dumped by participants as they are generated' (Cohen et al, 1972 cited in Kingdon, 2003, p.85).

The concept of the policy 'garbage can' may explain why it was that plans for the development of investigative practice advanced by Phillips (and to a lesser extent Vincent and Mark) that are assessed in this study, were favourably received. Perhaps the success of these 'policy entrepreneurs' can be explained in the context of an idea 'whose time has come'. At the right time and in the right political and social circumstances, an idea may represent an 'irresistible movement' sweeping over politics and society that 'captures a fundamental reality' about the public policymaking agenda (Kingdon, 2003, p.1). Kingdon's 'institutionalist' approach has been criticized on the basis that policy processes and systems are more organized than he suggests (see for example Hill, 2009). However, the reader has seen that the policy-making process in the context of the NIM was just as disorganized and haphazard as the process depicted by Kingdon.

Phillips' policy entrepreneurship was the key factor in the Home Office's acceptance of the NIM. The policy window was opened by the Home Office's mounting frustration with the police because of their seeming inability to reduce priority crime (even though the overall level of crime was declining). It calculated that it was politically necessary to do something to improve the situation and it welcomed the NIM as an almost perfect answer because it looked like a cheap option and, backed by ACPO and HMIC, it was unlikely to get ministers into political trouble. Phillips took full advantage of this opportunity.

Home Office senior official N065 said that his credibility as an operational leader and his powerful advocacy for the model meant that the case for the NIM was 'compelling'. Phillips' credibility was underpinned by his membership of an increasingly influential 'policy network'. Policy networks are founded on the principle of cooperation based on shared interests that may underpin policy networks. In this case, the key actors were ACPO and HMIC members and other senior police officers and officials.

Certainly, there are examples of the policing network's success in this context. However, reform or change in policing is far more difficult than may be supposed and there have been many occasions when the network has failed to influence public policy. Two recent examples are ACPO's efforts to prevent government micro-management of policing through its 'street crimes' initiative and the Police Federation's inability to influence government to remedy a perceived skills and experience shortage in general CID offices across England and Wales.

N065 was in no doubt about the importance of Phillips' advocacy of the model. He described Phillips as, 'a very powerful ACPO President by the standards of chief officers, very analytical ... [who] sounded like he knew what he was talking about, he probably did know what he was talking about'. He said that the NIM:

> also sounded logical because it was and is logical ... this was by far the clearest example ... where ACPO's own capability drove Government policy ... because actually David Phillips talked about the way you processed intelligence, the way in which you develop priorities as a consequence, in ways which were quite helpful to ministers because it wasn't about 'We need more money', it was about, 'We need to use what we've got in a much more effective way'.

Thus, the NIM became a plank in the development of policing policy at the beginning of the new century. Home Office official N013 said that the department took a calculated risk in embracing something that arrived out of nowhere and said '"This is the way that police should be doing things" not "This is the way they are doing things". There's a big difference between the two'. It was the 'synergy' between ACPO and the Home Office that was fundamental to the adoption of the NIM. N065 said that Phillips spoke a language that ministers could understand and easily accept. Ministers welcomed that Philips was honest; 'scathing' about the way the police service did not make the best use of its resources or people.

Former ACPO member N04 said that Phillips was certainly passionate about the NIM and that he became powerful through a 'confluence of circumstances' which included the ACPO presidency and New Labour's search for 'silver bullets', and also the 'the rising power base' of the specialist detective units 'NCS and NCIS and all things central'.

However, N065 refuted the claim that the NIM was yet another attempt to centralize public policing. He said that the model's appeal was that in a landscape heavily driven by a centralizing regime of targets it was police-led, service-owned and was unlikely to get Ministers into political trouble. Particularly when the other service-led initiative of the period, the National Crime Reporting Standard (NCRS) was seen as 'a disaster'. The senior official's words lend weight to Weaver's assertion that 'politicians are motivated primarily by the desire to avoid blame for unpopular actions rather than by seeking to claim credit for popular ones' (1986 cited in Hill, 2009, p.164).

N065 was candid in his assessment of Phillips' importance in convincing the department to support the model. He said:

> David Phillips is a very, very effective advocate for it. I'm not saying it's all about personalities, but I really wouldn't understate that if David Phillips hadn't been President of ACPO, if it had been someone there completely different ... I don't think NIM would have got formally adopted in that way.

However, he also felt that there were unresolved questions of resources, compliance and outcomes, and whether there was any evidence that NIM-compliant forces performed better than non NIM-compliant forces. He said that his sense at the time was that the model tended to be 'far too difficult', to have 'too many variables' but in principle ACPO and the Home Office were in complete agreement. He said that even though the model (just like the KPM) represented 'quite a leap of faith', he could not think of any other example in that era of 'ACPO and the Home Office coming together in quite such a unified way'. He believed in the model as a 'good way of managing business' and that 'almost as an inevitable consequence', it was bound to bring a new focus on achieving more successful outcomes. The senior official's words suggest that the Home Office recognized the potential of Phillips' vision for policing and offered the NIM its unqualified support. However, the reader will see later that even at this stage, the police elite's real support for the NIM did not match its rhetoric.

NCIS executive N102 said that in advance of the publication of the first National Policing Plan (NPP), the Home Office's increasing interest in the NIM was evident. He said that Home Office Minister of State Charles Clarke spoke at the ACPO conference to 'put some beef' behind the model. After Clarke's address, it was the NCIS executive's turn to explain the NIM. He said that he was not well received. 'I said,

"This is what it's all about" and it made the usual impact on ACPO, as you can imagine, "Oh yeah, very interesting, thank you"'. However, in his view, the Home Office was more serious about implementing the model than anyone realized because 'behind it came the requirement for a plan and an implementation date' (which as the reader saw earlier, ACPO member N01 negotiated 'behind the scenes' with the Home Office).

In November 2002, the NIM was included in the inaugural NPP presented to Parliament by then Home Secretary David Blunkett. N013 said that whether or not there was any real evidence that the NIM could deliver any of the improvements that it promised, the Home Secretary considered the model important enough to the future of policing to include it in the first NPP as the changes in police structures and processes that it presaged represented such a 'step change' for the police. ACPO member (NIM implementation) N03 said that 'There was no other way of conceiving it. It had to be in there. That was from the Home Secretary – it had to be in there'.

The NPP promised that the NIM would underpin 'ILP at force, cross boundary and national levels'. According to the Home Office, the NIM already had a 'demonstrated ability to improve the collection, analysis and management of police intelligence and the effectiveness of police deployment'. Though as the reader will see later that point is open to question. Reflecting the agreement between ACPO and the Home Office, the latter was unequivocal in its instruction that 'the NIM should be implemented by all forces to commonly accepted minimum standards by April 2004 *at the latest* (emphasis added)' (Home Office, 2002, Para 3.21).

N013 said that that given the level of investment the Home Office provided for the model there was 'no going back'. Whilst ACPO member (intelligence) N06 said that 'actually any model that allocates resources on the basis of risk, in line with objectives, is a damn sight better that anything we had before ... It is a rational model for policing. *What did we have before*' (emphasis added)?

5
ILP as a Catalyst for Policy/Knowledge Transfer

Introduction

Before moving on to discuss the implementation of the NIM across Britain's police service, I assess the influence of policy and knowledge transfer of ILP strategies in Britain and also the way in which Britain's ostensible adoption of ILP policies have influenced policymakers and professionals in other British public sector agencies, and in other nations and policy domains. I set the scene by examining one of the most significant drivers of those developments; the need in modern times to better manage risk.

ILP in the contemporary era

The contemporary era is characterized by reflexivity; individuals and communities are much more critical of social institutions like the police than they were in the past and this has significant consequences both for society and for those institutions. Unable to meet the expectations that their communities have of them in terms of crime control, police forces across the developed world have responded, at least at the level of rhetoric, by embracing new technologies and innovative, intelligence-led approaches that seem to offer better prospects of countering the new criminal opportunities presented by the technological and social developments of the modern era, and better prospects of managing risk.

Managing risk

Few sociological works in recent times have rivalled the influence of Beck's *Risk Society: Towards a New Modernity*. Beck's central thesis is that in post-industrial society, the state is less concerned with material provision than with public safety. Where the welfare state provided a safety net that mitigated the less desirable consequences of capitalism, the safety state provides security against 'the destructive side effects of modernization' (Delanty, 1999, p.150). At the heart of the risk society is information and information technology, which of course are central to ILP and which, ostensibly, allow the police to manage their resources in intelligent ways to deliver that security. The dramatic upsurge in the demand for information to better manage risk is a feature of modern times. That search for knowledge requires the police to collect information but, more importantly, also to interpret it to make sense of the social world. Risk therefore may be explained as an awareness of the dangers inherent in the social world and risk management as police action (sometimes police inaction) to mitigate that risk.[1]

In an interview, ACPO member (intelligence) N06 said that the NIM was 'ultimately about protection, and protection is about managing risk'. He said that he recognized the importance of the knowledge/risk nexus and that his view was shared by the rest of the police elite. However, he knew his own staff struggled to make the connection between the two (which says much about the action orientation of police officers and the continuing dominance of the reactive paradigm). Summing up that challenge of getting that message to the frontline he said, 'you have got to have information to manage risk. For me this is right at the heart of policing ... but people just don't get it'. N06 claimed that the NIM was 'a very simple model' and that it would help the police to improve that situation, to better use their knowledge to assess risk. I explore that idea of the NIM as a 'simple model' in detail later but it should be recognized from the outset that few in the police organization shared N06's view and, as the reader later will see, there was never a cogent and coherent plan to improve their understanding.

Managing risk through ILP

In recent years, criticism of the police as risk averse has grown exponentially (see for example Home Office, 2010 and Heaton, 2011). That criticism led ACPO to introduce a new National Decision Making Model, described as a 'values-based tool to provide a simple, logical and evidence-based approach to making policing decisions' (ACPO, 2011, p.2). ACPO claims that the model will help police officers and staff to develop their professional judgement and encourage a more positive approach to the question of risk. However, it has not yet been subject to any formal review and whether it does actually assist officers and staff in the way that ACPO hopes is moot.

In principle, ILP with its emphasis on the collection and analysis of information prior to taking action should lead to better decisions around the management of risk. Though for many citizens only the most abstract of notions, there is an important connection between corporate risk management and routine policing interventions. Ericson and Haggerty (1997) argued that the police have become information brokers to a diverse group of institutions such as insurance companies, vehicle licensing agencies, local authorities and other organizations whose operations depend to a greater or lesser (but in each case significant) extent on knowledge of risk. In turn, those institutions influence the ways that police officers think and act so as to create a 'risk society' where knowledge is used to control danger.

Researchers have criticized Ericson and Haggerty's thesis as overly simplistic. Campbell (2004, p.710) argued that Ericson and Haggerty's work fails adequately to explore the relationship between the police's risk management role and the 'prevailing structures of belief in policing's ability to actually manage risk'. Certainly, as the reader will see in the cases studied for this book, the police actually can be very bad at sharing information. For me, Ericson and Haggerty's argument is flawed, not because it necessarily is wrong in principle but because it posits a level of efficiency that is rarely achieved in practice in the maelstrom of the policing mainstream.

Jackson and Bradford argued that people think about their local police in ways that 'are less to do with the risk of victimisation ... and more to do with judgements about social cohesion and moral consensus' (2009, p.1). Even when there may be a heightened awareness of risk, people's confidence in the police to manage risk (given that they lack the extensive empirical data that would provide a 'scientific' level of reassurance) must largely be a question of a faith that is bound to shape those judgements. That faith is negotiated and renegotiated each day through the tens of thousands of routine interactions that take place between the police and public, which ordinarily involve frontline staff who, according to one of their leaders, 'just don't get' the link between knowledge and risk and probably would not recognize the image of themselves as 'information brokers'.

I earlier noted that in modern times the police largely have failed to maximize the return from their two greatest assets; their information

and their people. Given the emphasis that the architects and supporters of the NIM placed on information, it is puzzling that so little
thought was given to the role of frontline staff as routine collectors of
information. After all, they must outnumber intelligence specialists by
a ratio of 50:1. In my work as an intelligence manager, I came to
understand that if I did not tell people what I wanted; I should not be
disappointed when they failed to deliver it.

Unfortunately, many in the police service (including those who put
greater emphasis on the 'need to know' than on the 'responsibility to
share') have been unable or unwilling to recognize the benefits of a
more inclusive approach. That has had a significant impact on organizational cultures and on the training and development (more accurately, the lack of training and development) given to frontline officers
and staff. Inevitably, that has contributed to the continuing insularity
and 'task-focus' of frontline staff who are rarely encouraged to see the
'bigger picture' let alone to recognize their potential to contribute to it.
As the reader has seen, that has held true during a period of democratization of intelligence work through the development and expansion
of Britain's local intelligence system.

Embracing 'what works'

Policy transfer in the field of criminal investigation is nothing new;
Howard Vincent, the first proponent of ILP (though he would not necessarily have recognized his activities by that label), learned his craft at
the Paris Faculty of Law before becoming the chief of detectives. In the
1930s, members of the Home Office Committee on Detective Work
travelled to France and to the United States to study detective work
and brought back policies on records management and the use of
science in investigations.

ILP in Britain first emerged as a coherent and distinct strategy in the
1960s with the introduction of UBP but it is easy to see the influence
on its architects of much of what had gone before (for example, the
success of the Met's Flying Squad testified to the efficacy of mobile
patrol and rapid response; the Aberdeen Policing Scheme confirmed it
even though it was rejected by the police elite for reasons unconnected
with its utility). It was not until the 1990s that the term ILP entered
the policing lexicon, as a result of the work in Kent. Subsequently,
much has been written about the influence of the Kent model on
policing elsewhere. However, less attention has been given to the
external influences on that model.

Policing in the Netherlands

In the 1960s, the Dutch police recognized that in some areas 'owing to the increased use of police motor cars, officers were losing touch with the public and consequently, efficiency was falling off and morale was low' (Rand, 1970, p.14). Some forces took steps to improve police/public relations. One such scheme was implemented in Arnhem. The municipality was divided into discrete sections and specially selected, mature, area officers posted to those areas. The result was that the public [received] better service in the matters of petty crimes and complaints ... there was a drop in offences ... [and] information began to flow from quarters where previously there had been none' (Rand, 1970, p.4). The success of the Arnhem scheme meant that it was emulated elsewhere. By 1977, 50 percent of Dutch police forces had established a system of beat constables. Their primary task was conflict resolution, acting as 'the "ears and eyes" for the rest of the organisation, controlling public order, and solving problems that might otherwise get out of hand' (van der Vijver and Zoomer, 2004, p.255).[2]

When the UBP experiment was rolled out across England and Wales, elements of the Dutch schemes were incorporated into the new arrangements (Rand, 1970). In formulating their plans, Britain's police elite implicitly rejected Dutch fears of mobile patrol (which became a key element in the UBP arrangements). However, it embraced the idea of area beat constables (later to become known as 'home beat' officers in Britain) and the mature local record-keeper. Thus the collator, an individual tasked with evaluating the information collected by the beat officers, the service's 'ears and eyes' was born.

Conversely, an analysis by Dutch policymakers of Britain's UBP project might have pointed to some of the challenges that they might face in developing their own community policing programmes along similar lines. Too late, a study of one of the early experiments in Delft found that it had failed miserably. The evaluation found that:

> The change process started as an experiment in one area and if this was a success, teams were to be installed in the whole force. However, resistance ... grew with time, co-operation diminished, information was not exchanged, CID officers openly depreciated the work of the officers in the teams in the field of criminal investigation, tension between different departments grew, and within a year the experiment was stopped (Broer, 1982 cited in van der Vijver and Zoomer, 2004, p.262).

As the reader has seen, the same sentiments had been expressed about Britain's UBP project some 12 years earlier (see Williamson, 1971).

As a postscript to the above, it may also be significant that one of the NIM's architects spent several years prior to the creation of the model as a liaison officer in the Netherlands. Whilst in that post, he would have seen that the police were giving much more attention to crime mapping and to the emerging science of crime analysis. Certainly, both are central to the contemporary British ILP model.

The systems for investigation and detection (SID) project

Largely overlooked by scholars, the SID project was introduced by the Met at about the same time that Kent was developing its own model, the KPM.[3] Just like the KPM, SID explicitly was about crime control. Commissioner Paul Condon's vision for the project was that it would underpin 'new professionalisms of surveillance, targeting, intelligence and informants, things that will give us a better chance of catching criminals in the act' (Metropolitan Police, 2009, p.1). SID's stated aim was to deliver a long-term intelligence strategy that provided a sustained and focused proactive concentration on prolific offenders (Metropolitan Police, 1998). The force assembled a team of intelligence specialists (hereinafter, 'the SID team') to develop its plan. Grieve has noted that the phrase that epitomized the team's philosophy was 'lawfully audacious' (J. Grieve, personal communication, 27 April 2013).

The project was organized into four discrete work streams. The first involved piloting and evaluating a new divisional intelligence unit structure. The second involved determining and implementing a new organizational structure (fit to exploit the intelligence opportunities that the SID team identified) at the area (at that time the Met was split into five areas) and headquarters levels. The third focused on the identification and development of appropriate information technology. Finally, the fourth organized the work intended to lead to the introduction of an integrated intelligence system; the Met's first computerized criminal intelligence system (this finally was delivered in 1998).

Streams 1 and 2 were managed by the intelligence specialists of the Met's SO11 department (formerly C11) (whilst streams 3 and 4 were managed by the force's Department of Technology). This was significant because unlike earlier efforts, it meant that the interoperability of the force from top to bottom was considered from the outset. That was further reinforced by the establishment of a new management structure and by the standardization of the equipment issued to the intelligence units (although in some cases that amounted to little more than a set of binoculars and a camera to be used from static observation points). Grieve has noted that SID was very much bottom-up, emphasizing the local intelligence cell as the heart of the system and beyond that, the network of cells as fundamental building blocks of an enhanced intelligence system (J. Grieve, personal communication, 27 April 2013).

The new units represented a significant development of the local intelligence collection capability. The SID team recommended a staff of at least five people for each divisional unit; to be made up of two police officers, two members of the administrative staff and a civilian intelligence analyst. The distinction between the administrators and the analyst was made because in this period the Met had trained a small number of police officers to perform the analysis function. However, even then, the civilianization of posts that did not require a sworn officer was high on the organizational agenda and whilst some sworn officers were so trained, this was never meant to be anything other than a stopgap measure.

The SID team made the best effort it could to try to ensure that only 'capable, committed, and enthusiastic staff' were posted to the new units and went as far as specifying that the Divisional Intelligence Officer (Operations) (later re-designated the Intelligence Manager) should be an officer with 'active operational effectiveness ... the ability to communicate well ... the ability to instil confidence in others' and to be 'meticulous, tidy and methodical'. However, just as under the collator system, the new units became dumping grounds for officers and staff who, for a wide variety of reasons, could not work elsewhere in the organization.

Hayes (1998, p.20) (a high-ranking Met officer in the period), claimed the SID project allowed the Met to target resources at the 'six percenters'; prominent criminals who were believed to be responsible for approximately 50 percent of crime in London, and to resist calls to pursue the kind of zero tolerance strategies being pursued elsewhere in the developed world. He said that the project underpinned effective crime-fighting tools, particularly when it was accompanied by 'bursts of activity' intended to target particular crime types.

Examples of these were the 'Bumblebee' initiative against residential burglary and 'Operation Crackdown', which was targeted against drugs (Hayes, 1998). Perhaps a little idealistically to an objective observer but nevertheless clearly a heartfelt view was expressed by Griffiths (a colleague and contemporary of Hayes who like the latter visited New York

City to see COMPSTAT in action) argued that the British police should be 'proud of the enduring magnificence of a policing system that was laid down in the late 1820s and which sees its renaissance in the late 1990s as intelligence-led crime reduction, in partnership with the community' (Griffiths, 1998, p.136).

John Grieve, the Met's Director of Intelligence in this period said that there was a great deal of interest in what the Met was doing. In June 1993, he briefed a member of the Audit Commission in advance of its seminal report on ILP and in the same period discussed developments with David Phillips. In October 1993, those who were designing the KPM visited him to discuss his plans for the Met. He said that the Kent officers seemed impressed with what they saw and took away lots of information about the project and what they identified as best practice, particularly in the context of the organization and staffing of the local intelligence units (J. Grieve, personal communication, 27 April 2013). On one level, the fact that there was a sharing of information and ideas (amounting to a transfer of knowledge) between the Met and Kent about their intelligence structures and processes suggests that there was a willingness at the operational level to work cooperatively towards a common goal for their mutual benefit.

However, I find it perplexing that beyond that routine exchange of information, two neighbouring forces, under the same political and organizational constraints, broadly sharing the same view of the social world, pursuing the same aims, whose efforts were underpinned by the same ILP ethos, do not seem to have considered agreeing to a common strategy to achieve their purpose. That says something fundamental about the territoriality, the silo mentality, in British policing that seems to have existed throughout its long history and which was only confirmed both by my own experiences and by my research.

Problem solving and POP

The influence of both on ILP and on police practice is plain. POP (rather than problem solving) underpins some of the most frequently used tactics in ILP; the targeting of suspect individuals or communities and the identification of crime hotspots. Both of which usually are followed, where resources allow, by the deployment of an appropriate operational response. That may extend beyond patrol and may involve partners in the delivery, if not the formulation, of that response.

There is a clear difference between POP and problem solving. Eck and Spelman (cited in Clarke, 1997, p.31) have distinguished between a 'department-wide commitment' to an aggregated problem implied by the term POP. Whereas, problem solving usually is carried out at a lower (often individual) level and deals with the manifestation of individual problems without, necessarily, any demand on the services of the wider department/force. However, it is worth noting that, in British policing there is confusion over the applicability of each term; the effect is that they are used interchangeably.

I have already touched on the influence at the policy level of POP and problem solving on ILP in Britain. Both originated in the United States and are clear examples of the diffusion of policy; in this case from the US to Britain. Though policy diffusion may be apolitical (Peters cited in Stone, 2001), in this context the political dimension is extremely important because all policing is political. Used routinely in POP analyses, the Problem Analysis Triangle (PAT) emerged from the work of Cohen and Felson (1979), US authors of Routine Activity Theory; a realist perspective that posits that crime occurs as a result of the convergence of a motivated offender and a likely target at a time/in a place that lacks a capable guardian. Cohen and Felson's work was brought to the attention of the Conservative administration, which seized upon the theory as confirmation of the efficacy of its own law and order strategies that tended to focus on a criminal 'underclass'.

The notion that lawbreakers are usually to be found in discrete, readily identifiable, groups is a convenient one for policymakers and for police officers committed to the idea of policing as crime control, alike. I discussed earlier, the view that one of the primary purposes of Peel's new police was the control of the dangerous classes. That idea has persisted throughout the history of policing. As I discussed earlier, Rowan and Mayne, the first Commissioners of the new police were clear that some offenders could only be dealt with effectively whilst they were 'going in'; that is to say, whilst they were in the act of committing the crime. That suggests that the police had a good idea of who to watch out for in the first place.

The idea that criminals can be recognized by their physical appearance or by their behaviour was explored by the early criminologists (see for example Lombroso, 2006). The work of those early positivists continues to appeal to 'common sense' ideas of crime and criminals. The existence of 'habitual offenders' who required police supervision was recognized by statute as far back as 1869 (with the enactment of the Habitual Criminals Act). The Prevention of Crimes Act of 1909 introduced harsher penalties for habitual offenders and a system of 'preventive detection'. Those thought to be leading a criminal life and sentenced to penal servitude, served an additional period of between five and ten years imprisonment during which they were subject to 'disciplinary and reformative influence and employed on such tasks as are best fitted to make them able and willing to earn an honest liveli-hood on their discharge' (Leach, 1930, p.5). The result was that they became very well known to the police and in the event of a crime being reported; they were the first to be arrested by their erstwhile supervisors (see for example Leach, 1930).

Even if they were not always able to prevent crime or to bring every offender to justice, or to document and analyse crime trends in the way that modern analytical techniques allow, it would be wrong to think that the British detectives were not usually finely attuned to the places where crime commonly was committed and to those criminals who in modern parlance would be termed 'prolific offenders'. In an early example of ILP, around the turn of the twentieth century, detec-tives were in the habit of visiting prisons to view those inmates whom they reasonably might expect on release, to once again be their quar-ries. Ferrier (1928, p.9) (like Leach, a career Scotland Yard detective) described a 'crooks club', known to the police, where criminals were 'probably less harmful when assembled together than when scattered throughout the city'. Seen through that long lens of history, there are of course wider issues of 'labelling' and of 'guilt by association', which may be germane but they were of little consequence to the task-focused detectives.

The targeting of offenders and the identification of criminogenic spaces are as old as policing itself. In that sense, there is little new to problem solving and POP. Although both appear products of modern times, they merely exploit modern technologies to formalize and extend traditional practices rather than inventing new ones. Modern times in which police actions are subject to far more public scrutiny than ever were the investigations of Leach, Ferrier and the like. Perhaps the real strength of these 'scientific' methods that now are in use across the developed world is that they allow the police to demonstrate they are taking crime seriously and are acting decisively to reduce it using the tools and technologies of the age.

We may live in times when being seen to do the right thing, is just as important as doing the right thing and that makes new demands on the police. However, having stripped away the veneer of technology, it is questionable whether one would find that criminal investigation has changed very much over the years (as even a cursory examination of the first textbook on the subject of criminal investigation, Hans Gross's *Handbook for Coroners, Police Officials, and Military Policemen* published in 1893 will confirm). Ultimately, whether the adoption of POP and problem solving in Britain amounts to policy transfer or policy diffusion rather than to knowledge transfer remains open to debate. On the evidence available, it is the latter that is closer to the truth and that, whether transferred or diffused, neither problem solving nor POP has changed policing or criminal investigation in the paradigm-shifting way that some have claimed.

COMPSTAT

Few policing strategies in modern times have attracted the level of interest that has been afforded to COMPSTAT. Before assessing its influence on ILP in Britain today, it is worth examining exactly what kind of policing style COMPSTAT represents. In so doing, I also want to identify points of convergence or divergence between the COMPSTAT and NIM narratives. The name itself, derived from the term 'computerized statistics' suggests that measurement is central to the system. However, measuring police activity (in an effort to ensure that the service is doing the right thing in the right ways) is not novel. Certainly, that kind of scrutiny has always been considered important in Britain; particularly since the introduction of NPM principles into policing in the 1980s.

The term COMPSTAT entered the policing lexicon in 1994. It was coined by New York Police Department (NYPD) commanders and represented a shortening of the terms 'computer statistics' or 'comparative statistics'. (Maple, 1999 one of its chief architects has observed that nobody can be certain which of the terms is accurate). COMPSTAT supported a campaign by the new mayor, Rudolph Giuliani, to drive down crime in the city. Tough and ruthless management of operational resources was key to achieving that goal.

Giuliani appointed William Bratton as his police commissioner. Given a free hand to reorganize the NYPD, Bratton embarked on a programme of structural change underpinned by a belief in the new orthodoxy in American police-thinking espoused by, amongst others, Wilson and Kelling (Bratton, 1998). The COMPSTAT process was intended to ensure that information was gathered and managed in ways that allowed resources to be targeted at the most pressing policing problems (which was exactly the ACPO chief's ambition for the NIM). Bratton (1998) argued that internal accountability arrangements were crucial to the success of the project. Precinct commanders were given the authority to address the problems in their areas as they saw fit but were called to account for their decisions by the NYPD's executive. Weekly Crime Control Strategy Meetings, at which the commanders reported their results, took place in a 'data-saturated environment'; central to those meetings were the statistical analyses contained within the weekly COMPSTAT report (Weisburd et al, 2006).

COMPSTAT meetings increased internal accountability but they could be brutal affairs. Persistent failure to meet standards meant demotion or worse. Within 18 months of taking control, Bratton had transferred a third of his precinct commanders and fired four of the five NYPD 'superchiefs' (Maple, 1999, p.136).[4] Bratton's stated intention was that COMPSTAT principles went beyond statistics and should influence decision-making at all levels of the NYPD, not just at the elite or executive level. However, researchers have found little evidence to suggest that diffusion has taken place. Notwithstanding, the apparent success of the system drew the attention of police forces across the developed world.

In an interview, former ACPO member (N04) said that for a period in the 1990s, no transatlantic flight passenger manifest was complete without an ACPO member or other senior police officer on the way to or returning from a fact-finding mission to see Bratton's ideas in practice. The COMPSTAT message spread as the NYPD's commanders found prestigious jobs elsewhere. So that soon, members of the British police elite were travelling to a number of US cities. For example in 2002, the deputy chief constable of the Thames Valley Police visited Philadelphia, Pennsylvania to view COMPSTAT in operation in that city under the control of Police Commissioner John Timoney, recently arrived from New York (BBC News, 2002, p.1).

Hayes (1998) and Griffiths (1998) (two of the senior British officers who visited New York City) broadly welcomed the development of COMPSTAT and supported its adoption in the UK. Hayes (1998) believed that elements of the process could be implemented in the UK but that limited resources and the need to meet regional and national demands meant that it was unrealistic to expect the system to succeed in its entirety. Importantly in the context of the UK debate, both of those senior commanders saw COMPSTAT as an additional level of scrutiny rather than as a replacement for existing management and oversight mechanisms in Britain's police (Hayes, 1998; Griffiths, 1998).

Researchers found that COMPSTAT concentrated strategic decision-making at the top of the organizational hierarchy rather than promoting initiative among frontline staff in the mainstream (Weisburd et al, 2006), and a survey of US police agencies suggested that 'the rank and file remained largely oblivious to COMPSTAT and that it intruded little, if at all, into their daily work' (Willis et al, 2003, p.291). Tellingly, Willis et al found that COMPSTAT departed markedly from what had been promised and did not 'represent a radical transformation in the way these departments have done business' rather, they had 'transplanted some new ways of doing business without making much change to some very fundamental structures of police organizations' (2003a, p.77).

Arguably, COMPSTAT was designed to serve the NYPD and New York City's communities and it was never intended that it should play a part in addressing either state level or federal challenges (which may explain the complete lack of state or federal funding for the programme). In that respect, the process can be seen as rather inward-looking. Nevertheless, it was hailed as a success by many police commanders across the USA and it (or a variation of it) went on to be adopted in many police departments. Weisburd et al (2003) have argued that where COMPSTAT succeeded, it complemented existing strategic problem solving processes. However, perhaps the greater appeal of COMPSTAT for policymakers and the US police elite was that although it promised innovation in organization, strategies and tactics, in reality it did not 'demand a revolution in the organisational structure of the military model of policing' (Weisburd et al, 2003, p.449). Rather than offering real reform, it has been argued that COMPSTAT largely served to reinforce the traditional control elements of the rational-legal, bureaucratic, police organizational model in the United States in ways that made the system more palatable for US commanders (Weisburd et al, 2003).

I argued earlier that policies are very rarely implemented as their architects expect. One dimension to that debate is that often implementation may lead to unintended, and often less welcome, consequences. For example Eterno and Silverman (2013, p.1) surveyed 491 retired police supervisors, including 323 who worked during the COMPSTAT era. They found that while those working under that regime 'respected and honored the system's fundamentals', they also felt under 'enormous pressure to downgrade index crime compared with pre-COMPSTAT era's commanders'. The researchers concluded that the COMPSTAT system and a combination of heavy pressure to downgrade index crime and somewhat lesser pressure to maintain the integrity of crime data had 'contributed to manipulation of crime statistics'.[5]

Other research has shown that in some areas, COMPSTAT variations may provide positive results. For example, McElvain et al (2013, p.4) found that a strategy 'loosely based on the system' reduced some crime reported to the Riverside County Sheriff's Department in Southern

California. The mediation of the original system in that case is note-worthy. Moreover, most of the scholarly research of the system, over the period from its inception in New York City to the present day, suggests that COMPSTAT has not delivered the paradigm shift in policing claimed by its advocates. As Willis and Mastrofski have noted, 'predictive policing's core focus remains laser-like on crime reduction' even if the rhetoric suggests otherwise (2012, p.87).

However, one should never underestimate the power of rhetoric, particularly when it seems to offer law enforcement agencies a solution to previously unsolvable ills. I described earlier the transatlantic travel of the British police elite around the turn of the new century and also the views of some of those travellers about COMPSTAT. In the 11 years since the last visit I described, COMPSTAT has not revolutionized policing in Britain. However, some elements of the system have found their way into British practice. Many police forces have COMPSTAT style meetings that perform a scrutiny function and the system has also found its way, one assumes through police partnership arrangements, into public sector bodies.

For example, Wholey and Compton (2010) report that the Westminster CSP (made up of police and community safety partners in the London Borough of Westminster) uses CompStat local crime data to enhance accountability and scrutiny of the CSP's problem solving and POP work. However, the methods adopted both by the British police and by the Westminster local authority would (just like the Riverside Sheriff's approach) be more accurately described as 'loosely based on COMPSTAT' rather than as a clone of the system as it was originally envisaged by its creators.

As a postscript to this analysis, as the reader will see in the next chapter, the enthusiasm of the British police elite for COMPSTAT was displayed in a period when apathy for the NIM, ostensibly a creation of that same elite and designed to achieve the same purpose, was at its zenith. That may suggest that in this period the police elite were simply reaching out to explore 'what works' elsewhere that might be adapted for their needs. However, it might also say something about its real commitment to the NIM.

Beyond policing: Mapping the increasing influence of ILP in Britain

In this section, I examine the influence of ILP on the rest of Britain's public services and on research and practice elsewhere in the developed world. Soon after its introduction to Britain's police service, the

NIM was publicly acclaimed by central government as the means by which intelligence-led practice could and should be adopted across Britain's public sector. Those words were backed up by a 'Crime and Disorder Toolkit', later developed into a 'Partnership Toolkit', that was designed by the Home Office and made available to Community Safety Partnerships via the World Wide Web. Beyond that marketing of the NIM, it also came to the attention of scholars and researchers in Britain and elsewhere. Like COMPSTAT, the NIM seemed to offer the prospect of real reform and a new improved public police. Even though early reviews of the model carried out by Collier (2006) and John and Maguire (2004) were, at best, equivocal.

ILP's influence on Britain's local authorities

Beyond the police service itself, the most obvious 'beneficiaries' of Britain's ILP strategies were its local authorities. The first stage in central government's responsibilization of those authorities was the enactment of the Crime and Disorder Act, 1998 and their responsibility for the maintenance of 'safe and strong' communities was confirmed by the Local Government Act 2000, which called for 'integrated approaches' to the concept of community well-being. By the time that the first review of the utility of the Crime and Disorder Act (and associated legislation) was completed in 2005, Home Office plans had been laid to compel local authorities (as members of CSPs) to: implement a NIM-style framework to underpin their decision-making; produce annual three year rolling plans to reduce crime and maintain safe and strong communities; undertake regular strategic assessments of the challenges they faced; and, use intelligence-led problem solving approaches to support their performance, risk and financial management processes.

Unsurprisingly, some local authorities have been more enthusiastic about embracing those plans than others. Osborn (2012) found in his research that driven by centrally dictated performance targets, many CSPs delivered narrow crime reduction, rather than community safety, strategies. In some cases, not only have partnerships failed to deliver what was expected of them, they have even distracted their members from their stated purpose (Home Office, 2006). There are cases where the Government's plans seem to have been exploited with positive outcomes. For example, the Greater Manchester Against Crime, Partnership Business Model (GMAC PBM) has reported favourably on its use of the NIM (GMAC, 2010).

However, whilst praising it for its commitment to partnership working, John et al argued that in fact, GMAC was working according to an 'interpretation' of the NIM that suited their particular purpose rather than 'pure NIM' as the model was envisaged (2006, pp.1–2). We should not be at all surprised by that. Taken together with other examples of policy mediation discussed in this chapter, this simply provides further evidence of the ways in which public policy is mediated and translated when it leaves the rarefied atmosphere of the policymaking environment. That should give us cause to question if the adoption of, essentially, NIM-lite or COMPSTAT-lite, really amount to policy transfer albeit that some knowledge of what works may have been shared.

ILP's influence on other public sector bodies

Beyond Britain's local authorities, central government also has encouraged its own departments and agencies to embrace the NIM ideal. A diverse array of bodies including: the Environment Agency; the UK's Anti-Doping Agency; and the Driver and Vehicle Licensing Agency all, ostensibly, use the NIM. Osborn (2012) studied the putative adoption of the NIM by three of Britain's public sector institutions: the Department for Work and Pensions (DWP); the Identity and Passport Service (IPS); and the Driving Standards Agency (DSA). Each of those bodies has proudly proclaimed their 'NIM-compliance'.

However, Osborn found that in fact they were 'not compliant' with the NIM and that the model had 'not delivered any meaningful improvement in the consistency of process, investigative efficiency, improved partnership working, or in fraud reduction in those agencies' (2012, p.i). In other words, policy transfer had taken place only at the level of rhetoric. At the operational level, the model was unpopular with investigators who viewed it as 'unhelpful, inappropriate and associated with performance management and governance' (Osborn, 2012, p.124). Compliance with the model demanded levels of investment and of resources that simply were not made available by senior managers, and a commitment to cultural change that few in those bodies were convinced was necessary or desirable. At the strategic or business level, the senior managers responsible for the adoption of the NIM failed to recognize the need for that investment or 'the necessity to revise investigative processes and procedures to accord with the compliance criteria' (Osborn, 2012, p.121).

Osborn's study highlights something about the NIM that should not be overlooked. Even though one of its stated aims was that it should encourage partnership working, the NIM explicitly was designed by the police, for the police. Its structures and processes mirror those found in British policing and its intelligence products require intelligence specialists and a capacity to collect, analyse, and assess information in ways that few other organizations possess. Certainly, none of the bodies studied by Osborn had those structures, processes or anything like that capacity.

In that sense, attempting to lever the NIM into them was analogous to trying to fit a square peg into a round hole. Those seeking to encourage the adoption of the model might still have achieved a measure of success (in terms of the encouragement of knowledge transfer in the way I discussed in the previous section) had they made a sustained effort to demystify the model and overcome the obvious cultural resistance to it. However, Osborn found that no such effort was made and instead, that resistance was only compounded by a 'mismanaged introduction and an inaccurate association with unrelated organisational change' in the bodies he studied (2012, pp.140–1). Dolowitz and Marsh (1996) have argued that a transfer of policy may range from voluntary to coercive or may fall anywhere along a notional continuum between the two. The fact that the implementation of the NIM met such strong resistance, suggests that those being asked to adopt it felt that they were being coerced even if that was not the intention of their elites. That only fuelled the former's resistance.

ILP: The international dimension

Notwithstanding the lack of meaningful evidence that ILP could deliver what its British advocates promised; the consistency of their rhetoric, the policy entrepreneurship that had delivered political backing in Britain, and the popular view of it as the solution to policing's ills was a powerful combination. The notion that ILP is qualitatively better than the discredited reactive paradigm has taken root in popular discourse and has led others to emulate Britain's model. Walsh has argued that despite the many challenges the NIM has faced in Britain, it has provided for 'other policing agencies in Australia, Canada, New Zealand, and the USA, a framework that covers comprehensively all aspects of the intelligence business in policing' (2011, p.104). What is also significant about this group of countries is that they are likely to share what Stone (2001, p.21) has termed 'common patterns of understanding' established through a long history of joint working towards common causes.

I examine some of those different policy domains in which ILP is claimed to have prospered in modern times. I focus on the other four of the 'Five Eyes': the USA; Canada; Australia; and New Zealand. Not to measure ILP's influence on the business of national security, that is a separate area of study that is beyond the scope of my research, but to illustrate the extent to which Britain's ILP model has been emulated by other nations and increasingly has come to feature so strongly in policing around the world that a global discourse of ILP has been established.[6]

ILP in the USA

The 2008, US Department of Justice (USDoJ) census of US state and local law enforcement agencies reveals that in that year there were 17,985 state and local agencies employing at least one full-time officer (or the equivalent in part-time officers) in the US. That figure is broken down as follows: 12,501 local police departments; 3,063 sheriffs' offices; 50 primary state law enforcement agencies; 1,733 special jurisdiction agencies; 638 other agencies, primarily county constable offices in Texas (USDoJ, 2011, p.2) Though there are many large (usually metropolitan) departments, notably, about 8,800 state and local law enforcement agencies (49 percent of the total number) employed fewer than ten full-time sworn personnel, and about 5,400 (30 percent) employed fewer than five officers (USDoJ, 2011, p.1).

In that context, although in each case there is the commitment to problem solving, partnerships and the like, unsurprisingly that commitment is operationalized in many different ways. At the federal and state levels, many departments are committed to the National Criminal Intelligence Sharing Plan (NCISP), which was developed following the terrible events of 9/11. Similar in outlook and spirit to the NIM, which US officials studied in the aftermath of those events (Peterson, 2005, p.5), it is claimed that the NCISP coordinates the strategic integration of intelligence 'with an emphasis on predictive analysis derived from the discovery of hard facts, information, patterns, and good crime analysis (Taylor and Russell, 2012).

However, it is apparent that unlike the NIM which was meant to inform both local resource allocation, and the strategic and national pictures, the NCISP largely serves the higher level intelligence function and that intelligence to support ILP in the mainstream is managed very differently. That is to say, there usually are local arrangements to generate intelligence products that are designed to serve the commissioning department at an operational level; they do not necessarily contribute to a regional or national picture. Good examples of that in action can be found in the US Bureau of Justice Assistance-sponsored Smart Policing Initiative (SPI). The SPI aims to support law enforcement agencies in building evidence-based, effective, efficient, and economical data-driven law enforcement tactics and strategies in the mainstream.[7] It aims to harness the research capability of local universities to develop the ILP, POP, community policing and COMPSTAT-like strategies used in 33 sites across the USA.

That is an ambitious undertaking. Perhaps it is more accurate to say that the initiative aims to combine selected elements of each strategy in a hybrid approach (subtly different in each case) that exploits modern tools and techniques to improve the delivery of mainstream policing services. The initiative relies on some basic principles. Fundamentally, as SPI Project Director, James Coldren has argued, the initiative honours Robert Peel's principles of crime prevention and community approval. Echoing Peel, in Coldren's view, the test of police efficiency (and ultimately of the success of the continuing SPI initiative) will be the absence of crime and disorder and not the visible evidence of the police dealing with it (Coldren, 2013, p.1). I have argued throughout this book that police departments must know their past if they are to know their futures so I take some satisfaction from Coldren's words.

ILP in Canada

There are 380 policing agencies in Canada. I focus here only on the Criminal Intelligence Service of Canada (CISC) established in 1970 and Canada's national police department, the Royal Canadian Mounted Police (RCMP). Though not representative of all Canadian policing bodies, the latter has significantly influenced the development of policing in that country in modern times. Whilst, Hamilton (2006 cited in Walsh, 2011, p.22) has noted, that it is the 'common heritage' of the RCMP and the CISC that has helped to foster the development of ILP in Canada.

The RCMP established a Criminal Intelligence Directorate in 1991. The Directorate's assumption of overall responsibility for the collection, analysis and dissemination of crime intelligence brought an element of professionalism to (a previously inefficient) system and also demonstrated the RCMP's commitment to ILP (Smith, 1997, p.1). However, it seems that, just as in Britain, the path to a truly intelligence-led service has been far from smooth. Stewart (1996, p.1) has noted that in this period the criminal intelligence community in Canada was 'fractured and disjointed, with national and regional efforts not being entirely coordinated'.

Certainly in 2001, a further attempt to develop an ILP system along British lines was felt necessary (Deukmedjian and De Lint, 2007).

Walsh suggests that even that renewed commitment to ILP, did not deliver the 'truly comprehensive ILP model with national standards' that policymakers expected (2011, p.105). In his view, that was because those efforts were never 'optimal'. Arguably, that could have been due to fundamental inadequacies in the British model as much as to any deficiency in the Canadian efforts to implement it. That too says something about the wider issues of policy transfer and diffusion.

Reflecting political and organizational imperatives (it is very difficult to find anyone, anywhere, willing to argue that ILP is a bad thing), the CISC recently has begun to develop a new improved version of its existing Canadian Crime Intelligence Model (CCIM). Notwithstanding, that renewed commitment, Walsh argues that Canada will find it more difficult to reach its goal than Britain because it will not be able to introduce federal legislation to ensure compliance (2011, p.109). That is because policing largely is the responsibility of the provinces. Instead, he suggests that the CISC will have to negotiate the agreement it seeks over a period of years rather than weeks. In my view, that ultimately may be to the nation's advantage. As the reader will see, in Britain, legislation did not deliver the uniform system that was expected. Instead it encouraged a thin veneer of apparent compliance that masked some pretty non-compliant behaviour.

Given the inertia and the resistance (albeit largely passive) witnessed in the UK, perhaps negotiation and a longer lead-in to the CCIM may prove more fruitful in the longer term. However, at the time of writing, it seems as if the CISC and RCMP have some distance yet to travel to reach their goal. Reflecting on his attendance at an academic outreach event held by the RCMP's national security section to discuss ILP in January 2013, Forcese (2013, p.1) recorded that whilst he came away with the impression that the RCMP clearly valued ILP, 'in the eyes of its advocates, the concept has not to date been mainstreamed'. That suggests that Canada may be facing just as many challenges as everyone else in trying to turn the rhetoric of ILP into practice.

ILP in Australia

Australia has two federal agencies, the Australian Federal Police (AFP) and the Australian Crime Commission, and seven state police departments. On the surface, it too seems to have embraced the ILP orthodoxy established in Britain. Baldino (2010) has argued that in recent years , the Australian federal and state police have had little option but to adopt ILP practices to confront and challenge the interests of criminal networks and that the growing influence of those networks has led to increased cooperation, and intelligence-sharing, between those agencies. Moreover, Walsh (2011, p.123) has described 'Project Sentinel', an Australian Crime Commission project designed to remedy a 'thematic and bifurcated' view of organized crime that had resulted in a 'siloing' of intelligence and investigations.

Walsh provides a thorough critique of the project and I will not repeat that here but what seems to emerge from his evaluation is that in practice there is a split along similar lines as found in the US (2011). That is to say, that a federal body (in this case the Australian Crime Commission) serves largely to deliver the higher level intelligence function of the state (in its response to terrorism, drug and other organized crime, etc.). At that higher level, there has been a significant element of 'borrowing' from practice elsewhere (for example, Britain's Serious Organised Crime Agency's lifetime offender management programme has influenced the development of something similar by the Australian Crime Commission). However, at the state level, most of that borrowing has been of aspects of well-established US, POP and problem solving strategies. In Australia, just as in the US, there usually are local arrangements (in the form of local intelligence or problem solving units) to generate intelligence products that are designed to serve the commissioning department in its POP or problem solving activities.

ILP in New Zealand

Policing throughout New Zealand is delivered solely by the New Zealand Police (NZP). Even without the organizational and cross-cultural challenges experienced elsewhere, the path to a reflexive, intelligence-led police service seems to have been just as challenging for New Zealand as its other 'Five Eyes' partners. Walsh (2011) notes that it was not until the 1970s that ILP was integrated into mainstream practice. Even then, progress in implementing a coherent strategy at the local level was slow. In 2001, an inquiry by New Zealand's Controller and Auditor General (NZCAG, 2001) concluded that local intelligence had a very low profile, difficulties in recruiting and retaining staff, and were often side-lined in business planning. In 2005, a review of that original inquiry found that the police had started to make greater use of ILP and that intelligence units had raised their profile and reach.

NZCAG attributed much of the improvement to the implementation, in 2003, of the New Zealand Crime Reduction Model (NZCAG, 2005). Unsurprisingly, given events elsewhere, the aim of the model was to encourage a more systematic approach to crime reduction that involved targeting prolific offenders, hotspotting – the identification of crime prone areas, and regular strategic and tactical meetings. The NZCAG professed itself encouraged by the results of its review but recommended that the effectiveness of ILP should be formally evaluated, given the strategic and operational importance of the model to the police (NZCAG, 2005, p.22).

Walsh (2011) argues that the ability of the NZP to use intelligence to direct its activities was greatly improved in 2007 when an intelligence specialist from the Police Service of Northern Ireland (PSNI) was appointed to lead a national intelligence development project, which subsequently became the NZP Policing Model (NZPPM). The similarities between Britain's NIM and the New Zealand framework are obvious (particularly in its tasking processes and its use of 'knowledge products'). That perhaps was inevitable given the involvement of the British specialist. However, it would be unfair to describe the NZPPM simply as an emulation of the NIM. The NIM has been adapted and developed to meet local needs. A good example of that is the development of the NIM's Prevention, Intelligence, and Enforcement menu of options into the NZPPM's Prevention, Intelligence, Enforcement, Reassurance, and Support credo). Provided with the resources and framework that it asked for, the NZP is now coming under scrutiny to deliver results (Walsh, 2011). Given, the model's similarity to the NIM, Britain's police chiefs should be just as interested as the NZP's elite, in the outcome of the programme.

Summary of the 'Five Eyes' evaluation

This evaluation shows just how broadly the term ILP is interpreted around the globe. Even on the basis of 'common patterns of understanding' using essentially the same toolset, these five nations have each operationalized ILP in their own way; to meet their specific needs. The arrangements made in Britain and New Zealand share many features. Both national models seek to link intelligence work and resource allocation at all levels of policing, which in the case of the New Zealand model is unsurprising given the antecedents of a key actor in that process. Conversely, in the US and Australia there seems to be a growing acceptance of the need for a separation of national and local intelligence on the basis of an understanding that one size does not necessarily fit all. In respect of Canada, the literature presents a confused picture of a system that is very much in flux; a commitment to ILP in principle but confusion over how that may best be achieved in practice.

It also highlights the challenge of assessing whether policy transfer (or some variant of it) can ever be said to have taken place. It is easy to generalize about the export or import of ideas; particularly those that are so fully formed as POP and problem solving. However, it is much more difficult to accurately assess the interpretation of events by those actors intimately involved in the transfer process. What this again seems to confirm is that policy implementation is always context specific. It is always shaped by local conditions, by existing networks of influence, by the strength of the diffusion from one domain to the next, and by the institutional structures and politics of the relevant domains.

The European Criminal Intelligence Model (ECIM)

Before leaving the subject of policy transfer, it should be highlighted that there is one policy that certainly has been influenced by the NIM and that is the ECIM. The background to the ECIM is that it was first imagined by those who were working in Britain, largely within the NCIS, to establish the NIM. Those individuals very quickly came to the conclusion that the NIM could also be a vehicle for the coordination of intelligence work across Europe. In interview, ACPO member N02 said that during Britain's Presidency of the EU, when the NIM 's star was in the ascendancy, Britain had lobbied to have the model accepted as *the* European intelligence model.

Brady (2007, p.4) has noted that the increasing problem of organized crime challenged policymakers to find a solution. The policy window was opened by Britain's presidency of the union and Britain exploited that to 'sell' its ready-made solution, the NIM. In 2005, Britain's proposal was approved by the EU's interior ministers who were persuaded of the need for something that could coordinate intelligence-led investigations throughout the EU. N02 said that the approval of the ECIM was the product of a huge amount of work by NCIS and ACPO via Europol. N02 expected that once the agreement had been signed off, Europol would develop the systems and processes needed to institutionalize the model.

However, Brady (2007) has observed that whilst the adoption of a Europe-wide model was a significant step forward for the EU and for Europol, the initial evidence suggested that neither the governments nor the police services of member states were taking the ECIM seriously enough. Further studies by Wolff (2009) and Zarkadoulas (2010) revealed the situation to be little changed. Zarkadoulas (2010, p.64) highlighted that EU law enforcement agencies mirror those of the member states in that they continue to be 'fragmented and obstruct effective communication and collaboration'. Inevitably, that has influenced the Europol's adoption of ILP. On that evidence, it must be concluded that an effective ECIM remains an aspiration for the EU rather than a reality.

6
Evaluating the NIM: Challenges to the Model

Introduction

This chapter continues the ILP narrative by evaluating the putative implementation of the NIM in the police forces in England and Wales. The chapter highlights ACPO's inability to coordinate the activities of its fiercely independent membership. It explains the diminishing influence of its supporters on NIM implementation. It also analyses senior commanders' opposition to the plans for the model. These are important next steps in explaining ILP in Britain because the contrasting ways in which the NIM was received by senior commanders explains why ILP took the shape that is revealed in the case studies explored later.

Models of policy implementation

Of course, in determining whether or not a policy can be considered to be adequately implemented, one should first recognize that few are implemented as their architects anticipate. Most policies are mediated, negotiated or translated in unexpected ways as they enter the 'real' world. That makes establishing the criteria by which the success of any policy should be judged, extremely difficult. Skogan (2008) argued that management-inspired programmes must be relevant to officers in the mainstream and that unless they are underpinned by regulation, they are almost bound to fail. That usually means that otherwise 'abstract concepts must be converted into 'lists of practical, day-to-day activities enshrined in enforceable orders' (2008, p.26). It follows that the mediation I have described is an essential element in making the conceptual; real and practical.

Policies often are revised during implementation to reflect 'real world' demands. To achieve success, those tasked with implementation must be flexible, resourceful and willing to reach compromises (Sabatier, 1986). It is by these criteria, taken together, that the real commitment of the police elite to ILP via its implementation of the NIM may be judged. The model was underpinned by a statutory code of practice; it was funded by the Home Office and had clear and consistent objectives that were set out in the code and the accompanying minimum standards.

The reader will see later that with the backing of ACPO, the NIM was integrated into the police hierarchy and satisfied the service's decision rules. It also was supported by an ACPO implementation team and further officers and officials in police forces, tasked with ensuring compliance. Therefore, it met both Skogan's 'regulation' and (substantially) Sabatier's 'structural' criteria. However, the reader will also see later that the model's implementation was characterized by inflexibility, an unwillingness to reach compromises with those expected to work with it, and an inability to make the model relevant to the wider police service.

ACPO's lack of influence over its members

Even though the NIM had been approved by the ACPO council, many members resisted the model. Earlier, I described ACPO's practice of taking decisions in its council meetings on the basis of what Savage et al (2000) called a 'presumption in favour of compliance'. Whilst the researchers found no evidence that members failed to comply with decisions taken in that way, they noted that the principle of chief officer's independence was given prominence by the organization and that it was clear that 'chief constables at no stage have to comply with ACPO policy' (2000, p.83). The reader will see that the NIM provides a clear example of an apparently binding decision made by the ACPO council, being resisted by wider ACPO membership. Savage et al's questioning of ACPO's ability to coordinate the activities of '43 fiercely independent chief constables' when the Association's sanctions for rule-breaking were so limited, was prescient (2000, p.62).

Shapland (1988, pp.189–90) argued that 'territoriality', the protection of individual fiefdoms in this way is a significant factor in the policymaking process in the criminal justice arena. Criminal justice agencies (including the police) see themselves as individual bodies rather than as parts of an interconnected and efficient system. Those who control fiefdoms jealously guard their independence and work-load and will not easily relinquish either no matter how 'sensible' (or in this case intelligence-led) the alternatives presented to them may be. She argued that NPM-inspired reforms aimed at making criminal justice agencies more 'business-like' may actually have encouraged further division and strengthened those areas of control (2000 cited in Crawford, 2001). This phenomenon is not limited to the criminal justice arena. For example, similar concerns have been expressed about those whom criminal justice agencies turn to as partners (Crawford, 2001). The Audit Commission (2000) too has highlighted how the activities of departmental fiefdoms restrict local councils' room for manoeuvre.

In the modern era, the line of accountability for Britain's chief officers has tilted increasingly to the centre, with the result that the Home Office is seen by senior commanders as the most powerful and influential of the institutions of policing. Given the obvious strength of that argument, senior commanders' resistance to the NIM in the face of the department's codification of the model is surprising. However, in my view, their ambitions for their forces often outweighed their concerns about any sanction from the Home Office for breaching the NIM's code (but perhaps explain the 'veneer' of compliance that ultimately was applied to the implementation process). Even though Phillips, the President of ACPO gave it his full backing, he did not outrank any other chief officer and he could not direct other chiefs to comply with his plans. Instead, he had to rely on the force of his argument, his powers of persuasion and, his policy entrepreneurship. The case studies that follow, show that ultimately those were not enough.

Challenges to NIM implementation

This section analyses the challenges that the NIM's supporters faced, in persuading the wider ACPO membership and others in the police service to accept Phillips' vision for policing in the new millennium. To Phillips, the NIM was no more than a 'profoundly simple set of fundamentals' for policing in England and Wales (Phillips, 2006, p.4). However, as the reader will see, few others saw or understood it in those terms.

Home Office performance targets

The NIM highlighted pre-existing tensions between the policing of local crime problems and of national/transnational crimes (such as terrorism) and also between the service's responses to 'priority' crimes measured by the Home Office which are particularly significant for BCU commanders, and those harms that are of the greatest concern to local communities. There is evidence that the NIM encouraged the police to focus on priority crime at the expense of second-order criminality. For example, John and Maguire (2004) found that police managers applying NIM principles were putting too great an emphasis on meeting centrally-imposed performance targets (that measured performance against Home Office-proscribed priority crime) and were taking insufficient notice of local concerns.

In interview, former detective inspector N055 said that he too felt that community concerns were too often ignored. He said that in a training session for police executives, he was told by a BCU commander that his NIM strategic intelligence assessment reflected only those problems measured by the Home Office and for which he would receive central funding. N055 said that in the same session, a BCU superintendent confessed to a kind of conspiracy between the police and the local authority to obtain the maximum possible amount of Government cash. He said that the superintendent told him that:

> He had persuaded his local authority chief executive that, if asked, to reply that his problems are street crime and drugs. He said 'We all know that the real problem is anti-social behaviour but the Minister has said we're focusing on street crime so we're focusing on street crime because that is what will bring us the funding'.

County chief inspector N029 said that from senior commanders' perspective, the decision to focus on performance rather than outcomes was a wholly pragmatic one. Commanders who failed to 'get the job done' risked their bonus payments from their police authorities. Referring to chief officers' bonus payments, which hitherto had not been widely reported (though which since has received media attention, including one report that chief officers had received annual bonuses of up to £74,000 – O'Neill, 2009), N029 said:

> The police authority, in negotiating their contracts, sets them a bonus target. The policing plan is about priority crime because it's about Government objectives and very clear targets to hit ... and they are going to receive 10 or £20,000 bonus if they hit certain bits ... Their heart might be more in what their bonus targets are about, rather than what the actual people really want.

This was not a view expressed by any other respondent but it does nevertheless add an interesting dimension to the debate.

In September 2004, ACPO felt obliged to admit that a focus on 'priority' crime measured by the Home Office (which has come to be associated with the NIM), at the expense of those issues of greatest concern to local communities, meant that neighbourhood policing in many forces was 'at best, patchy and under-resourced' (2004, p.3). Neither programme was introduced in a policy vacuum and it probably is as simplistic to blame the NIM for the ills of neighbourhood policing as it is to blame neighbourhood policing for the failures of the NIM. However, ACPO's statement highlights the failure of the Home Office and the police elite to 'join up' policing policy in this period.

ACPO member (NIM implementation) N03 was concerned that in some BCUs, performance had assumed so great an importance that COMPSTAT-type meetings replaced the NIM meetings. He said that too great an emphasis on current performance could undermine the forward planning element of the NIM and that could 'directly and singularly influence tactical delivery'. However, performance really mattered. He said:

> You would be living in 'cloud cuckoo land' if you didn't think that the meeting of targets and performance wasn't going to drive tactical delivery. However, if that was the only influence on your decision-making around tactical delivery you would be unable to see what is coming up and what's going to bite you significantly in the future.

He said that nominated individuals should be held to account for their decisions but that process and outcomes should not be confused. He said it would be 'pie in the sky, nonsense' to think that performance targets would not affect tactical delivery but balance was essential if longer-term challenges were to be met. BCU commander N027 said that in his experience the need to meet performance targets forced BCU commanders to put short-termism before long-term planning. He said that they were always under pressure to 'live in a day' because 'in the long run you're all dead. Short term [performance] is where you're at'. He said that this was one of the greatest weaknesses in policing. ILP was meant to transform police work, to allow the police to make better use of their intelligence to address policing problems in more cost-effective and efficient ways However, as the reader can see (and as the case studies which follow demonstrate), being perceived to be doing a good job rather than actually doing a good job, was the default position for many in policing; performance measurement continued to far outweigh any other consideration.

Ideological resistance

Perhaps the most significant of the challenges that confronted the NIM's proponents was the intransigence of the police elite. Manning has argued that 'attempts to reorient policing to information-based or evidence-based operations implicitly challenges many assumptions about how policing ought to work' (2008, p.163). On that very point, ACPO member (NIM implementation) N03 said that chief officers were divided over the NIM from the beginning. Many in the Association did not welcome Phillips' plans and there was a significant section that saw no role for it in their own forces.

Surprisingly, there was even resistance within NCIS where the NIM had been developed. For example in May 2002 at the ACPO annual conference, an NCIS executive argued that the model was 'contrived'. ACPO member N06 said that criticism of the NIM at that time was 'a sin worse than death because this was David Phillips' baby because it had come out of Kent and it was *fantastic* (respondent's emphasis)'. He said that Phillips had 'gone bananas' over the NCIS executive's complaint that the NIM was 'over engineered, too complex' and that because of Phillips' reaction the NCIS official 'probably learned to be more guarded in his critique' after that meeting.[1]

N06 said that even after the model's incorporation into the NPP, the implementation process was characterized by resistance and antipathy. In his view, those early attempts to persuade some chief officers to implement the model were frustrated by resistance based on competing policing ideologies. Though many chief officers saw the value of making a new commitment to ILP and intelligence work, others were more attached to POP and problem solving and they just could not make the links between those strategies and the model.

He said that one force which resisted the NIM was Humberside Police which had a 'real issue about how it fitted in with their [neighbourhood] policing model ... because they believe[d] in Bobbies on the beat in big hats and that intelligence didn't fit in to all that'. There are some rather obvious implications to be drawn from this statement in the light of the Soham Murders and the Bichard Report (Bichard, 2004). Those words also highlight that there were indeed (at least) two 'camps' within ACPO; one which supported a crime control agenda and another which was committed to policing strategies that sought to address the root causes of crime.

Many in that rival camp supported the plans for a 'neighbourhood policing' programme and in November 2004, just six months after the NIM was announced in the NPP, the Home Office set out its plans for just such a programme in the White Paper, *Building Communities: Beating Crime*. This was a significant policy document, which set out plans for the 'democratization' of policing, encouraging 'active cooperation' rather than the traditional doctrine of policing by consent (McLaughlin, 2007). On one level, that programme could be seen simply as a natural development of the community policing arrangements introduced by the CDA. In the context of this research, it was significant because it suggested that the policy entrepreneurship of Phillips' rivals in ACPO, although not quite as visible as Phillips' own, may have been equally effective. However it also suggests that, despite the support it had given Phillips, the Home Office did not necessarily understand his plans or share his vision for the NIM.

Implementing the neighbourhood policing programme and the ILP-inspired NIM at the same time, was bound to be problematic because if a force used the NIM correctly (according to its original plan), it would continually move resources around the force to the areas that its intelligence assessments indicated, needed them most (that is to say, that resource allocation would be intelligence-led rather than being dictated by circumstance). Whereas, the underpinning ethos of neighbourhood policing was that community teams remained with their communities no matter what the level of demand elsewhere (effectively, they were 'ring-fenced'). It was this kind of tension that ACPO member N06 acknowledged as existing in Humberside, and which Oakensen et al (2002) identified in many other forces in England and Wales.

It should have been obvious to senior commanders that NIM principles (even if they were implemented faithfully) would contradict some of the fundamentals of neighbourhood policing. Both ACPO and the Home Office should have considered plans to reduce the tension between the two before the demands on the service implicit in NIM implementation were mandated by the NPP. It was only after this development, when the service's room for manoeuvre was much more limited, that either ACPO or the Home Office acknowledged a potential conflict. Former ACPO member N04 said the implementation of such obviously competing policy initiatives at the same time simply was not strategic.

The NIM represented a 'Big Idea' for policing in the new millennium. However, what seems clear is that neither the ACPO membership nor the Home Office ever really appreciated what the plans for ILP really involved. During the period of the research, the NIM was not seen by either party as a way of bringing together these disparate strands of policy or as a means of coordinating strategy. As a result, operational policing policy remained fractured and disjointed. The 2004 White Paper demonstrates as much as anything in this research that the Home Office never saw ILP as the means by which operational policing would be revolutionized. Instead it suggests that it was just the latest fad that was being 'bolted-on' to existing structures.

The NIM's association with NCIS

Earlier, I discussed the attitude of the police service to NCIS. In the light of that discussion it is clear that the NIM's subsequent association with NCIS also was a barrier to its acceptance by chief officers. ACPO member N01 said that initially, the consensus within the Association was that NCIS was the logical place to complete Phillips' vision for policing but in hindsight it was the wrong choice. Because of NCIS's involvement, ACPO members' associated the NIM only with intelligence gathering. Whereas it was intended to be much more than that; it was intended to be the cornerstone of operational policing in the new millennium. ACPO member (NIM implementation) N03 said that the NIM was not just about intelligence, it was about 'much more than that, a grander plan than that'. These are really important statements because they establish the true standard against which the success or otherwise of the NIM, according to its architects' plans, should be judged.

N03 said that though NCIS was the national intelligence service it lacked credibility in the eyes of operational police officers. He said:

> It did not have ... the sort of leverage you would expect an intelligence agency to have. That goes back to slightly before 1992 when NCIS was started up. It was going to be all things to everybody and ended up not doing anything like as much as people hoped because there weren't the funds and resources there. So people always have been disappointed in NCIS.

He said that this manifested itself in many of the meetings that the NIM implementation team held with force elites:

> They said 'You can give us advice and guidance but don't tell us what to do. You are a national agency. You're working at level three (national and international crime). This isn't going to work at level 1 (volume crime). Thanks a lot, leave us alone'.

Senior intelligence official N050 questioned ACPO's resistance to something which appeared such a 'simple and sound model for policing'. She said that confusion stemmed from a lack of clarity about the areas of policing the model was meant to drive, about whether it was an overarching business model or whether it simply was meant to drive proactivity (rather than response or demand-based policing) in the mainstream. It is worth noting here that the NIM achieved even less success at the national level; the model effectively was ignored by senior commanders and the high profile national specialist detective agencies. In interview, NCIS executive N102 said that NCIS' successor, the Serious Organised Crime Agency (SOCA), also completely rejected the NIM as a model for its business.

N01said that the NIM's identification with the Kent force was a significant factor in member's resistance to the model. ACPO member (intelligence) N06 agreed some of his peers found it difficult to accept the model into their own forces. Problems were exacerbated by the failure of ACPO's NIM team to realize the need to translate something intended for an internal audience in Kent, into something that would be acceptable to the other police forces in England and Wales. Though senior intelligence official N050 questioned whether the police elite recognized the value of the NIM as an enabler; a process for delivering operational policing strategies (of whatever form) more effectively.

N01 said that perhaps the NIM was presented in too complicated a manner for busy chief officers who at that time were under no obligation to implement the model (or at least under no stronger obligation than was represented by their 'presumption in favour of compliance') and who were 'busy doing other things'. Some ACPO members' complied with the NIM more in spirit than in deed (N06). N03 said that believing they could ignore the model without any real sanction; many chief officers did just that.

ACPO member N053 criticized NCPE doctrine because it was developed in a 'rarefied atmosphere' far above the reality of the environment in which people actually had to deliver. In his view, the doctrine developers (including those who added to the extensive library of NIM guidance) had moved so far ahead of the frontline of mainstream policing that 'the people who are left can't understand what then comes out of it'. Doctrine should be about 'Let's make it as simple as possible as opposed to as complicated and detailed as we can'. Former ACPO member N04 said that the service became so overwhelmed by doctrine that it arrived on his desk 'like London buses'.

Inadequate implementation strategy

According to ACPO member (intelligence) N06 the Association took a conscious decision to use a 'top-down' approach to implementation because it lacked the full support of Centrex, the national police training organization (now part of the College of Policing). He and his colleagues on the project board directed Centrex's National Specialist Law Enforcement Centre (NSLEC) to deliver training in the model's processes. ACPO member (NIM implementation) N03 said that the Association took a further decision to use NSLEC's limited resources to persuade only senior and middle managers of the model's benefits and hope that the message would 'cascade' down to the frontline. NSLEC executive N054 said that this meant that there was no meaningful engagement with the detective force. Indeed the national detective agency, the National Crime Squad, played no part whatsoever in the NIM's introduction.

N06 said that as a result of those decisions, NIM implementation was wholly senior management-driven. Goals and objectives were not agreed with senior or middle managers or frontline staff. He said that this caused problems 'down the line' in persuading operational staff in the mainstream to accept the new processes required for compliance with the model and that those staff failed to 'buy in' to the model's aims. He said that 'We were trying to get people at the top of the organisation to understand [the model's aims] ... Now, that is like anything. You can push for a certain length of time but really you need to be pulling don't you'? In other words, because there was no process of negotiation with those who were meant to implement the model, the 'abstract' concepts of the NIM were never translated into the lists of practical, day-to-day activities that would have meaning for frontline officers.

Comparisons may be drawn with the implementation of UBP in the 1960s. In neither case, was the knowledge and expertise of the detective force enlisted appropriately (the specialist detective force, which by most objective analyses would be expected to have the greatest investigative expertise, appears to have played no part in either process) and the goals and objectives that accompanied the new policies were never properly conveyed to frontline staff. In that sense, the arrangements made for the implementation of the NIM, just as they were for UBP must be considered wholly inadequate.

It is worth stressing here that the failure to train the very staff who would be expected to use the model's processes on a daily basis was a deliberate decision taken at the highest level of the police. The inadequacy of that strategy was soon recognized. In its written evidence to the Select Committee on Home Affairs (29 July 2004), Centrex blamed its 'lack of capacity' for the delivery of intelligence training which it admitted was a 'real limitation and a matter of concern' (NCPE, 2004a, p.7.3). There was 'a pressing need' to provide a range of training for 'intelligence specialists' because even though the NIM was 'at the heart of police business, the training of intelligence managers, analysts, field operators and assessors [was] piecemeal and inadequate' (NCPE, 2004a, p.8.2). NCPE expressed a desire that training would begin before the end of 2004. However, N06 noted in August 2005 that Centrex still was at least five months away from delivering on its training promises.

Two ACPO members (N03 and N06) regretted Centrex's inadequate support of NIM implementation. N03 observed that the amount of NIM training that Centrex eventually offered was extremely limited, amounting only to a series of presentations for student constables and intelligence managers. Though the NIM team delivered some workshops for commanders, these were on the specific subject of tasking and coordinating and not on the wider aims of the model. Even then, because of limited staff and resources it was unable to sustain the training it offered. N03 said 'We never ever had the ability to take it further than grass-roots, bread and butter stuff really'.

N054 blamed ACPO for the delay. Its training requirement was poorly defined and the Centrex training staff was unable to clarify it because of poor communications between Centrex and the ACPO project team. He said that he had contacted six members of the ACPO project team for guidance or direction but had received only one response. The bottom line was that those who would actually implement the model knew the least about it. As an individual tasked with actually delivering the training, he felt marginalized and unsupported. He said that the NIM team, 'talked about strategic assessment, they talked about tactical assessment, they talked about all the different problem and target profiles [but] no one knew what they looked like'. In his view, NIM training was no more than 'an afterthought'.

N03 defended the Association. He said that as an emergency measure, 5,000 CDs (detailing the NIM's structures and processes) were produced and issued to police forces but he also conceded that this did little to raise standards or to ameliorate concerns about the lack of classroom-type training available. N054 decried the issuing of the CDs as a token gesture that 'didn't actually persuade, motivate or convince anybody about what [the NIM] actually looked like'.

N03 said that a combination of the pressure to implement the NIM by the Government's April 2004 deadline, and the lack of training support either from the NIM team or from Centrex meant that some forces resorted to delivering their own training, which was of a variable standard. He said that the training was 'not necessarily nationally qualified and accredited and may not [have been] the right stuff which then in turn means that people are getting the wrong message locally and will continue to do so because there's no quality assurance mechanism on it'.

Few police trainers understood the NIM. Even though ACPO wanted to do more to explain the model to frontline staff; the 'national expertise pot' was just too small. The few trainers with sufficient knowledge were either attached to forces whose chief officers would not allow them to be released (a prime example of protectionism) or because of competing demands on their time, were able to offer only an ad hoc service. ACPO member N06 said that NSLEC eventually provided more support in the form of seminars for BCU commanders only but this was no more than 'Band Aid training'. He wished, with hindsight, that he had been more robust in pushing Centrex to deliver what ACPO needed. However as the foregoing analysis has demonstrated, it is questionable whether he would have got the support he needed from his ACPO peers.

Earlier, N03 argued that the model could not work effectively unless the commander, the intelligence manager and the analyst were working together in harmony. However, the obvious inadequacy of NIM training meant that two of those three were completely unprepared for the demands made upon them and the third was provided with only the most basic of knowledge. Given the recent history of high profile intelligence failures, the reader may question ACPO's strategy. The consequences of failing to train people for these key roles were never properly considered. Even though the police service lacked the necessary knowledge or expertise, it would be reasonable to surmise that it might be available in some other government department and might be readily obtained via a process of policy or knowledge transfer. However, those alternatives seem never to have been seriously considered. That provides more evidence of the insularity, the 'silo' mentality that dominated the police organization in this era.

N03 and N06 said that despite the lack of training, the NIM delivered some improvements in intelligence work. N03 said that intelligence assessments had improved marginally since implementation but further development was dependent on improvements in information technology. N06 noted that whilst the overall standard of intelligence assessments had improved, he continued to see a 'mixed bag' that were 'overly crime related' and that ignored those problems of concern to local communities. However, O'Connor has argued on the basis of assessments seen by his inspectors that the picture was uniformly poor. NIM intelligence assessments had only 'a narrow base and [that] in many places the analytical and other products appeared to have had only a limited influence on decision making' (2005, p.36).

A further example of that fractured and disjointed approach to strategy and policymaking is provided by efforts to estimate the scale and extent of policing problems in BCUs and in forces. As the reader has seen, police intelligence units produce the NIM intelligence assessments but the crime audits required by the Crime and Disorder Act 1998 (that are used to formulate a three-year plan of how the local crime reduction partnership will address crime and disorder in their area) were produced by completely different departments (usually those with responsibility for community relations). Forces also were obliged to produce annual policing plans which often were written by a third department.

One can only speculate on how forces managed their business well enough to respond to a NIM strategic assessment refreshed every six months, the National Community Reassurance Plan (NCRP) refreshed every three years, crime audits refreshed every three years (but not according to a pattern that coincided with the NCRP), and the annual policing plan prepared for the police authority – now the PCC (see Fletcher and Stenson, 2009 on the growing complexity of those arrangements). That neither those involved in the creation nor implementation of the NIM appeared to have considered these requirements provides further evidence of ACPO's failure to reflect 'real world' demands.

The NIM structures and processes could replace some if not all of these other strategic plans and indeed, proposals to merge the NIM strategic assessment and the crime audit set out in the 2004 White Paper seemed eminently sensible. ACPO member N03 said that he held a series of meetings with representatives of the Association of Police Authorities (APA). According to an APA official who participated in those meetings (N05), there was an expectation that the model would become ever more important as a business plan for police authorities. N05 said that the APA saw the NIM as being capable of strengthening accountability in ways that pointed 'fundamentally to a better relationship' between police and partners.

There is some evidence that in some areas there has been such a development. For example, established at the end of 2003, the Greater Manchester Against Crime (GMAC) Partnership Business Model is based upon an 'interpretation' of the NIM (GMAC, 2011). The GMAC model aims to provide common methods for the ten Community Safety Partnerships in Greater Manchester to manage their core business. However, interviewed for this research, respondent N08, an information officer employed by the County local authority, highlighted that plans to develop those arrangements in his force area were developing much more slowly than he wanted and that other authorities he worked closely with, including Greater London, had abandoned their plans because they found them unworkable.

The NIM's language and style

Factors in the resistance to the NIM that I have not yet properly acknowledged were the language, style and even the name of the model. John and Maguire (2004) in their study found that there were large 'knowledge gaps' amongst all ranks and some resistance to the NIM based on ignorance and on dislike of its 'academic' structure and language. Many of my respondents cited the management jargon and exclusive language contained within the NIM as impediments to comprehension of the model in mainstream policing. A typical observation was that the model was 'too full of terminology and was not user friendly'. Senior intelligence analyst N039 said 'It just blinds you with the language and the unnecessary jargon'. ACPO member N053 said that the NIM had earned a bad reputation because it was 'overly bureaucratic ... and overly complicated'.

The NIM's inaccessible prose gave insufficient consideration to the reader. Jargon and exclusive terms may be common currency in policing but the NIM raised their usage to new levels of obfuscation and impenetrability; this was a classic example of the medium obscuring what was meant to be a very simple message. ACPO member N01 said that:

> with the benefit of hindsight, the 20/20 ... I think that had it been written in simpler terms, had it not been so elegant, elegantly written, if it had been conceptualised in a different way I think it would have taken off much easier.

ACPO member N03 said that for the ordinary police officer the model was, 'very high-powered, very high-level, and principally sound without question ... but little practical application within it'. In interview, NCIS executive N102 accepted that he had made mistakes in formulating the NIM. In writing the model, his central aim had been to describe a management process that put intelligence at the heart of policing activity but he had assumed a level of knowledge that just did not exist in mainstream policing. He said:

> I acknowledge that we wouldn't start from here now. Of course we wouldn't ... I suppose, this is inevitable, not only was [the NIM] a child of its time, it was a product of the people of that time. Even though we were being innovative, I joined the cops in 1964 so I've kicked around it for 40 odd years and inevitably times change.

'Management speak' of the kind found in the NIM is one of the curses of modern times. Often it is used to make something seem more impressive or complex (and therefore exclusive) than it really is. The model is littered with examples. For instance, the NIM terms 'knowledge products' and 'system products' mean, respectively, 'knowledge' and 'systems'. The knowledge and systems described by the NIM possess no attributes beyond those commonly understood but their meaning is obfuscated as a means of elevating the terms and inflating their importance. As many respondents in this research commented, elaboration of this kind is neither desirable nor necessary and it certainly was a barrier to understanding, yet examples like this are sprinkled throughout the model.

The case against management or marketing speak of this kind perhaps was put best by Sir Ivor Roberts, formerly the British ambassador to Italy. In 2006, on leaving his employment with the Foreign Service, Sir Ivor noted wearily:

> Too much of the change management agenda is written in Wall Street management speak which is already tired and discredited by the time it is introduced. 'Synergies, value for money, best value, benchmarking, silo working, roll-out, stakeholder, empower, push back, deliver the agenda, fit for purpose', are all prime candidates for a game of 'bulls**t bingo' (in Parris, 2009, p.1).

Readers of the NIM and its associated codes and manuals of guidance will sympathize with Roberts' sentiments. Disappointingly, even though ACPO eventually recognized the challenges that the model faced in that context, ACPO member N06 confirmed that it made no effort to change the NIM's prose. ACPO's subsequent efforts, through NCPE, to produce doctrine for the police service demonstrated that it learnt little from this failure.

Even though the NIM essentially described a business or planning process, several respondents in this study referred to the inappropriateness of the term. To many, it suggested an unwelcome association with particular policing styles or specialisms (that is, criminal intelligence or crime control) and in the minds of many confirmed the NIM's role in what Reiner (2010, p.206) has called the 'managerialist-cum-populist stress' on crime-fighting, prevalent in this period. ACPO member N03 said that the model was named 'incorrectly'. In his view, the NIM was 'a policing model that is all about resourcing; all about information' but the inclusion of the word intelligence 'skews things a little bit'. He suggested that more accurate names for the NIM would have been the 'National Information Model' or the 'National Resourcing Model'. NCIS executive N102, agreed that the NIM was 'very much a business model rather than an intelligence model' as the term implied. N06 agreed that the model's designation was misleading. However in his view, the debate on that topic already had been fruitlessly rehearsed 'a zillion times'. He said, 'Yes the name is misleading but would I change it at this stage? Probably not'!

UK intelligence architecture

The reader has already seen indications that the police intelligence architecture in England and Wales has always been fragmented and inefficient. Even if senior commanders had been completely committed to the NIM, by no means a given, the inadequacy of that architecture would have prevented the model from making the impact that its architects anticipated. In this section, I highlight some of the most significant inadequacies and inefficiencies.

During this study, national responsibility for managing criminal intelligence was vested in NCIS. Police inspector N016 said that most forces managed their responsibilities for local and regional intelligence through force intelligence bureaux. A significant exception to that rule was the largest force in the country, the Metropolitan Police. This led NCIS executive N102 to suggest that the Met was 'hazarding its future' because without that single point of access it was unlikely that it could fulfil its information management responsibilities, under the Data Protection and Freedom of Information Acts.[2]

In the mainstream, local intelligence units have long since replaced collators. However, former detective inspector N055 said that the notion of local intelligence staff as less capable and less valuable than their operational colleagues persisted. N102 said that the lack of training and support offered, meant that those who worked in BCUs probably were the least well trained in the police service and also the least well paid for the work that they did. In his view, the service was simply 'not geared up' to intelligence work at the local level because the service had 'never seen it as an area for people investment'. He cited as an example, the intelligence failure connected to the murders of Holly Wells and Jessica Chapman by Ian Huntley. He said that the systemic failure, in every one of the 43 forces in England and Wales, to properly train and support intelligence staff meant that an event like Soham had been 'an accident waiting to happen'. Though in his view it was no coincidence that it was Humberside, a force that had 'invested so little in its intelligence and information management' which had suffered the most.

Cope et al posited that the shift to ILP demanded an intelligence system based on network principles that employed a 'production line' approach in which intelligence units 'function as "knowledge centres" within the "intelligent organisation"' (2003, pp.29–30). In such systems, the unit takes responsibility for developing information on individuals or groups which it then passes to other units who enact the investigation. This approach has a compelling logic in the modern era and, at least in part; it is consistent with contemporary practice. However, Fielding highlighted that it was difficult for the network logic to overcome 'the established values of the occupational culture, together with the tradition of hierarchical organisation' (cited in Cope et al, 2003). Events following the putative implementation of the NIM demonstrate that Fielding's words were particularly insightful. N102 said that instead of applying that kind of logic, the service just used the intelligence system as a place to 'chuck everything you haven't got a home for'.

In the aftermath of the Soham murders, the Bichard Report identified fundamental errors in police intelligence processes and *inter alia* recommended the establishment of a national intelligence database and protocols for the management of intelligence. ACPO's response; the IMPACT Programme, was formulated to encompass a comprehensive change in police information management. This included the computerized IMPACT Nominal Index (to enable forces to establish whether data of interest in criminal investigations might be held elsewhere) and the Police National Database (meant to provide a single access point for data held across all of the police's local and national information systems). The programme also established a new code of practice for the Management of Police Information (the MoPI) (NCPE, 2006a).

N102 said that Bichard should be a catalyst for a major change in policing because 'the one thing that the cops are responsive to is getting smacked about the head and Bichard has given them something to think about'. However, he was critical of NPIA over its MoPI guidance which approached the problem of information management 'from the old police perspective ... you pile all the stuff in a pot somewhere and ransack it at will'. NPIA failed to recognize that police systems did not provide the fundamental integrity in records management required. That made the service intensely vulnerable around information not managed properly according to the law. Interviewed in August 2005, ACPO member N06 regretted that he had not been more robust in his response to the Bichard Report. He said that the opportunity to talk about the failure of intelligence was missed. Data protection was only a small part of the problem yet this is what, in the main, Bichard had focused upon and ACPO had not challenged this effectively enough.

The capability of intelligence staff should have been a matter of much greater concern to ACPO. In an interview, former detective superintendent N051 recalled his experiences as a teacher at Bramshill Police College during 2008. He found that his students (in the main, senior police officers) complained that their intelligence units were made up of 'the sick and the lame'. In that context, the situation clearly had improved little since the Audit Commission (1993, p.37) made that same observation some 15 years earlier.[3] He said that the officers' comments demonstrated that there was an inability amongst senior officers to understand that 'if you don't make any investment in intelligence then you will get back exactly what you put in'.

ACPO member (NIM implementation) N03 believed that the police service could resolve the situation by creating a national career pathway for intelligence officers (just as Phillips had done in Kent). He questioned the need for sworn police officers to hold intelligence posts. He said that the precedent of 'civilian' intelligence officers was well established in 'the security services, the military and in NCIS'. However, there is a certain irony (given the support of the President of ACPO and another key figure in intelligence in the Association) in the fact that ACPO does not appear to have made any move to develop this as policy and also that none of the services that N03 identified, was called upon to resolve the intelligence training deficit in policing he identified.

According to ACPO member N053, the inadequacy of police intelligence work could not be attributed to a lack of resources. He felt that the 'generosity' of successive governments, meant that the police had sufficient resources to meet most challenges they faced in this context but (in his view) the police needed a model based upon the service's twin strengths, its people and its information. The failure to train staff in the NIM was symptomatic of a wider malaise in police training; forces did not tell their staff how to use information. Police training was all about 'training to respond to incidents and being able to deal with incidents in a capable fashion'. Training needed to be approached in a more holistic manner.

Senior intelligence official N050 said that the police struggled to use their information effectively. She felt that the service did not have the necessary infrastructure. Essentially, in her view, policing was hamstrung by the 'response' culture. She was critical of the police's information-gathering processes observing that, 'policing doesn't think about what information it wants to gather … most of the information is brought to it by the people who use its services. It still doesn't do an awful lot of pro-active information gathering'.

A further problem was the reluctance of officers to share the information that they collected (which could of course also be attributed to the failure of the training regime). N053 said that even though some key individuals stood out like beacons and 'realised that actually understanding the information is critical', the general level of resistance was 'just truly, truly magnificent'. He considered that Centrex's introduction of the MoPI had failed to achieve its intended aim. It had gone some way to persuading officers that they should not conceal intelligence from their supervisors. However, the hoarding of intelligence by different units and departments remained problematic for the police organization. He said:

> It may have moved beyond the individual but it's now very clearly in teams, units, stations, boroughs … and it's exactly the same argument, magnified up. It's exactly the same as it was in the 1970s. It's now actually much bigger on an organisational level. If the organisation wants to embrace information-led rather than intelligence-led policing then it needs to actually find a way to get rid of all those cultural barriers, all that protectionism, that exists.

N053's words reflect both the findings of Manning and Hawkins (1989) who noted that 'the social organisation of police work ensures that information ... remains located primarily in the heads of officers, and secondarily in their own case files, private notes or log books' (1989, p.145). According to N053, the new infrastructure that Centrex had attempted to establish (through the MoPI and other intelligence doctrine) had been only partially successful in overcoming the cultural resistance to the sharing of information. The hoarding of intelligence in the ways described is not only significant in the context of police culture but it could have serious implications for the service in terms of its compliance with a range of legislation from the Data Protection Act 1998 to the Human Rights Act 1998. The issues described in the foregoing paragraphs should have been of much greater concern to police managers. That they were not, suggests a lack of understanding of the consequences of inadequate and inefficient data management.

Phillips' retirement from the police service

A rather obvious question that arises from the foregoing analysis is, if there was so much resistance to the NIM then how did it achieve the measure of success claimed in the previous chapter? The most important factor in that context was David Phillips' policy entrepreneurship which allowed him to overcome his colleagues' objections and to secure ACPO's mandate. Phillips exploited his influence on the Home Office to persuade it to codify the NIM as *the* model for mainstream policing in England and Wales. However, with hindsight, it is now obvious that his position as President of the Association was critical to his success and his departure from that post in March 2003 meant that his star (and the prospects for ILP and the NIM) soon began to wane.

The Home Office senior official who lauded Phillips' advocacy of the NIM and the impression that he made on the department (N065) said that Phillips' influence on the Home Office was diminished by his retirement from the police service. He said that the model:

> Started to lose its focus when David Phillips moved from being ACPO President to NCPE because NCPE for him was all about applying NIM in practice even more rigorously and demonstrably ... the whole lustre if you like of being President of ACPO and a full time chief as well – you know, going to a quango like NCPE – he was very frustrated in that role because the influence was nothing like as significant.

Following Phillips' departure, lacking its former President's personal commitment to ILP and the NIM, the priorities of the Association seemed to change. The latent resistance to the NIM came to the surface. Thereafter, individual ACPO members gave greater priority to their own ideas, their own ambitions, for policing in the modern era (for example, those ideas captured in the neighbourhood policing programme) and to other challenges that were emerging (at least at the rhetorical level, these included the need to deal more effectively with cross-border crime and questions about force restructuring).

However, by persuading the Home Office to codify the model (under section 39A of the Police Act 1996, as inserted by Section 2 of the Police Reform Act 2002); Phillips had set the service on a path from which it could not easily deviate.[4] This presented ACPO members with a problem. Few matched Phillips' enthusiasm for the model but the NPP and the statutory NIM code of practice meant that they could not easily ignore it. As the reader will see, the compromise solution favoured by the service elite was to adopt a policy of 'NIM compliance' that ticked boxes but which paid little meaningful regard to business outcomes.

Cross-border crime

The service's inability to respond effectively to cross-border crime undoubtedly was a complicating factor for those advancing the NIM as the solution to the challenges of the twenty-first century. In 2005, HMIC identified a significant gap at this level and questioned the ability of the service's 30 year-old, 43-force structure to provide a solid platform for a future policing environment that it considered to be characterized by 'widespread, enterprising, organised criminality; proliferating international terrorism and domestic extremism; a premium on intelligence, expertise and smart use of capacity and an increasingly risk-concerned public and intrusive media' (O'Connor, 2005, p.7).

In an interview, ACPO member (NIM implementation) N03 said that cross-border crime was 'something which will significantly hurt you if you take your eye off it and if you don't police it because you're concentrating on performance targets and [local] issues'. He said that an example of a force that 'took its eye off' the emerging problem of cross-border crime with significant consequences was Nottinghamshire. In the first few weeks of 2005, the force's command team had publicly acknowledged that they had done so. He said that as a result the force's performance around local crime was 'completely off skew' because it took commanders all their resources to try to resolve the cross-border problem. In turn, that meant that local problems began to build up because the force did not have sufficient resources to police them effectively (see Ford, 2010 on the difficulties of the Nottinghamshire force in that context).

In my view, the distinction between cross-border and local criminals is false and it is a barrier to effective intelligence work and investigative practice. Former detective inspector N055 said that in his experience 'professional' criminals (usually associated with cross-border offending) fell into one of two categories, either they were 'lifestyle criminals; people who found that they had no other alternatives in life' or they saw life as a challenge and made 'a conscious choice to engage in crime'.[5] He said that popular representations of professional criminals failed to acknowledge that individuals can operate at any level depending on the circumstances that pertain at any given time. He said:

> Individuals exploit opportunities. Someone who is involved in international drug trafficking today, can be involved in illegal gambling tomorrow and at the same time be buying other types of drugs for their personal use, getting involved in pirate DVDs or fiddling their VAT or income tax. All these activities present law enforcement with opportunities.

In my experience, those opportunities are rarely capitalized upon as well as they might be. The reader need only consider the lived reality of many local communities facing for example; widespread drugs problems or gun crime, to see that *a priori* there are clear links between those 'professionals' and local policing problems. Every professional criminal, every gang boss, every member of every criminal network lives within a community and on some local police officer's 'patch'. Properly exploited, the local intelligence opportunities routinely afforded can be useful adjuncts to the more sophisticated intelligence gathering methods that one might associate with specialist detective squads. This would go some way towards achieving a single service approach.

The closing of the perceived gap between local and cross-border crime was one of the drivers of the plans for force reorganization that emerged in 2005. HMIC argued that the policing environment required a service that could deal effectively with 'volume crime [and] the current performance focus, but [would] also have demonstrable readiness to tackle complex, volatile threats to individuals, neighbourhoods and businesses'. To achieve this, the police service needed not only to change its structure, but the 'whole configuration of policing' (O'Connor, 2005, p.6).

Ultimately, Home Office reorganization plans were shelved due to opposition from police authorities. However, that debate has rumbled on with ACPO tending to favour replacement of the existing structure with larger regional bodies that may be better placed to tackle national and international serious and organized crime and finding support from ACPO chief Hugh Orde (BBC News, 2009, p.1). Force restructuring as a means of reforming the service to make it 'fit for purpose' in the twenty-first century remains firmly on the agenda and it can only have been given further impetus with the recent merger of the eight Scottish forces to produce 'Policing Scotland'.

In the context of that debate ACPO (2008) argued, perhaps counter-intuitively given the foregoing analysis, that the NIM is a cohesive model that is capable of coordinating operational activity from the national to the local and from the local to the national. According to ACPO the NIM can also enable 'information to move freely between local level community intelligence and "developed intelligence" to trigger covert investigations' (2008, p.56). Arguing against, as it saw, the effective disintegration of the service, ACPO cautioned the Home Office that future mechanisms for 'funding, governance and accountability' must recognize 'that the whole spectrum of policing activity must be given due priority in parallel' so that the service is not 'balkanised [sic] into separate structures for neighbourhood policing; cross border policing activity and national security' (2008, p.57). There is logic to ACPO's argument. However, the reader has seen in this study that the commitment of many ACPO members to ILP and the NIM was questionable. Whether the Association's claims for the model amounted to a Pauline conversion of its membership to the NIM's aims or whether it simply was enlisted as a means of influencing policy is surely open to question.

7
Evaluating ILP and the NIM: Urban Case Study

Introduction

This chapter, the first of two case studies, evaluates the extent to which the introduction of the NIM in 'Urban' represented a genuine effort to mainstream ILP in that force. I examine the force's bifurcated approach; its decision to reject the NIM as an organizing framework for corporate business but to mandate its local policing units to implement the model.

Intelligence and investigative practice in the force are analysed through an assessment of the work of a local policing unit. The analysis is based on my own observations of business meetings, on interviews with officers, police staff and policing partners, and on the views of a broad range of frontline officers that were collected from focus groups.

Reaction of the Urban elite to the NIM

I chose Urban as a case for study because it has often taken the lead on policymaking, has a long history of 'going it alone' and was likely to offer a significantly contrasting perspective to the second case 'County'. Against the background of: the resistance to ILP at the national level; the inadequacy of the national police intelligence architecture; the seeming inadequacy of the implementation process; and Urban's pre-existing commitment to neighbourhood policing, mainstreaming ILP was always going to be a challenge for the force.

NCIS executive N102 said that whilst it never showed any inclination to do so, Urban's size and influence meant that the force could have 'killed off' the NIM at birth. Given ACPO's 'presumption of compliance' in favour of the model, one might believe that talks between the NIM team and Urban's leaders over implementation would be straightforward However, providing further evidence of ACPO's lack of cohesion, N102 said that the negotiations were a 'long painful process'. He said that at one stage of the negotiations he was offered the job of implementing the NIM in Urban. His response that he was 'not looking for a fast track to the grave', indicated his view of the challenge ahead.

In 2002, following those meetings, Urban established its own implementation team. Ostensibly, its role was to prepare the force to accept the model (both in structural and marketing terms). However, team members quickly recognized that despite the ACPO agreement, its senior commanders were not persuaded of the merits of the model. Senior intelligence official N050 said that personally she supported intelligence-led, evidence-based, practice but she was far from certain that the chief officer would accept it and that there was never a chance that Urban would restructure in the same way as the Kent force. There was an obvious lack of unanimity at the elite level of the force. Some of the command team (one may reasonably assume, those who were not party to the NCIS meetings) believed that the model was being foisted upon them without adequate negotiation. Urban senior official N015 said that the key issue in the force became that the NIM 'wasn't invented here and therefore they (members of the force elite) just would not have it'.

Respondents, including ACPO member N098 and N050 said that some opposition was founded on the NIM's perceived conflict with Urban's own strategic plans. A section of the elite expressed doubts about Urban's ability to dovetail the model into existing management processes (N050). Those doubts only increased as they learned more about the NIM. Naturally, this research was unable to capture every development in Urban but according to N050, with limited input to its elite decision-making forums, she was unable to sustain the elite's interest in the model even though members' private reservations were never expressed publicly.

N050 said that eventually she too came to the realization that the NIM was 'fundamentally flawed' as a business model. She said that many of Urban's elite believed its advocates just had not fully appreciated the complexity of business planning in policing. That *de facto* rejection of the model meant that Urban's executive (the level below the elite team) made little effort to embed it in the force's business processes. Tellingly, N015 said that he perceived the resistance to the

NIM to be so great at the elite level, so entrenched, that he made a decision not to refer to the model in any corporate plans because to do so would mean that command team would not sign them off.

Predictably therefore, the NIM played no meaningful part in coordinating activity at the corporate level and it made no impact whatsoever on any of the force's major decision-making forums (senior intelligence official, N050). N050 said that no NIM intelligence assessment 'worthy of the name' was ever produced at the corporate level of the force. According to an inspector charged with the responsibility of allocating Urban's centrally-held resources (such as the mounted section, police dogs, etc.) (N016), the very best that could be said about its impact on Urban's elite was that it was 'extremely limited'.

In an interview, a member of that elite (N031) said that its focus on other priorities took precedence over any planning for the NIM. He said that as someone committed to streamlining Urban's management processes and to finding solutions aimed at preventing the force 'hurtling in crisis mode from one issue to the next' he should have been the NIM's strongest supporter. However, he said that he had done nothing to encourage discussion of the model and his 'honest observation' was that he could not remember the NIM coming up 'in any meaningful way in any measurable discussion' he had been party to. He said:

It is interesting that we have just not confronted [the NIM] in any meaningful way. So even in the context of where we were looking very carefully at how to get a more rationalised joined up effective way of using our intelligence, NIM has been invisible.[1]

Interviewed in 2007, a member of Urban's police authority (N052) said that he had been briefed on the NIM in 2004. Initially, he had been concerned about Urban's ability to adopt the model because it represented such 'a revolutionary approach' to managing the force'. Three years on, his sense was that it was the norm in policing and had become 'embedded' in Urban because, since that briefing, the model had been referred to so rarely in his meetings with Urban's elite. What seems clear now is that regardless of the National Policing Plan (NPP) and ACPO's support of the NIM, to all intents and purposes it was ignored at the elite level of this force.

ACPO member N098, a self-declared advocate of the NIM, expressed his frustration with some of his peers. In his view, the greatest problems were 'the cultural barriers [and] protectionism' that existed in the force. He said that even if the earlier rhetoric (that emerged from the NCIS meetings) suggested otherwise, most of the elite were unwilling to embrace the changes that the mainstreaming of ILP were bound to bring. Moreover, some simply would not share their information and resources. He cited as an example, his peers' attitude to plans then being made for a new intelligence structure which included at its apex an FIB controlled by the specialist detective branch.

Even though the chief officer and deputy were persuaded that a new structure was needed, the majority of the elite were ambivalent and some were implacably opposed to the plan (N098). He said that the ACPO member with responsibility for local policing was 'dead against it' and the member in charge of the force's Special Branch was 'vehemently and venomously against it'. In N098's view, the former feared that he would lose staff and resources to the new bureau and the latter would not surrender to the new unit, SB's exclusive access to the intelligence received from the security services. Territoriality; manifested in an unwillingness to cede power and influence, is often found in police organizations so it is no surprise to see it feature here. Gill's analysis of information as a valuable commodity that can define an individual's power, seems apposite here in this case study (2000). Though, considered against the background of recent COMPSTAT-inspired reforms in policing, it is easy to see how a police manager might be sensitive to any changes in their departments that reduced their resources without also diminishing their responsibilities.

A member of the Urban elite (N031) said that the model had little effect on the force and its impact even on the FIB, when it eventually was introduced, was limited. That was substantiated in 2008 when an inspection found the bureau was applying the model inconsistently and had even unilaterally determined that the NIM model was 'not compulsory' for some categories of the intelligence it managed. That was entirely predictable – FIB executives were simply following their commanders' lead.

NIM at BCU level

I argued in the previous section that the NIM simply was not implemented in Urban at the elite level. However, senior intelligence official N050 said that even though she believed that the model could not help to organize the business of the force (as an individual entity), she was persuaded (and in turn, persuaded senior commanders) that it would have some value for local policing. Urban's senior management mandated its NIM team to work with its BCU commanders to introduce the model at the local level.

I am no conspiracy theorist but it has to be recognized that the result of that decision was to demonstrate to the Home Office and to HMIC (which was tasked with monitoring NIM implementation) that Urban was fulfilling its duty under the NPP to implement the NIM even though its real impact on the force would be, at best, marginal. The reader has seen that, together, the NPM-inspired management ethos (a feature of policing since the 1980s) and the HMIC inspection regime encouraged commanders to demonstrate compliance over any meaningful consideration of outcomes. In that context, the decision may be just another example of the way in which public policy is translated by those tasked with implementation and the reader should not necessarily be surprised by that.

Local commanders generally were unaware of the tensions surrounding ILP policy at the highest level of the force. For them, there was no negotiating; the NIM was just the next thing they were obliged to implement. Just as at the highest level of the force, views on the NIM were inextricably bound up with attitudes and beliefs about the broader topics of ILP and intelligence work. The local commanders interviewed broadly welcomed its emphasis on, and support of, intelligence work. However, they had reservations about whether the changes they were obliged to make to their operating practices could be effective in the long term.

BCU commander N033 said that the model brought structure to their operational planning. She said that it meant that officers better understood how their individual efforts fitted into the broader picture of intelligence, which Urban collected to support its investigative activity (though little evidence was seen in this study to support that belief). Detective chief inspector N035 said that the NIM meeting structure offered more accountability and the chance of better engagement with partners, and it also allowed the command team to demonstrate that it both understood the policing problems it faced and that it was managing its resources effectively. Though as this chapter will show, at least in terms of partnership and resource management, that analysis was flawed.

The Senior Management Team (SMT)'s commitment to intelligence work was evident in its resourcing of its local intelligence unit which was made up of approximately 40 staff. Headed by a detective inspector as the intelligence manager, the work of the unit was divided between a number of 'focus desks' overseen by sergeants (some detectives, others police sergeants), staffed by civilian analysts and researchers, and sworn police officers as FIOs.[2] Though CID officers accounted for most of the supervisory posts, they represented only a very small minority of the staff (only four out of the 40 staff in the unit during the period of the research). In the BCU chosen for the study, the NIM meeting cycle was followed faithfully, and the BCU's analysts prepared NIM intelligence assessments in the recommended manner. On the surface at least, the NIM was in place and was fully operational.

According to an inspector charged with the responsibility of allocating Urban's centrally-held resources (N016), similar arrangements were in place across the force. Though he acknowledged that levels of efficiency and effectiveness were inconsistent. A member of the force elite (N031) was more direct on that subject. During his visits to BCUs, he found that intelligence capability was 'very variable' and the whole picture of NIM implementation was not as 'clear-cut' or positive as he had expected to find. There was no consistent approach to the NIM and it had not provided a framework capable of developing much consistency. He was particularly concerned that what he observed seemed to contradict HMIC's endorsement of the implementation process. This once again raises questions about inspection regime that values process over outcomes.

Few frontline officers were able to relate either ILP or the NIM to their daily work; those that attempted to do so discussed the model only in the vaguest of terms. Given the lack of NIM training highlighted earlier, it was entirely predictable that this would be the case. Intelligence team leader N042 said that on balance he felt that the model was a positive development. Though it should be noted that intelligence staff had a better understanding than most of what the NIM was intended to achieve because intelligence managers and analysts had been provided with some, albeit limited, training.

Senior intelligence analyst N039 said the NIM provided her with clarity, structure and common points of reference. However, like many before her, she criticized the delivery of that information. Echoing the views of some senior commanders, N035 said that the NIM had been imposed without sufficient consultation and without sufficient account being taken of local differences (that is, without reference to context); this made the NIM 'a very difficult beast'.

Tensions between the intelligence manager, the analysts and local commanders were revealed by N038, who should have been a key figure in the process. However, he said that he felt marginalized by the NIM and that he had been cut out of the chain of command (and the information loop) by the local commander who tasked the analysts without any reference to him. There certainly was disharmony in the unit and an element of 'picking sides' in blaming who or what was the cause of that conflict. The net result was that it perpetuated the inefficiency of the intelligence unit (for example, in terms of its prioritization of analytical work and the standard of the intelligence assessments it produced).

Another consequence of the manager's disillusionment was that, without official sanction, he maintained his own intelligence database (using a stand-alone computer) containing information on those suspected of crime in the BCU area. Essentially, this amounted to a reinvention of the collator system but with a personal computer rather than a rolodex and card indices. This breached both the force's data security rules and data protection principles. FIO N045 said that the database was insecure and amounted to a 'ridiculous duplication' of the official records and it was clear that this too was a continuing source of tension between the intelligence manager and the rest of the unit.

The NIM process in Urban

Having established the environment into which the NIM was introduced, I now want to examine its influence on intelligence work and investigative practice at the local level.

Intelligence collection in Urban

The intelligence unit's primary purpose in the new environment was to collect intelligence around local priorities. However, what may appear to be a simple task for 40 intelligence unit staff was complicated by poor supervision of those frontline staff who contributed much of the unit's data, and by a continuing focus on generating performance data rather than intelligence analyses.

The unit relied too heavily on police data for those analyses. Many intelligence reports were entered into the intelligence database by patrol officers via any one of the more than 100 data terminals located across the BCU. This was convenient for the officers but gave the unit little control over what was entered. Cope et al highlighted that in the modern era officers provide so much extraneous information in their reports that it creates an 'information glut' that proves problematic for analysts (2003, p.26). This was confirmed by chief inspector N035 who said that the NIM encouraged the collection of so much data; it was difficult to extrapolate essential intelligence from 'the mire'; the huge number of intelligence reports did not necessarily translate into useful intelligence.

Intelligence manager N038 attributed this to poor supervision and the insistence of local commanders that the quantity (rather than the quality) of reports submitted should be a performance indicator. N038 and a patrol constable (N049) detailed the effect of that decision. Duplicate reports could be entered by officers from the same team for the same incident or, where multiple persons were stopped at the same time, separate entries for each person could be made without them being linked. So for example, where four officers stopped three individuals, in theory, a total of 12 intelligence records could be created. The result was no more useful intelligence than would have been generated by a single entry. N038 said this was a significant factor in the perception of the unit as a 'black hole' into which much data entered but little came out again.

Collation, analysis and evaluation in Urban

The NIM was expected to focus the work of intelligence analysts. An individual piece of analysis is often the product of hours of work by analysts and researchers. Therefore, analysts should produce assessments around identified priorities and only otherwise if directed by their manager. In the Urban BCU, much of the analysts' work reflected those priorities but a significant proportion did not. Analyst N044 said that the manager and senior analyst tried to filter requests but protocols often were not followed and the system was not robust enough to support analysts who did not acquiesce to those extra demands.

Many examples of crime pattern analyses and subject profiles were seen during the fieldwork for this research. No results analyses (the analytical technique recommended to commanders as providing the best means of evaluating their operations) were carried out by the intelligence unit. Gill (2000) has described an ideal model of an intelligence system in the modern era. That system orientates around information and control and utilizes feedback to steer future action. However, Innes and Fielding have argued that Gill's system represents a 'normative model of what should happen, rather than a descriptive model of what actually occurs in practice' (2002, p.14). In particular, they argue that the feedback loop that is fundamental to the model usually is missing. The lack of results analysis carried out in Urban lends weight to Innes and Fielding's criticism and suggests that in this case the NIM did not make the BCU any 'smarter' in evaluating its operational endeavours than it had been under the previous regimes.

Presentation of evidence in Urban

Strategic analyses were prepared by the senior analyst and every six months they were presented at the strategic meeting to the BCU commander. After three months, the assessment was reviewed at a further meeting (so that there were a total of four strategic meetings each year). The intelligence unit produced a NIM tactical assessment for the weekly tactical meeting. To that extent, the BCU faithfully followed the NIM guidelines. However, both commander N033 and senior analyst N039 questioned the value of those assessments.

The former said that the requirement for each BCU to complete a strategic assessment did not represent 'best value' because they were completed too frequently. She too said that the standard of the assessments was variable and inconsistent. In her view, Urban should establish a strategic analysis unit to compile thematic assessments for the force. N039 questioned whether commanders understood that the assessments were intended to provide a basis for a discussion about future priorities, rather than simply confirming what the SMT already knew about its policing problems. She said there was a danger that it saw the assessments as 'paper exercises' that did not influence the day-to-day business of the BCU; assessments that would be referred to for administrative purposes but otherwise were 'shelved'. The need to meet Home Office performance targets meant that the control strategy would always include burglary and robbery. Those were the crime types that would attract its scarce proactive resources because the BCU commander directed it, no matter what the intelligence assessment recommended.

This forcefully demonstrated that the NIM did not overcome those established values of the occupational culture and the hierarchical tradition of the police organization. A former ACPO member N04 said that the 'big push' on performance management was 'inimical' to the NIM and that in his experience if 'strategic and/or tactical assessments indicated anything contradictory to national priorities, the latter held sway'. That HMIC inspectors did not identify this as an issue in their inspections of the force, suggests one of two things. Either, this issue was unique to the selected BCU or, it was of little concern to the inspectors. The foregoing analysis (which highlighted inspectors' enthusiasm for compliance) suggests that the latter is much more likely to be true.

Earlier in this study, ACPO member N03 argued that failing to see the 'bigger picture' could allow new threats that may have been just over the operational horizon to emerge unchallenged. That warning was not heeded in this BCU (in the next chapter the reader will see that County was similarly unprepared to meet those challenges). The setting of the BCU's control strategy according to centrally-imposed priorities rather than according to local intelligence assessments demonstrates as convincingly as anything in this research, the reality of ILP.

That is, that intelligence is often ignored in favour of compliance with performance standards. In my view, the NIM would have struggled to gain acceptance in the mainstream even if the antipathy of the force's senior commanders had not been a factor because the tensions between the model and the neighbourhood policing programme and between the reactive and proactive policing paradigms, together with the pressure to hit performance targets, manifested themselves just as forcefully in BCUs as they did at the force level.

I have already highlighted that training (specifically, the lack of it) was a significant factor in the failure of the NIM. Senior analyst N039 said that she struggled to write intelligence assessments because of lack of guidance. Assessments seen during the research period were weighty documents that clearly had taken a great deal of time and effort to prepare; the shortest seen was 73 pages long. At the end of the study, looking back at the previous year, N039 said that assessments remained too long and complicated because best practice had not been shared. She continued to prepare lengthy and complex assessments because she simply did not know what to leave out. Her concerns about the assessments were shared by other intelligence unit staff.

Something that received little attention was the NIM intelligence requirement. In interview, NCIS executive N102 said that the intelligence requirement was 'terribly, terribly, terribly, terribly difficult' to explain but he felt it was important to get right so that local intelligence could be fed into the fight against serious and organized crime. However, that message was not understood in Urban. Senior analyst N039, the only respondent to refer to the requirement in this study, said that its completion effectively was a paper exercise to ensure compliance with the standards set by ACPO. She said that the intelligence requirement 'stays in the PowerPoint and the Word document and doesn't really go any further than that ... I think we write the intelligence requirement because we need to – that's all'.

The willingness to continue to expend organizational time and energy in demonstrably inefficient and ineffective ways like this, even when the shortcomings of the NIM process were obvious to everyone, reveals much about the organizational culture of policing. It was hard to escape the conclusion that at every level of the BCU, individuals and groups carried out activities simply because they were told do so by those above them in the hierarchy. The compliance imperative pervaded the whole organization and few were willing or able to challenge that orthodoxy even when the incompatibility of the model and the existing structure of the force was obvious. Wright has argued that effecting any behavioural change in police organizations is a long-term process that requires 'a clear understanding of the pervasive culture ... and the individual and collective needs it fulfils' (2007, p.605). He highlighted that it is not enough that change programmes (like the NIM) adhere to a 'compliance agenda', they must also 'be highly credible to experienced practitioners and address the real difficulties inherent in the job' (2007, p.606). As the reader can see, there was little evidence of that in this case.

It is difficult to escape the conclusion that the collective failure to challenge the obvious inefficiencies identified here, suggested that the model was not made sufficiently credible to practitioners. It also suggests that there remained a substantial gap between the realities of day-to-day police management and the rhetoric of the NPM business ethos, with altogether too much emphasis placed on compliance at the expense of a proper examination of inputs and outcomes. This provided further evidence that Urban failed to grasp what it really meant to be intelligence-led.

Consultation with partners in Urban

The NIM contains some guidance on partnership working. Subsequently, NCPE has published further advice, which sets out clear directions to commanders to consult a range of partners when deciding on priorities and on the allocation of operational resources. However, in the BCU selected for this study there was only very limited evidence that the NIM contributed to that inclusive model of decision-making.

Many commentators have expressed concerns about police/community partnership interactions. Byrne and Pease (2003) argued that the police became frustrated with the partnership experience because it did not deliver what they expected. However, Gilling (2005) highlighted that this frustration is born out of a simplistic approach to that relationship. He argues that many fail to recognize that partnership represents a complex social phenomenon. Individual actors bring to it their own 'baggage' in the form of their professional ideology, and occupational and organizational cultures. He argued that partnerships require the investment of time and energy from all, if they are to be effective (Gilling, 2005, p.737). Gilling's argument that the advance of ILP has seen partnership become a one-way street with non-police bodies increasingly being used to address 'second order' problems that usually would come under the heading of anti-social behaviour (ASB), was certainly borne out in my study.

In theory, the NIM should have offered the BCU's partners a chance to influence policing priorities in much more effective ways. However, the practice fell short of the theory in a number of ways. Relatively few partners attended the NIM meetings which were dominated by the police. I saw no evidence of any meaningful effort to discover why partners did not attend or of what they needed from the police. Whilst the views of those who did attend were sought, on no occasion were police plans changed to accommodate their needs. This partly was due to the fact that partners made few demands on the police.

One particular issue of concern to the local authority was ASB. It was raised at each strategic meeting I observed but was dealt with perfunctorily. In one of the meetings, a complaint from the local authority's crime reduction department, that the BCU was ignoring ASB was dismissed by the commander. Providing a perfect example of the tension between priority crime and those harms of greater concern to communities that I discussed earlier, senior analyst N03 said that despite the local authority's request for ASB to join the 'few crumbs' for partners included in the police control strategy, it was not included because of the police's focus on achieving performance targets for priority crime.

In reality, there was little to discuss in the meeting in that context. N039 said that the commander decided the priorities in advance. It was the SMT's expectation that meeting the performance targets for priority crime would always be more important than anything else and therefore there was little room for manoeuvre. N039 wanted the commander to follow the NIM guidelines, and to seek the views of staff and partners in the meeting. However, she said that her lack of training and her inexperience meant she never had the confidence to challenge the latter on that point.

On the evidence of the strategic assessments seen in this research, an objective appraisal of the intelligence would have led to the inclusion of ASB in the BCU's control strategy. However, decisions on priorities were set by the commander before the meeting. Therefore, partners were excluded from the decision-making process. N039 expressed her sympathy for the local authority. She said:

It's like they are coming to be informed about what we are discussing rather than them being involved in the discussion. It is the process that is wrong. They always raise anti-social behaviour and want to know why it is not on the control strategy. I get the feeling that they go away thinking that they are all out of the loop. I get the impression that they don't get much out of it.

DCI N035 suggested that this debate masked fierce competition for resources between priority crime and the 'key public issue' of ASB which, as I will show later in this chapter, was being played out, outside of the strategic NIM meeting. Chief inspector 'partnerships' N036 said that some in the BCU recognized that the same individuals who committed the robberies and burglaries were responsible for the ASB and that they could be targeted through anti-social behaviour orders and the like. However, there was little evidence of this in the strategic meetings observed. At those meetings, senior analyst N039 presented the BCU's future priorities; they changed little in the research period.

It was obvious from the exchanges observed, that the BCU's performance against Home Office-imposed targets was by far the most important consideration for the commander. Unsurprisingly, she allocated a disproportionate amount of resources to those areas in which the BCU was under-performing. N036 said that although this went completely against the principle of the NIM, 'borough commanders live and die by their performance targets' and they could not afford to do otherwise. That tension was apparent at the first strategic meeting observed and was never resolved during the period of the research.

The conflict between demands on the police to deal effectively with 'priority' crime and at the same time address those areas of concern for local communities has long been recognized. Like Gilling, Crawford highlighted the competing agendas of partners. He argued that the managerialist reforms of the last 20 years not only encouraged individual introspection on the part of the police but also strengthened intra-organizational control at the expense of collaboration (2001, p.63). They may also have hindered the cause of partnership by buttressing 'baronial fiefdoms' in the criminal justice arena. Indeed, Shapland (2000) has argued that these managerialist reforms may actually have strengthened those spheres of influence.

The NIM tactical meetings also demonstrated the imperfect application of the model. These were large meetings chaired by the BCU commander and, unusually, divided into two phases. The first phase (known by participants simply as 'the tasking meeting') was attended by around 25 police officers and staff and representatives of the local authority's crime reduction department. They were lengthy affairs, often lasting longer than two hours. As in the strategic meeting, there was a heavy emphasis on the BCU's performance throughout this phase, although the NIM tactical intelligence assessments were also given some prominence in discussions.

Once again, local authority crime reduction staff were the only non-police attendees. Local authority crime reduction manager N058 said that she was always made welcome at NIM meetings. However, she recognized that her ability to influence the police was extremely limited because her contributions amounted to no more than 'chipping in a comment about this or that decision'. She believed that decisions made in the meetings were police decisions and there was not the 'genuine shared responsibility' that the NIM's advocates envisaged. Interviews with the BCU commander and the Crime Reduction Manager (CRM) confirmed their shared commitment to partnership working but the CRM did not view the NIM as important to future success in that context. In her view, the NIM meetings were largely irrelevant to her work. Therefore, she was happy to see her role as that of an observer.

Other members of the BCU SMT expressed their support for partnership working. For example, DCI N035 said that she wanted more engagement with partners and much more effort put into working together to find solutions to policing problems. Both DCI N035 and CRM N058 welcomed Home Office plans for the preparation of an assessment that merged the NIM and CDA reviews.[3] However, no progress was made in that regard during the period of the research.

The most significant partnership forum established in this BCU was the Joint Action Group (JAG) which, puzzlingly, had absolutely no connection with the NIM. The JAG was meant to coordinate multi-agency working by the CSP (of which, the local police and local authority were key members). Nominally, the JAG was headed by the BCU commander and the local authority's chief executive. However, in practice it was overseen by the Superintendent 'Communities' and the authority's Director of Environmental and Cultural Services. Monthly meetings were hosted by the local authority and were broadly equivalent to the NIM tactical meeting. They represented the 'practical' meeting recommended to local authorities by the Home Office in its web-based crime reduction toolkit *Using Intelligence and Information* (Home Office, 2003). The attendees included local authority housing managers, licensing officers, council ASB officers, Parks Department representatives, the local fire and rescue service, representatives of the BCU's neighbourhood policing teams, drugs action team members and environmental health officers.

The JAG was informed by an intelligence assessment written by the local authority analyst. He relied principally on the authority's databases but was also permitted full access to police data records. As a former police analyst himself, he was well-informed both about local crime problems and the pressures on police analysts to focus on priority crime. However, lacking the police's obsession with performance, the local authority's assessment was much more about local problems. The meeting oversaw a number of joint activity sub-groups which were largely focused on ensuring the delivery of projects funded by the local authority. These operated according to action plans agreed by the BCU in its annual policing plan rather than in its NIM plans.

Chief inspector 'partnerships' N036 said that initially, some officers had seen the JAG as a threat to their monopoly on operational decision-making but that most had come to realize that it presented a 'massive opportunity' for the police to engage more effectively with their community partners. CRM N058 said that the JAG was still developing (there had been only four meetings) but that it complemented the NIM meetings and offered a useful indication of the path that the partnership could take in the future. She said:

> I would say that there's a huge amount of work to do ... the theory is all there but in terms of really genuinely, hand on heart, being able to say that everything that we do is driven by intelligence. That is a long way away. There's still far too much of, 'This is what we do because this is what we always have done' – on both sides.

On a practical level, it was difficult to see how the NIM meetings could fit with the CSP, JAG and policing-plan forums. Arguably, three sets of partnership meetings were already too many. BCU commander N033 said that the NIM was helpful because it provided structure and that any suggestion otherwise simply highlighted the need for it to be marketed more effectively. However, N058 felt the NIM overcomplicated what at heart was a very simple process and, in effect, she ignored the model and its processes. Gilling has argued that the development of police/community partnerships often relies on the individual agencies getting to know one another and establishing 'the antecedents of trustworthiness' in each other (Gilling, 2005, p.751).

The JAG seemed to offer some hope in that regard but, in contrast, it was difficult to see how the NIM would help to build a more constructive alliance because the absence of partners meant there simply was no opportunity for trust to develop. In this case, the obvious step forward would have been to merge the NIM tactical and JAG meetings. There would of course be a number of practical difficulties to overcome; particularly in satisfying the police's obsession with performance indicators. However, police territoriality and their inability or unwillingness to challenge traditional practices meant that such solutions were never seriously considered. During the period of this research, the merging of the meetings simply was not discussed.

Monitoring problems in Urban

The operational plans made in the NIM meetings did not conform to the NIM code of practice (NCPE, 2005b). In none of the strategic meetings observed were middle managers given responsibility for operational plans. In another example of police orthodoxy, chief inspector N036 suggested that this could be explained, at least in part, by the fact that each SMT member already knew their responsibilities and therefore did not need to be reminded of them. However, senior intelligence analyst N039 said that the failure to identify operational heads in the way envisaged in the model led to a duplication of effort and a waste of scarce resources.

The inspector charged with the responsibility of allocating Urban's centrally-held resources (N016), who usually was based at Urban's HQ, said that he previously had visited a NIM meeting at this BCU and was concerned that managers seemed to take so little responsibility for the activities of their staff. He said:

> I was sitting there ... [wondering] 'Where are all the chief inspectors and inspectors?' Inspectors in particular are getting paid a lot of money to perform that role aren't they? I know it sounds awful and I don't mean to have a go at them but I was thinking 'Well why aren't they here?' and 'What could they do if they were here?' and 'Would there be more effective delivery if they were here?'

However, for reasons known only to him, he never raised this point with the BCU commander and the meetings continued according to the same format.

In the first phase of the NIM tactical meeting current proactive operations were reviewed and new operations (usually to reduce crime in newly identified hotspots) were commissioned by the commander. The second phase of the meeting was attended only by the commander, the DCI, a representative of the BCU's duties office and the supervisors of the BCU's proactive teams. The aim of this second phase was to assign operational staff to various operations over the forthcoming week. The commander and DCI used a weekly 'duties planner' prepared in advance by the duties office. Some tasks and commitments had already been entered into the planner. In those cases, the commander decided on the number and type of resources that were to be assigned to the task. Supervisors then 'bid' for the remaining operational resources. For example on one occasion, an inspector in charge of a neighbourhood policing team asked for extra staff to be assigned to assist in an eviction. Disappointingly, as no partners attended this phase of the meeting there was no opportunity to enlist their help in solving the BCU's problems.

Crucially these meetings highlighted just how few resources the BCU was willing to devote to proactive policing. Its own assets amounted to approximately 50 uniformed officers (divided into small teams) and a 'crime squad' made up of detectives and uniformed officers employed in plain clothes. This represented less than 5 percent of its staff. The rest were allocated to core teams (responsible for responding to all emergency calls and for routine patrol activity), 'ring-fenced' neighbourhood policing teams, or support duties.

The BCU was able to bid for certain categories of extra resources from Urban's HQ and each week entering a competitive bidding process with other BCUs and departments for Urban's HQ resources (such as the dog section, mounted branch, or other tactical support). Applications were assessed in the light of the current performance of the BCU and then passed to an operations group meeting at Urban HQ overseen by the specialist detective branch. Inspector N016 said that the group relied almost exclusively on performance data to reach its decisions. Bids were usually assessed 'on the basis of need'. If a BCU or department's performance was dragging down the performance of the force for a particular crime type then it was almost certain to be granted that assistance. However, he admitted that there was a consensus within Urban that the process was dysfunctional; resources were not being deployed where they were most needed. Because of this, the system was in a state of almost permanent flux. It had been changed on a number of occasions and he expected it to change again when the force's new FIB was introduced. It was striking that not one respondent in Urban suggested that the NIM might be the vehicle to effect that change.

In another illustration of the protectionism that this research suggests is endemic in policing (perhaps indicating that in policing, there are fiefdoms within fiefdoms), NO16 explained that it was both the structure and membership of that group that were issues. Its chair (to which he himself reported) was subordinate in rank to many of those applying for assistance. Decisions taken by the group were often criticized for favouring the specialist detective branch and there was constant squabbling over resources. NO16 said that he felt that the conflict could be resolved only if one of the highest ranking ACPO members of the force (the chief or their deputy) chaired the meeting to provide greater objectivity, transparency, and authority to the process.

As this section has shown, both local and corporate systems of resource allocation were made to work (it is significant that NO16 commented in interview that this BCU was considered to be one of the best in the force) but the processes described here not only represent a significant departure from the NIM ideal but also a diversion from the ideals embodied in POP, community policing, the principles of best value, and the normative rules of bureaucratic hierarchies that police managerialism was meant to address. Collectively, they provide further evidence of the service's misconception of what it is to be 'intelligence-led'.

A central principle of the NIM is that the BCU commander should make all operational plans in the strategic meeting. In that way the commander has all the resources of the BCU at their disposal. However, senior analyst NO39 described how a separate system, completely divorced from the NIM process, had emerged. Ironically, under this parallel system, police middle managers *were* identified as operational heads and given defined action plans for the reduction of priority crime. However, those plans were never discussed at the NIM meetings. NO39 said that she was 'completely in the dark' because the SMT had:

> been having meetings that I haven't been going to because I didn't know about them. Apparently, they have burglary, robbery and motor vehicle action plans but I don't know if those are the action plans that are supposed to come out of the control strategy or something else. I don't know what they're basing it on. I don't know what is going on.

This case shows that compliance with the formal rules introduced by the NIM was largely presentational and did not significantly affect orthodox practice. Operational activity was coordinated through action plans because that was the way that the BCU traditionally had worked. What was clear was that in this period the intelligence unit was marginalized and excluded from discussions about the allocation of a significant amount of the BCU's resources because the BCU SMT prioritized the meeting of performance targets over any other consideration. The NIM simply was ignored. Moreover, the deployment of resources certainly was not intelligence-led.

The arrangements described here raise questions both about the efficiency and the accountability of the management processes and about the extent to which the formal rules established by the NIM and the NPP (which ostensibly were accepted by the Urban elite and the force's executives for Urban's BCUs) were merely presentational, justifying conduct but not affecting practice. Police rhetoric suggests that these kinds of inefficiencies have been ameliorated by changes in management practices and in new commitments to transparency and accountability in the new millennium. Yet, as this section has shown, there remained a substantial gap between the rhetoric and the realities of day-to-day police management.

In summary, I have shown that despite the introduction of the NIM, the picture of policing in Urban basically remained unchanged. The specialist detective force's contribution to mainstream policing in Urban was as limited as it had ever been and the police continued to pay lip-service to real partnership working. Ninety-five percent of the police resources remained undisturbed and the model remained at the periphery of operational policing. This, of course, was very far from the vision for the model.

NIM and neighbourhood policing in Urban

The selected BCU was a 'pathfinder' site for the implementation of neighbourhood policing. Each of the 43 Home Office forces had selected one BCU as its neighbourhood policing pathfinder. Forces were expected to focus their implementation activity on those sites so that they could identify implementation problems before they rolled out the programme fully. According to chief inspector 'partnerships' N036, the Urban BCU had struggled to reconcile the NIM with neighbourhood policing. He said that competing and contradictory demands were often made upon the SMT and that accommodating two new policing models at the same time had resulted in the division of the BCU's operational resources.

A challenging situation was made more difficult by senior commanders' decision to 'ring-fence' the new neighbourhood policing teams. This meant that they could not be deployed outside the wards to which they were assigned and this often limited the options available to local commanders. As a result of a force directive (which was intended to demonstrate Urban's commitment to its neighbourhood strategy), the neighbourhood teams were not counted as BCU assets and could not be deployed against priority crime. This made it much more difficult for the BCU to reach its Home Office-imposed performance targets. This also was completely contrary to the NIM ethos which essentially is to put all of one's assets into one pot and then use them according to a single set of priorities.

DCI N035 admitted there was a bifurcation of the BCU's resources and energies which somehow had to be devoted both to the NIM and to neighbourhood policing. That was usually played out in the tasking meetings where the BCU's 'bottom up' NIM assessments which highlighted anti-social behaviour (the explicit focus of the neighbourhood policing programme) usually were overlooked in favour of priority crime. N035 said that she recognized the need to get more from her staff to somehow reconcile those competing demands. BCU commander N033 said that this had been made more difficult because neighbourhood policing was considered 'a soft option' by staff and this had undermined the BCU's overall investigative effort.

She said that the neighbourhood teams were not as effective as they should have been because they neglected the crime fighting element of their role. She said that some teams also had a tendency to neglect their intelligence-gathering duties, to believe that simply providing a visible presence in communities was enough and they ignored their duties to carry out the intelligence-led identification of community concerns and to take effective action against them. Certainly few acted as the BCU's 'eyes and ears' in the community as proponents of the neighbourhood programme had anticipated. Kleiven (2005) has argued that the neighbourhood programme has not improved the police's ability to collect community intelligence. N033's comments may explain, at least in part, that failure.

Urban's intelligence architecture

Many respondents discussed shortcomings in the intelligence unit and in Urban's intelligence systems. The failings highlighted should have been obvious to commanders from the outset. However, problems in the intelligence architecture extended from the top to the bottom of the force. There were many challenges to the development of the force's FIB. The fiercest came from Urban's Special Branch (SB). DOI N098 said that the branch was unwilling to share its information with the rest of the force because it took the 'need to know' principle to a ridiculous extreme. For example, shortly after the London bombings of 2005, he had challenged the branch to identify the threat posed by the radicalization of young Muslims but his request was refused on the basis that 'it might just let people know that we're interested'.

N098 said that SB simply failed to recognize the challenges that Urban was facing but he also saw in the branch's reluctance, the reaffirmation of 'the little boundaries, people working in their own little areas as opposed to seeing the force as a whole'. It also demonstrated forcefully that seeing over the operational horizon is not just a question of box-ticking or compliance but can have real consequences for communities.

At the local level there was a consensus amongst uniformed officers, interviewed for this research that the local intelligence unit was not up to its task. Cope et al found that perceptions of intelligence units often are associated with 'unrealistic expectations about what intelligence could produce and what could be achieved based on intelligence' (2003, p.27). Urban FIO N045 was candid that the popular perception of his unit by frontline patrol officers was that it was 'completely shit'. BCU uniformed sergeant N066 suggested, rather more diplomatically, that the intelligence unit was seen as taking up too many resources so that something that was no more than a support function was detracting from the 'real' policing of the streets.

Predictably, this contrasted sharply with the view from within the unit where the main complaint was that it simply did not have enough of a proactive capability to use the intelligence it received. Intelligence team leader N042 said that too few of his officers were capable of being deployed to support operations, and that his staff often were taken away by the SMT to spend time 'doing performance and compliance'. Intelligence manager N038 said that the unit suffered from having far too few healthy, sworn, police officers. Even after the extraneous material had been filtered out, the unit did not have enough of the right resources to work on the intelligence that remained.

N042 said that half of the police officers in the intelligence office were on 'restricted duties'; the force's medical department had determined that they should have only limited contact with the public. N045 said that whilst most of the unit's supervisors were willing volunteers, many essentially were conscripts. That is to say, they were limited to office duties by ill-health or infirmity. The result was that the operational capability usually amounted to no more than two or three constables. This is a common complaint about intelligence work in mainstream policing. However, it was never resolved in Urban. For example, N045 described a 'really frustrating' deployment where, because no other intelligence unit staff were allowed to leave the office, two field intelligence constables (including N045) were supervised by three sergeants.

Office manager N040 said that weekend cover also was a problem. The commander had decided there should be skeleton coverage of the office but few staff had the skills necessary to cover all its functions. The result was that the same two 'multi-skilled' people were always called on (more often, directed) to provide that cover. Readers may find it difficult to reconcile those statements, which to my mind raise questions about the structure, perceived value and, ultimately, purpose of the intelligence unit.

The kinds of deficiencies in the police intelligence architecture described here were first identified in the 1930s by the Dixon Committee. Its continuing inadequacy was a significant factor in the failure of the UBP system almost 40 years later. Despite those failures, as the reader has seen, internal reports and external research have continued to highlight: the police's failure to invest sufficient resources in intelligence; to use those resources properly; to really value intelligence work; and to embed the intelligence process 'intelligently' in mainstream policing. The introduction of the NIM seemed to have made little difference in any of those contexts.

Over and above those problems, in this particular case the BCU SMT's indifferent attitude to the physical integrity of the unit perhaps indicates better than anything else the standing of local intelligence work. Intelligence team leader N042 said that he was obliged to leave the office open 'around the clock' even though unit staff were present for only 16 hours a day and the office walls were covered with confidential maps and plans and there was no clear desk policy. He said:

> You come into our office on a Monday morning after the [uniform teams] have used all our computers. You've got kebabs rotting on people's desks, Coke cans everywhere. They treat it like a dump. But it's not just that, you've got the cleaner who walks in whenever she wants and you've got operational targets everywhere and plans written everywhere and maybe a subject profile on somebody's desk that shouldn't be on that desk.

FIO N045 said that the SMT accepted that the physical security of the unit was a problem but it had failed to address it as such because it was considered a long-term accommodation problem. The implications for the security of the unit's information should be obvious. Certainly, failing to store personal data in a secure environment is a breach of the Data Protection Act and it is difficult to conceive that allowing unrestricted access to such material would comply with Urban's own operational security protocols. This case suggests that in mainstream policing, relations between patrol officers and intelligence workers and between middle managers and their intelligence units need fundamental reappraisal. Without such a review, a single service approach can never be considered to be anything more than a pipedream.

8
Evaluating the NIM: County Case Study

Introduction

This second case study examines the extent to which a largely rural police force in England, referred to here as 'County' implemented the NIM. It was significant that County's relatively small size meant that it simply did not present the same organizational issues evident in Urban. County differed from Urban in that even before the NIM emerged it had sought to demonstrate its commitment to ILP. That was an important factor in the NIM story in County because (at least superficially) the force was much more prepared than Urban to accept the model. Just as in the Urban case, my analysis is based on my own observations of business meetings, on interviews with officers, police staff and policing partners, and on the views of a broad range of front-line officers that were collected from focus groups.

Force reorganization

In 1995, County implemented a new crime strategy in the force which was inspired by the KPM. It introduced local intelligence units to its divisions. They were expected significantly to improve intelligence work in the mainstream. However, later that year, an inspection found that the units were not achieving expected standards, intelligence analysis was rudimentary, the tasking of operational resources was 'inconsistent, slow and bureaucratic' and the assistance the force's specialist detectives offered to BCUs was limited.

County BCU commander N027 (who became a significant figure in the subsequent development of the NIM in County) said that the policing style which evolved in this period 'hamstrung' the force with unnecessary bureaucracy; there was too great an emphasis on 'the administrative function' instead of 'positive investigative outcomes'. N027 said that in 1997, the new (Labour) Government's renewed focus on performance management persuaded County that it needed to change that approach and operate within a new culture. He said the force elite finally recognized that crime fighting, community safety, and reassurance should be given greater priority. The most obvious manifestation of that recognition was further restructuring with the aim of delivering an intelligence-led force.

In October 2001, the force's operational policing arrangements were completely reorganized, boundaries were realigned and ward-based teams introduced. Officers were reassigned either to intervention, roads policing or neighbourhood policing teams. Senior commanders also enhanced the proactive capability of each BCU and increased the size and capacity of its intelligence units. Each was provided with additional reactive crime investigation and proactive resources (though those available for proactive work represented less than 10 percent of County's human resources). Case investigation units, crime management units and minor crimes units were created as well as new area intelligence units that were intended to gather and analyse data, enabling crime patterns to be identified more quickly and operational resources to be targeted more effectively.

The reorganization of intelligence work was not universally welcomed. In HMIC-facilitated focus groups, a recurring complaint was the remoteness of the new intelligence units from the bulk of operational work, and the relative invisibility of intelligence staff. This resulted in a significant deterioration in relations between the units and mainstream officers. County DOI N032 said that the criticism indicated that County perhaps had 'missed a trick' in realigning its staff. Too much emphasis was placed on getting the operational policing teams right, and too little on developing the intelligence units (that were needed to support the operational teams) to the same standard. She said that:

> What tended to happen [was that] the sick, the lame and the people who they couldn't redeploy anywhere else got put into intelligence because that was quite a large office with lots of computers that they think 'Well as long as somebody knows how to type they can sort out the intelligence'.

The same complaint has regularly been made about intelligence workers so it was no surprise to see it expressed here. N032 said that in developing its intelligence units, County focused on selecting IT-literate people rather than those who could make 'really good sound and rational decisions on things', which should have been the greater priority. That opportunity was missed. Consequently the perception of the units was that they were simply concerned with 'housekeeping' and that real intelligence work would be done elsewhere.

I have highlighted at several points, detectives' lack of involvement in intelligence work in the mainstream. As the reader has seen, that has been a feature of local intelligence work since the 1960s. The County DOI suggested that the deployment of skilled and experienced detectives in local intelligence work would provide the obvious solution to a persistent and seemingly intractable problem. However, Chatterton has argued that the divisional CID is already under huge pressure to meet the demands made upon it in the face of the 'haemorrhaging of detective experience and expertise through transfers to specialist units, squads and major incident teams' (2008, p. viii). It seems unlikely that police managers would welcome further abstractions from core policing. In an interview, both Phillips and ACPO member N03 argued in favour of the direct recruitment of civilian specialists for intelligence roles. Whilst civilian analysts and researchers have been directly recruited to intelligence posts by many forces with some success, the problems described in both cases suggest that a more fundamental re-evaluation of mainstream intelligence work is surely long overdue.

County elite and the NIM

Though County's senior commanders were more receptive to the NIM than their Urban counterparts, implementation was delayed at the highest level (and was hamstrung at the BCU level) because of continuing deficiencies in the force's intelligence structure and processes. According to County's principal intelligence analyst (N026), despite the reorganization that was intended to make the force truly intelligence-led, there was 'no strategy for intelligence at all' in County. This had to be addressed before the NIM could be embraced.

In 2003, N026 was appointed as the intelligence 'champion' for the force. Her brief was to develop the systems and structures needed to accommodate the NIM. However, the establishment of that post in a department that oversaw administrative tasks, rather than in either the crime management department or the specialist detective division (where most of the intelligence functions were located) was problematic because it removed her from the day-to-day business of intelligence. N026 said that implementation of the NIM was further set back when an assistant chief constable (ACC) who had been a great supporter of intelligence and analysis in County was promoted out of that post. When the ACC moved on, County lost its focus on intelligence because 'that moved with him and it all just ... slipped off the agenda'. In the absence of the ACC, there was no one at the elite level who truly believed in the value of intelligence.

I have previously highlighted the importance of an effective advocate for change with sufficient power, authority and energy to drive the change process, so it was perhaps inevitable that with the ACC's departure, the momentum for change was lost. The principal analyst said that even though the NIM processes were in place:

> Two and a half years down the line, we still can't get even the tactical tasking and coordination to work. We have a lot of structures in place and we have a lot of process but ... we're saying to ourselves that it doesn't actually make a great deal of difference ... You know, would it make a difference if we didn't have it?

The County elite's understanding of what it truly was to be intelligence-led is brought into question by the principal analyst's words. Though there was not the outright resistance there was in Urban, there was little appreciation of what the NIM meant for the force. Even the most basic of the NIM's procedures failed to operate effectively and although there was lots of NIM-related activity, the model made a negligible impact on the business of the force. Once again, this demonstrated the way that police organizations prioritize administrative competence over outcomes.

At the beginning of 2004, County's elite appointed a detective superintendent (N032) as DOI. N032 tried to change the perception of the NIM in County but the impact she made was limited by senior commanders' lack of commitment to the substantial changes that the model required. Rather unusually (*a priori*, uniquely), the DOI's responsibilities in County were limited to intelligence policy, the authorization of covert policing activity by the detective force, and the management of local intelligence units. All key intelligence functions above BCU level were managed by someone other than the DOI. To complicate the situation even further, she was of course separated from the person who should have been her key lieutenant, the force's principal analyst (who remained in the corporate affairs department).

N032 attributed those irregularities to a coup by her immediate predecessor that was designed to put power in the hands of the specialist detectives. She said that as a result of poor communication there was duplication and wasted effort because 'If something came in that was vaguely NIM, vaguely intelligence, vaguely analytical, it would get tasked out three different ways'. N032 said that she was slow to remedy a wholly unsatisfactory situation but she recognized that she had to resolve the constant conflict with other senior managers over intelligence issues.

N032 wanted to resolve those difficulties and to ensure that intelligence actually supported the operational work of the force. She introduced a pilot scheme, briefing virtually all the supervisors in the force about the NIM. The success of the pilot persuaded senior commanders to approve its introduction. In September 2006, a new intelligence directorate (that included all the force's intelligence assets) was established with N032 at its head. Interviewed at the end of this study, she said that the new system allowed her to bring a more consistent approach to adding value through intelligence work to mainstream policing. However, coming as it did at the end of the fieldwork, that statement was not tested in this research.

NIM at BCU level in County

Just as in Urban, County's BCU managers were largely unaware of the tensions around the NIM at the highest level of the force. The SMT members interviewed, said that they welcomed it as a further development of the force's ILP strategy. BCU commander N027 said that the NIM was welcomed unequivocally at BCU level because commanders felt it organized their business in a more effective way. He said that he felt it would underpin a new body of knowledge, an institutional memory, for a police service which in his view, had 'no tradition of any sort of professionalism'.

He said that the NIM symbolized the police service's desire to change. Though in my view the commander's analysis was flawed; the major problem for the NIM was that the actual proportion of the service that really wanted change was relatively small. N027 contrasted the service's approach to its institutional memory, with that taken by the British Army:

What are the courses at Bramshill for ... not to look at a body of researched historical experience around policing? We never do that do we? You know, trying to work out what works. Who lectures at Bramshill? Generally, pretty hopeless people. If you go to the Army Staff College, the lecturers are the people that have won battles.

Reflecting the Urban DOI's comments, N027 said that he hoped the NIM would help to create a body of professional learning which could provide a structure that would remove County's reliance on 'inspired individuals' for results. In that regard, the commander was echoing the NCIS executive's demand for policing doctrine. Earlier, I referred to criticism of doctrine as unnecessarily complex for frontline staff. Not a single respondent in either case study had read even one page of NIM-related doctrine so their understanding (or otherwise) of those documents was not a factor in this study. However, given that at the time of the study there were over 600 pages of NIM doctrine, it is reasonable to suggest that the sheer volume of instruction and advice was overwhelming for staff who also had busy 'day jobs'. The Westminster Coroner's criticism of doctrine in the case of Mark Saunders suggests that the Urban senior intelligence official (N050) may have had cause to fear the 'programmed responses' that doctrine can deliver.

N027 said that because it described the social and policing environments within which he was operating, the NIM allowed him to better manage his business. He was a great advocate of the model and his support was evident in the way that he tried to embrace the NIM's structures and processes. As much as anyone in County, he was the policy entrepreneur that the model needed. His support for local intelligence work was evident in his resourcing of his intelligence unit which was made up of approximately 35 staff performing broadly similar roles to their Urban counterparts.

The unit was headed by a DI (who initially, was the only detective officer so employed, though later he was joined by a Detective Sergeant (DS)) but in a departure from the NIM ideal, the title of intelligence manager was given to a civilian member of staff who oversaw the day-to-day running of the unit. Intelligence researcher N021 said that the unit suffered from a lack of continuity in management, that there had been continuous and ongoing change. He said that problems with the unit had never been properly addressed. In his view, the unit was 'given first aid when it needed surgery'.

Intelligence manager N019 represented the unit at the NIM meetings. She said that she recognized that as a member of police staff, she was not qualified to make decisions on operational matters but she provided support to the unit's police staff and bridged the gap between those staff and the police officers in the BCU's intelligence world. However, given her (admitted) lack of knowledge of operational policing, it could be argued that she was not able to mediate between the operational and intelligence worlds as well as the model required.

Focus groups held with frontline BCU staff in this study were very poorly attended so it was possible only to assess a limited range of views on the NIM from the uniformed branch. However, it was clear that the BCU commander's views on the importance of the NIM to the policing mission had not been fully embraced on the frontline. Perhaps the youth and inexperience of the research respondents was a factor in that context but the similarity with the Urban case was obvious. Of the three patrol officers interviewed (N075, N076 and N077) the longest-serving had been a police officer for only 15 months.

None of those officers expressed any view on the local intelligence unit nor did they possess any knowledge of the NIM. They were completely task-focused, their days taken up either with responding to emergency calls from the public or carrying out work allocated to them by the force control room. A 'fire brigade' or 'AA patrolman' style of policing typically was the norm. According to officer N075, 'We do whatever's in front of us'. Schools liaison officer N074 had a rudimentary knowledge of the model. As a former collator, she had some understanding of the intelligence cycle and the fundamentals of intelligence work. She said that she applied them to her role; a substantial part of which was feeding intelligence on problem children and families to her operational colleagues via the intelligence unit.

Just as in Urban, the intelligence unit staff broadly was supportive of the NIM. Intelligence researcher N021 argued that it made the unit much more efficient and cost-effective whilst intelligence manager N019 welcomed the consistency and uniformity that the model brought. Senior analyst NC22 said that she was optimistic about the effect of the NIM on the profile of intelligence in mainstream policing but she could no more attribute any fall in crime levels or increases in detections to the model than others before her. She said that she questioned the influence of analysis on operational outcomes 'because it's still the same names coming ... up all the time, the same crime issues we are dealing with all the time so are we actually any further forward than we were back in October 2001'.

The NIM process in County

This chapter now moves on to examine the model's influence on intelligence work and investigation in County.

Intelligence collection in County

There was a huge divide between County's specialist detective force and the rest of County's investigative resources. The specialist detective force maintained complete control over its own operations and had gone a step further and enlisted County's FIB as an auxiliary. The DOI N032 said that the FIB worked almost exclusively for the specialist detective force and it took no part in the preparation of the NIM intelligence assessments for the wider force.

At the BCU level, intelligence meetings were held according to the NIM timetable. The meetings departed from the NIM ideal in that all reported crime was discussed, rather than only those crime types that were included in the BCU's control strategy and intelligence requirement. As a consequence, the intelligence meetings did not correspond to the normative rules of the NIM. Senior analyst N022 said that the unit focused on collecting intelligence around priority crime but this was not borne out by my own observations.

During the course of the fieldwork for this study the commander adopted anti-social behaviour (ASB) as a BCU priority. This meant that the unit had to cast its net even more widely for intelligence. BCU commander N027 described his inclusion of ASB in the control strategy as 'one of the most fundamental strategic decisions this force and I have made in terms of resource deployment'. He said that the decision demonstrated his personal commitment to public reassurance and there is no doubt that it represented a significant change in focus for the BCU. For her part, N022 was not convinced that the inclusion of ASB in the control strategy was justified by her intelligence analyses. Of course, the requirement to collect more data also contributed to the 'overloading' of the BCU's intelligence databases (analyst N023).

Notwithstanding N022's findings, according to N027, his 'professional judgement' was that meeting the needs of his communities took precedence over the intelligence assessment. Coming from someone who had expressed such support for intelligence analysis, it perhaps emphasizes that even the most 'enlightened' commander may exercise their prerogative to take decisions regardless of what their intelligence tells them.

Collation, analysis and evaluation in County

Just as in the Urban BCU, analytical activity was organized around focus desks. However, rather than being delineated by crime type as in Urban, four focus desks represented each of the BCU's CSPs. N022 said that intelligence analysis was central to the work of the focus desks. As in City, crime pattern analysis and network analysis were the techniques used most frequently. The SARA model was used extensively. Cope et al (2003, p. 14) have suggested that analytical products may be 'subject to objectification and reification by the officers who they are provided to' but this was not the common experience in this or the Urban case.

County DOI N032 said the NIM's 'demystification' of analytical products led commanders to believe that they needed to demonstrate their knowledge (and control) by specifying the product they wanted rather than allowing the analyst to decide on the most appropriate product for themselves. However, all the analysts interviewed in County agreed that it was their lack of credibility that was central to this debate. Loveday has suggested that the failure of police officers to recognize the value of police staff is a wider issue that may suggest 'a continuing cultural problem' (2005, p.6). He noted that the negative perceptions of police staff amongst junior officers previously identified by HMIC (2004) may be emulation of hostility present at the highest levels of the service. A continuing antipathy between operational police officers and civilian intelligence staff may perhaps be inferred from the statements of Urban's intelligence staff in the previous chapter. In that case the intelligence unit was seen as taking up resources that otherwise could be used in the 'real' policing of the streets. In this case, the hostility to civilian staff was overt and pointed to a continuing cultural divide in policing. The NIM did not seem to ameliorate that conflict.

Analysts N023 and N024 said that they were often seen by police officers simply as people who could provide IT support or act as minute takers. Though both noted that their relations with colleagues outside the intelligence unit improved as they became more skilled, they commented on the challenge of convincing police officers to accept their analyses. Senior analyst N022 said that in time, analysts' concerns were addressed by the introduction of formal processes that obliged officers to justify requests for analytical support. However, planning meetings continued to test analysts' patience and fortitude.

N023 said that when she attended fortnightly planning meetings, her judgement was often mistrusted and her reports were routinely ignored. Future priorities were decided without any reference to her analytical products. This left her feeling demoralized and frustrated. A second analyst (N024) also expressed concerns over the meeting. She said, 'I used to go ... it was just a chance to rip the analyst to pieces. It was horrendous'. That meeting might have been the 'worst' example of police officers' belligerence but other interactions with officers could be equally challenging. She said:

> We go to meetings and we just get ridiculed, laughed at, continuously spoken over when we are trying to present our work. Spoken down to, to the point that I've had to have a chief inspector come and apologise to me for the way he has treated me in a meeting because it was so blatantly rude. That I would say is the main problem in our job.

Analyst (N023) conceded that lacking experience of operational policing, she and her colleagues sometimes struggled to balance analytical theory with police practice. However, the attitudes and behaviours described by the respondents suggested that sworn officers sometimes made it only too clear to civilian staff that their views were not valued. I have highlighted both in this and in the other case, the need for a capable and credible intelligence manager to support the intelligence unit's police staff and to bridge the gap between them and the operational milieu. The events described by the analysts in this case demonstrate the paramount importance of that management function.

Just as in Urban, the techniques used most frequently were network analysis and crime pattern analysis. Given the difficulty of assessing the success of ILP; the fact that results analysis rarely was used was disappointing. The consensus amongst the analysts interviewed was that other demands on their time meant that they could not reflect on the consequences of operational activity. However, not being consulted early enough in proactive operations and the failure of commanders to set out clear objectives in the planning stage, also were factors. Whatever the reason, normative expectations of the intelligence cycle were frustrated. In particular, just as in Urban, the feedback loop that is fundamental to the intelligence cycle was broken. This only adds weight to my argument that in this period the NIM did not make BCUs any smarter in evaluating their work.

Presentation of evidence in County

The difficulties in separating the measurement of performance from operational outcomes extended to the preparation of the force strategic assessment. Principal analyst N026 said that initially the force assessment was an organizational rather than a strategic assessment. That is, the finished document contained priorities identified by the force elite (top-down) rather than an evidence-based, intelligence-led analysis of County's policing problems as envisaged by the NIM.

N026 questioned the intelligence value of a document that senior commanders authored themselves. She said that the document was 'just a long list of all the issues that concerned commanders. At the time this research was carried out, the document afforded the title of 'strategic assessment' remained a top-down list of priorities. County were not alone in adopting this approach albeit that the hazards attached to it should have been obvious to commanders. The setting of priorities in County in a way that rejected the normative values of the NIM, simply adds weight to the argument that in reality the police were unwilling or unable to fully commit to ILP.

Senior commanders' continuing focus on those issues that were of greatest concern to the force rather than to local communities (usually because they had a significant bearing on performance) was raised by many in this case study. In the view of DOI N032, information about ASB was equally as important as information about organized crime even if it 'just goes off in different directions and we prioritise it slightly differently and risk-assess it slightly differently'. She believed that (just as in Urban) County had to overcome its paternalistic 'mother knows best attitude' to its partners and allow them to play a greater part in decision-making.

Local authority CRM N09 was unhappy with the assessments. He said that at around 100 pages, the documents were 'far too long ... packed with police jargon' and had improved only marginally over time. They lacked the 'richness' of other data sources. He said that the police needed to see 'the bigger, wider picture'; the link between the environment and people's wellbeing. The force assessment was 'not within the spirit of partnership ... and not fit for purpose' because the process was managing the people rather than *vice versa*.

Foster has argued that practitioners may construct an 'assumed and oversimplified world' that ultimately may sabotage efforts to work with communities and establish effective partnerships (2002, p.174). The categories of data that N09 referred to would have allowed the police to construct a much better informed assessment that included just the kind of data that advocates of the NIM wanted the police to collect. The failure to do so was yet another example of the police's inability to break out of what I have termed an investigative orthodoxy.

DOI N032 said that she had worked hard to persuade the County elite of the merits of the NIM. She believed that the new force intelligence strategy was focusing operational activity more effectively, although senior commanders still demonstrated a degree of autonomy 'because the chief constable is the chief constable', which suggests that for all policing has changed since Reiner (1991) wrote his seminal text *Chief Constables*, even the most enlightened chief officer may from time to time exhibit the territoriality and mission-focus of a 'Baron'.[1]

At the BCU level, County's analysts compiled all of the assessments required by the NIM. As the only one to have attended a strategic analysis course, senior intelligence analyst N022 took sole responsibility for producing the strategic assessments. She said that the finished product took a huge effort and this was evident in the assessments seen, which ranged between 61 and 69 pages of data analysis, evaluation and recommendations. The senior analyst said that she received excellent feedback on her assessments but, just like the senior analyst in Urban and the local CRM, she felt they were too long and too complex. Despite her reservations, the assessment met the BCU commander's needs and, of course, his wishes prevailed. Like her Urban counterpart, the County analyst felt this undermined her professional credibility. Interviewed at the end of the research, she said that she eventually had persuaded the commander to take more account of the intelligence. However, her words add yet more weight to the argument that the NIM struggled to overcome those established values of the dominant occupational culture and the hierarchical tradition of the police organization.

Consultation with partners in County

Unlike Urban, County held a force NIM strategic meeting. It was chaired by County's Deputy Chief Constable. Many members of the force elite were present. They were joined by senior managers from the specialist detective force, senior detectives, County's BCU commanders, DOI N032 and principal analyst N026.[2] Partners were represented by the chair of the local police authority (N011), the local authority CRM (N09), representatives of the local Crimestoppers organization and members of local drugs action and youth offending teams and the probation service. This suggested that the County elite was more supportive of the NIM than others. However, as the reader will see, this did not necessarily translate into meaningful outcomes.

There were two distinct phases to the meeting. The first was given over to a presentation of the intelligence assessment by the principal analyst. At the conclusion of this phase, the partners (including the police authority chair) left the meeting to the police 'professionals'. It was in the second phase that key decisions about investigative pathways and the allocation of resources were made. Interviewed in 2006, County police authority chair N011 spoke positively about his relationship with the force elite but expressed his reservations about the structure of this meeting. Reflecting arguments about the ability of criminal justice agencies to control their fiefdoms, N011 said that the division demonstrated that despite the rhetoric, the police wanted limits on partnership working. They wanted to separate the 'professional' from the lay perspectives. He said:

> I'm not sure what the gain is from them having it in two parts. I think they would probably get a better buy-in, better engagement, if they ran it as a general meeting ... I think there is too much mystique, too much mystery. You know 'let's keep the public out. This is professional, this is ours'.

Police respondents believed that dividing the meeting in this way helped senior commanders to develop strategy and formulate action. They did not anticipate that the division would cause any concerns. However, police authority chair N011 said that by keeping too much of its work secret, County limited real public engagement. He said that senior commanders should be exploiting every opportunity to gain 'insights' into policing problems from their partners, and that partners' exclusion from the most important phase of the strategic meeting indicated that senior commanders did not afford those community insights the importance they deserved. Under the existing arrangements, partners could not be convinced that their views were being properly considered. He questioned whether County simply was paying lip service to the notion of public engagement as 'a box ticking function'.

The relationship between force elites and police authorities has been much debated. Reiner argued that in this period the lack of adequate local accountability was 'a major factor undermining police legitimacy' (2010, pp.682–3). In this case, even though the NIM provided a forum for the police authority chair to question a decision he was unhappy with, he spurned the opportunity. In my view, this demonstrated one of the major failings of those arrangements. Even if the mechanism of accountability was in place, it was not always used to scrutinize police decision-making in the way either that Parliament planned or an objective assessor might expect. It will be very interesting to see how the relationship between chief officers and their PCCs develops. Certainly, the Government's hope is that the PCCs will be far more proactive in their engagement with their chief officers.

Strategic tasking at the local level was a much more focused and inclusive affair in the County BCU, than that observed either at the elite level in County or at BCU level in Urban. Two of the three strategic meetings held during the period of the study were observed. BCU commander N027 said that he wanted to embed the NIM processes to such a degree that each successive year's plan would represent 'exactly the same picture of fundamental business process'.

Each strategic meeting was chaired by the commander and in each case the strategic assessment was presented by the senior analyst. However, it was there that the similarities between the County and Urban meetings ended. Whereas the Urban meeting was open to a range of attendees (even though most declined to attend), the County meeting was limited to senior managers and key decision-makers. In County, there was the same obsession with performance in the context of priority crime as there was in Urban. Senior analyst N022 began each meeting with an overview of the crime recorded by the BCU in the last period and continued with a presentation of the identified priorities. In stark contrast to what had taken place in the Urban case, N027 stressed that the future operational focus of the BCU was up for discussion. He said that in the short term, priorities would be set on the basis of information contained in the assessments prepared by his intelligence staff *and* on his own professional judgement. However, he anticipated that would change as the process became more participative.

Interviewed after this first meeting, a second local authority chief executive (N010) said that his relationship with the BCU commander was 'a real partnership arrangement'. Referring to the control strategy, chief executive N010 said that (just like the chair of the police authority) he trusted the commander's professional judgement. Gilling has argued that 'trust may be the most important commodity in establishing good working relations' (2005, p.737). Both N010 and N027 stressed the significance of building trust and of their personal relationship. However, they both highlighted that they wanted to establish an underpinning structure that went beyond that relationship and did not rely on it. Properly implemented, the NIM could have provided that structure.

Just as at force level, N027 had established a practice of holding the strategic meeting over two sessions; one attended by the police and the other drawing in partners. However, during the period of this research, N027 recognized that structure limited participation in the decision-making process and he changed it so to be more inclusive in attendance and content. The second meeting observed was attended by the police SMT, the senior analyst, two local authority chief executives, six members of the police authority and three local councillors. In the first meeting, the BCU's control strategy comprised 'the usual suspects' of burglary, robbery, violent crime, street crime, class 'A' drug supply and theft from motor vehicles. However, 12 months later, it had developed so that it included ASB, criminal damage, and violent crime (particularly alcohol-related violence in town centres).

The meeting also developed in that N027 (rather than the analyst), took more obvious ownership of the BCU's plans for the next period. That ownership seemed to generate much more discussion than previously and this seemed to make the meeting more of a coming together of equals. However, in another example of the 'compliance culture', it was noticeable that partners continued to defer to the 'professional judgement' of the police and their influence on the decision-making process was as limited as it was on the first occasion.

To summarize, at the force level NIM meetings, though there was not the level of resistance to the model observed in Urban, operational priorities were decided in the traditional manner. The police alone decided how resources would be distributed and it was clear that the NIM had not overcome the established values of the occupational culture or the hierarchical tradition of the police organization. Both the chair of the police authority and the local authority's CSM questioned the police's strategic decision-making process. Arguably, the significant difference between the two was that the chair of the police authority possessed the executive authority to at least challenge the process. However, neither attempted to remedy the defects that they observed.

At the local level, the BCU commander's enthusiasm for the NIM was evident. He had established and was maintaining clear lines of communication with both the police authority and the local authority and for their parts, the representatives of each expressed their complete support for the commander and the NIM process. However, as cordial and participative as they were, the meetings did not operate according to the normative rules of the model because, just as in Urban, decisions over priorities and resources were taken in the traditional manner outside the meeting by the BCU commander and his staff.

NIM tactical meetings were held each fortnight at force and at county levels. The force tactical meeting is discussed more fully in the next section. Briefly, principal analyst N026 said that there was no consultation with partners at these meetings as none were invited. In the BCU selected for study, BCU commander N027 chaired the meeting and senior analyst N022 presented the tactical assessment but otherwise County's tactical meeting was in complete contrast with the tactical meeting held in Urban. Attendance at the County meeting was consistent and was limited to the SMT and middle management. No representatives of partner agencies attended any of the five meetings observed. In other words, in terms of its attendance, the tactical meeting was conducted in a traditional manner.

Monitoring problems in County

Chatterton (2008) argued that the promotion of ILP in general and the NIM in particular led to the development of 'a new dynamic' in the 'squad imperative'. In his research, respondents referred repeatedly to the 'haemorrhaging of detective experience and expertise through transfers and long-term secondments' to specialist detective squads and the prioritization of the needs of those squads over the needs of their divisional colleagues (2008, p.viii). Chatterton points up one of the greatest paradoxes of the NIM; the model was forced through with some vigour at the BCU level yet the specialist detective force was allowed to ignore it.

I argued earlier that commanders in the mainstream seemed content to accept the management data that was a by-product of the administrative function associated with ILP but were unwilling or unable to deploy the resources needed to secure positive investigative outcomes. The force's tactical meeting provided compelling evidence of that inability, and of the tensions Chatterton has described. DOI N032 said that the meeting was meant to provide an opportunity for both the force's specialist detective units and its BCUs to bid for the force's headquarters-based resources (such as surveillance). However, she said that the two did not meet on a level playing field because the FIB and the other specialist detective units had developed a covert, mutually beneficial relationship, detrimental to BCUs.

She said that those units held their own meetings in advance of the main forum so that they were able to monopolize the force's proactive assets. The limited proactive resources of the force usually were deployed against serious and organized crime (which may have been perfectly proper) but there was never any real debate about the challenges faced by BCUs. Principal analyst N026 said that whether this was an appropriate use of County's scarce resources was never really considered and the investigative resources that might have been available to County's BCU's simply were dispersed elsewhere without any real discussion. Her comments mirror Morgan et al's (1996) observations about the lack of real debate in the police service on the continuing utility of the squad system and also, once again, demonstrate the durability of the established occupational culture and the hierarchical tradition of policing.

N026 wondered why nobody was prepared to challenge what she termed this 'investigative orthodoxy' which seemed to operate to the detriment of the wider force. By the normative rules of the NIM, the tasking meeting chair should have taken account of the demands on the whole force; to ensure that its limited resources were allocated to the priorities identified by the force intelligence assessments rather than those identified by the specialist detectives and to deliver that single service response that Phillips envisaged the model would deliver. However, certainly during the research period, there was not enough of a challenge to the power of the detectives. The perpetuation of the 'closed shop', described by the senior analyst, meant that BCUs were unable to obtain additional resources even when they had a pressing need for them.

DOI N032 said that the specialist CID controlled the tasking process to such a degree that if a BCU put in a request for assistance, it would be blocked before the tasking meeting. The effect was that BCUs just 'wouldn't bother any more'. N026 agreed with the DOI and said that BCU representatives failed to make bids for assistance because they thought 'well what's the point, it's only going to get knocked back anyway'. N032 said that lacking this central support, BCUs had been forced to become self-sufficient and to develop their own strategies (which rarely included proactive investigations). One can only speculate whether the commanders' failure to challenge the force elite to limit the influence of the specialist detectives was an example of their innate conservatism or a general reflection of the difficulty of challenging senior officers. Whatever the reason, local commanders did what they thought best served their own needs. The result was that County's specialist detectives carried on unimpeded, and the force's intelligence structures developed so that they lacked both a corporate identity and a common method of working.

I argued earlier that senior commanders have always afforded the specialist detective force the freedom to operate independently in the ways described in this chapter. This case shows that senior commanders have continued to give priority to the resourcing of the specialist detective force over mainstream policing into the modern era. In County, principal analyst N026 saw this simply as 'investigative orthodoxy', doing things the way they always had done but there may be good reason for that orthodoxy. Senior commanders have always been able to rely upon the specialist detective force as that 'safe pair of hands' that they can call upon to rescue almost any situation. In interview, chief inspector N028 colourfully described the specialist detective force as policing's 'Praetorian Guard – ready and willing to march out and save Caesar' whenever it was needed. County's commanders seemed to have little enthusiasm for any change to that *status quo*.

Though the force tactical meeting departed from the normative rules and values of the NIM (as set out in its Code), the BCU's meeting operated much more closely to the NIM ideal than any other arrangements observed. At the beginning of each BCU meeting, local commander N027 reviewed the actions he had previously allocated and held the plan holders to account for their operational plans. The meeting did not progress, until the results obtained were explained to his satisfaction. Most of the proactive resources available to the BCU were tasked from the tactical meeting. Just as in the Urban case, in none of the meetings observed, was any reference made to obtaining the assistance of the force's specialist detectives or other law enforcement agencies.

N027 said that he had worked to get the right people at the meeting. This meant that he needed only to press 'one button' if he wanted something to be done. In the meetings observed, each element of the control strategy was discussed in turn. This was followed by a discussion of 'non-control strategy' items and 'special' events. Meetings always ended with a formal tasking of the BCU's tactical resources and a final iteration of the meeting's key points by the commander. The overriding impression was of a very structured and focused process that achieved exactly what the BCU commander intended.

The commander was keen to emphasize, very much the majority view in policing, that any BCU commander's freedom to deploy his or her tactical resources, was limited by the ordinary expectations of the police as an emergency public service. The challenge for commanders was to carry out those routine policing functions (referred to by a chief inspector (N028) as 'the background policing' and by Goldstein (1979, p.238) (as 'the conglomeration of unrelated, ill-defined, and often inseparable jobs that the police are expected to handle') but also to bring 'relatively small' amounts of resources to bear against high-priority areas. He believed that '85–90 percent' of police business would be carried on irrespective of any attempt to manage it strategically. He explained:

> It is all about focus ... In effect there's just loads of stuff happening which you have no control over, detectives going to scenes ... officers arresting people ... You don't really have control. What I think the essence of the NIM is – is the 15 percent that you can control, we do control in terms of resources and where you place your emphasis in terms of tackling crime.

These were particularly revealing comments in this study because they came from an avowed supporter of the NIM, who demonstrated real commitment to the model's aims. They suggest that even though the commander was open to a degree of change in the BCU's policing style, he was not prepared to contemplate modifying his patrol or investigative strategies. I have argued at several points that in the policing mainstream the service is locked into an investigative orthodoxy that prevents it from using its intelligence and investigative resources in the most effective, efficient and economic ways. The commander's comments provide further evidence to support that argument and for all his claimed commitment to the model (albeit those claims were made in good faith), they demonstrate that there were always limits on the extent to which the NIM would be applied in County.

N028 said that despite the BCU's workforce being comparable to that of the smaller police forces in Britain, its tactical capability was limited and was far from 'the huge pot of tactical resources' that others might imagine. He said that those resources amounted to one inspector, four sergeants and 30 constables. He said that the BCU also was able to deploy its roads policing units to certain defined tasks (such as road checks and road blocks in high-crime areas) but their primary objective was road safety and the BCU was reluctant to over-use them outside that role. BCU commander N027 said that shortage of resources demanded that those available had to be targeted against the BCU's priorities. The really crucial question in this context was 'How should those priorities be decided'? This was exactly the question that the NIM was designed to answer.

NIM and neighbourhood policing

CSP chief inspector N029 said that initially the NIM processes seemed to work well in County. However, there was tension between the force's neighbourhood policing programme and the NIM because the requirements of one detracted from the other (for exactly the same reasons outlined in the Urban case). He believed that in County those tensions were exacerbated by the fact that each CSP had its own philosophy and way of working. He said that whilst the model encouraged a commitment to crime reduction 'across the board', the BCU commander was more concerned to achieve a reduction in priority crime and that meant the NIM (as it was applied in County) would always be in conflict with neighbourhood policing with its emphasis on local problems.

Second CSP chief inspector N028 said that he was concerned that the NIM did not take account of the crime reduction targets set for CSPs. Instead it sought to meet priority crime targets such as 'sanction detections'. He felt that the NIM made the BCU more focused, so that it was 'pointing all the ships the same way' (a rather interesting way to describe the single service approach) but he was concerned that applying the model in its purest form ultimately would mean that the needs of communities were disregarded. He said that it was 'unfortunate' that the same amount of energy expended on the introduction of neighbourhood policing had not been put into the NIM so that the tension between the two 'which should have been obvious' could have been resolved from the outset.

Oakensen et al (2002) argued that at a conceptual level there is no such tension, the NIM can provide a framework within which neighbourhood policing may operate but forces struggled to reconcile the two. In 2006, ACPO issued *Practice Advice on Professionalising the Business of Neighbourhood Policing*, which was intended to 'integrate neighbourhood policing into mainline [*sic*] policing by adopting the principles of NIM' (NCPE, 2006, p.6). However, this did not appear to have garnered much attention in the research cases and, certainly, nobody seemed to understand that the conflict between the two might be ameliorated if the NIM was implemented in the way in which it was conceived.

County's intelligence architecture

Analyst N023 felt that the NIM allowed her to make 'informed' rather than 'random' decisions. Analyst N024 said that the NIM had the potential to make the BCU more intelligence-led. However, she highlighted that this relied on the BCU receiving 'good quality intelligence' which it generally lacked. Intelligence researcher N021 said that the increasing fragmentation of the BCU's staff (into the cell team, tactical teams, intervention team etc.) had meant that it was even more difficult to get good intelligence into the system because of poor communication between the teams and the intelligence unit. He said that the unit had to take the information it was given because it would take too much time to train frontline staff. N024 said the result was an overloaded system with information of very little intelligence value. She said, for example, that over a six-month period she received just 17 pieces of intelligence on dwelling burglaries (a control strategy priority).

This 'clogging up' of the intelligence system with extraneous information was also a problem in Urban and across the police service. Moreover, this was one of the major complaints about the old collator system. This highlights that the change from the collator's card indices to computerized databases did not necessarily bring with it the filtering or the focus that was needed. However, and perhaps more importantly in the context of this research, it also demonstrates that commanders are not always as effective as they might be at conveying their priorities and intelligence requirements to their staff. At the very least it indicates that County's internal communication was not as efficient as it needed to be.

CSP chief inspector N029 felt that an intelligence void had developed because the service profile of the force had changed so much. Older detectives, wedded to traditional reactive practice, did not want to change. Younger uniformed officers simply did not understand the intelligence cycle. All of the uniformed officers interviewed said that they understood the need to pass information to the intelligence unit but the training they had received was limited to the inputting of information to the intelligence database. Schools liaison officer N074 was the only one of the four, able to articulate why that might be important. In Urban, uniformed officers had been contemptuous of the local intelligence unit. However, in County the majority of uniform officers interviewed simply had no opinion either of the unit or of intelligence.

Relationships inside the intelligence unit generally were harmonious. However, senior analyst N022 said that the relationship between the civilian and police staff could be fractious. Trained and experienced sworn police officers resented being tasked by the civilian intelligence manager even though she was the administrative head of the unit.

N022 said that the FIOs also complained about the increasing civilianization of the unit. There may be a variety of motives for the civilianization of police posts. Commonly, posts in intelligence work are civilianized because it is thought that they can be filled more economically by civilians and the officers they replace can be released to operational duties. Respondents in both cases (sworn and unsworn staff) questioned whether the balance of intelligence units had been allowed to tip too far to the detriment of the unit's proactive capability.

Jones et al (1994) highlighted that for the police, civilianization has always meant growth. The increasing civilianization of intelligence work may explain, at least in part, the size of modern local intelligence units. The senior analyst said that there was a noticeable change in the officers' attitudes when, in a change of policy, intelligence manager N019 was promoted out of the unit and was replaced by a detective sergeant. As this change was made towards the end of the study period, the reason for it was not fully explored. However, the obvious antipathy between police and civilian staff described here may well have been a factor.

In County, some training was provided for some staff. The intelligence manager attended Centrex's National Intelligence Manager's Course. The senior analyst and all of the unit's analysts completed the National Intelligence Analysts Training (NIAT) or the alternative Research and Intelligence Support Centre (RISC) courses. They also completed a variety of short developmental courses. Analyst N023 said that though she had attended the former, she had not received any training in the basics of intelligence work. Analyst N024 attended the RISC course but found that it ignored the practicalities of the work and the production of the NIM's key intelligence products.

The extent to which anyone can learn a job simply by attending a training course is debatable and that was recognized by both the principal intelligence analyst N026 and senior analyst N022 who at their respective levels provided ongoing support programmes for analysts and other intelligence staff. However, there was evidence that despite their best efforts, problems remained. In a further example of the shortcomings of the police's intelligence structures, a local authority analyst tasked with collecting incident data for the county council (N08) admitted that he regularly received police data that breached the 'need to know' principle and that in some cases revealed personal data or sensitive personal data (within the meaning specified by the Data Protection Act 1998). This included data that identified police sources, that had not been accurately risk assessed and that was transmitted without regard for the Government Protective Marking Scheme (GPMS). This demonstrates that, just as in Urban, despite County's efforts to professionalize their intelligence processes, some fundamental inefficiency lingered.

9
The Prospects for ILP

Introduction

At the beginning of the twenty-first century, policing is once again under intense scrutiny. Questions about the capacity and capability of forces around the world to respond effectively to the challenges of organized crime and terrorism, whilst meeting the crime-fighting and security needs of local communities drives further, albeit in some cases well-rehearsed, debate about the capability of the service. The Coalition Government's decisions to: cut police spending; replace police authorities with elected Police and Crime Commissioners; overturn more than 150 years of tradition to appoint an outsider as HMIC; and begin to make concrete plans for direct recruitment to senior ranks, add many new variables into the policing mix.

The previous chapters have demonstrated the failure of ILP in Britain as its architects conceived it, even if it is probably too early to say what the eventual contribution of its most recent iteration, the NIM, to British policing will be. There has been a huge amount of organizational energy invested in the model and I am sure that there are many in the police service, and who care about the police service, who would like to see some return on that investment. Even if it has been demonstrated that few want the substantial structural changes inherent in intelligence-led practice, within the service there remains some enthusiasm for the NIM as an organizing framework for intelligent practice.

In this chapter, I want to briefly summarize where I feel that British policing is today in terms of its policing, investigative, and intelligence practices, as a base for a final reflection on what the ILP narrative tells us about policing and the police organization.

Examining policing practice in Britain

As the reader has seen, attempts to fundamentally change British policing; to shift the policing paradigm, usually have fallen far short. Britain's police service is not the only one to have struggled to deliver on their promises in this regard, which perhaps points to the real scale of the challenge that police commanders in democratic societies face in this context. Perhaps, beyond the obvious organizational and structural challenges, there simply is no mandate for change from a public conditioned to policing arrangements configured according to Peelian principles.

Policing practice

In the earliest days of Britain's police, its elite emphasized the force's safeguarding and peacekeeping roles as a way of securing its legitimacy. The police's objectives would best be achieved by ensuring the safety and security of persons and property and by the preservation of public tranquility (which to modern eyes and ears may be a rather quaint expression but personally is one I find reassuring). That established the principle of 'policing by consent' that has underpinned British public policing for almost 200 years, and which has inspired democratic policing arrangements around the world. It also created what later became identified as the reactive mode of policing, which has dominated British policing throughout its history.

As the reader has seen, the police periodically have attempted to break out of a mode that some have found too restrictive. In modern times, the reactive paradigm has been subject to sustained criticism but on at least one level it has served policing well. Bittner (1974) summarized communities' normative expectation of the police. That is, that immediate police attendance is required when an undesirable situation arises, which is unlikely to be resolved unless executive authority is brought to bear. Other researchers have developed that idea. For example, Waddington (1993) has highlighted that reactive policing largely relies upon members of the public deciding when a situation has become so intolerable as to require police involvement. By that assessment, policing activity that arises as an immediate reaction to a request for assistance from the public has an innate legitimacy that other forms of policing may lack. That may begin to explain the persistence of the reactive paradigm and the relative failure of ILP, which entails the imposition, by the police, of their conception of order on communities they purport to serve.

This research certainly suggested that the culture of the police organization is a factor. In the cases I studied, police commanders in the mainstream only saw ILP as a factor in planned proactive activity. In both cases, the reactive paradigm dominated. Despite their ILP rhetoric, police commanders continued to put their faith in an orthodox approach that combined a 'fire brigade' response style for the bulk of mainstream policing with a reliance on specialist detective squads to combat serious crime.[1] In the light of my analysis above, I contend that may not be a bad thing, it has at least the merit of meeting normative expectations of communities.

Certainly, that approach has allowed the wider service to meet the performance targets set by central government, to avoid administrative sanction, and to satisfy the normative expectations of the communities it polices, without serious or sustained challenge. That is not to say that there has been no challenge to that position. Most recently, criticism of the service's response to the riots that broke out across Britain in the summer of 2011, raised questions about the continuing capacity of the service to meet those expectations. The appetite for change, that was stimulated in large part by those events, ultimately led to the appointment of Bernard Hogan-Howe as Commissioner of the Met and the transplantation and reinvigoration of the 'Total Policing' arrangements he had supported in his former post as chief of the Merseyside force.

Hogan-Howe described Total Policing as a system that recognizes the value of a single service approach (albeit that proved to be more a reified concept than a reality in Britain), in which the component parts of the force work together to deliver its strategic aims. The similarities with earlier ILP strategies are obvious. Hogan-Howe seems to share the enthusiasm and determination of Kent's commanders; the KPM and NIM experiences suggest that he will need both in abundance. Particularly as the scale of the challenge he faces in London is exponentially greater than that faced in Kent. Moreover, just as all Britain's police commanders have found, his success ultimately will depend on factors that are largely beyond the police's control.

I do not want to appear dismissive of Hogan-Howe's plan. However, the Commissioner will need to ensure that his force is reflexive and that traditional concerns over performance do not outweigh the search for positive outcomes. He will need to maintain his focus against a sea of troubles; some of which lie before him and some of which are well over the operational horizon. I have noted elsewhere (James, 2013) that if the Commissioner can send a consistent message; achieve marginal gains in terms of crime reduction and public confidence and deliver meaningful improvements in operational efficiency, his efforts should be considered to have achieved success. As the reader has seen, that will be no easy feat but experience has shown that it will be made easier if the Total Policing rhetoric focuses on the evolutionary rather than the revolutionary aspect of the force's plans.

Investigative practice

I have argued throughout this book that just as partners have deferred to the professional judgement of the police, so too have the uniformed branch's commanders deferred to the professional judgement of specialist detectives without a sufficiently rigorous challenge. This allowed the detectives to maintain control over a system which largely remained unreformed since the 1960s. In the process, the 'class system' in policing that I described earlier, was perpetuated and affirmed to the detriment of a single service approach.

Resistance to change has been a characteristic of the CID and the specialist detective force, just as (with some notable exceptions) a reluctance to enforce change in detectives' practice has been characteristic of the uniformed branch. For example, the service elite's failure to force the CID to engage with the UBP experiment ultimately meant that it was unable to harness the experience and expertise of the detective force to achieve its ambition. Instead, detectives (particularly those in the specialist force) continued to emphasize their separateness and their class superiority over the rest of the service and continued to operate in keeping with their own priorities. In at least one case, commanders in the mainstream were complicit in this because they allowed the detective force to monopolize resources that their uniformed colleagues needed.

In the modern era, until very recently, perhaps the most notable exception to that charge was Sir Robert Mark's whose efforts, in the 1970s, to root out CID corruption challenged the power of the CID and had the effect of reforming some aspects of specialist detective work. However, in failing to reform detective work more broadly, Mark never fully confronted the isolation and elitism of the specialist detectives. Consequently it was allowed to continue to the detriment of the wider service. That failure was problematic in a number of ways. Firstly, it perpetuated an action-oriented crime control culture that prioritized arrests and seizures of illicit commodities over crime prevention, problem solving and other community-focused activities. Secondly, it encouraged the perpetuation of orthodox organizational responses to policing problems and largely ignored the public service reforms of the modern era.

That being said, the detectives' position is now under sustained challenge and its power base undoubtedly is being eroded. That process can probably be traced back to the interchange and other scrutiny arrangements introduced by Mark in the 1970s. Though in themselves, Mark's changes were substantially accommodated by the CID without fundamentally changing practice. In recent years, changes in legislation (for example, the Police and Criminal Evidence Act, 1984), in prosecution process (with the introduction of the Crown Prosecution Service in 1986) and in policing practice (particularly and perhaps surprisingly, in the changes to the shift system of working of the uniformed branch, which have made a career in uniform a far more attractive prospect than it once was) have significantly altered the investigative milieu.

Although, as the reader has seen, researchers such as Waddington (1999) and Loveday (1998) had already signalled the cracks in the CID edifice, it was Chatterton (2008) (who had been commissioned by the Police Federation to investigate the increasing burden on divisional detectives) who presented the first really detailed analysis of the challenges faced by the detective force in modern times. Chatterton's (2008) contention that the divisional CID was under huge pressure to meet the demands made upon it due to staff shortages across the board, and that it suffered the periodic loss of its most experienced and capable detectives to the specialist squads, certainly squared with my experience.

However, that analysis largely overlooked the fact that in the longer term, that would inevitably have consequences for the specialist detective force and for the wider service. The Met's recent recruitment campaign for specialist detectives to make up a shortfall in its ranks, discussed earlier, provides evidence to support that view. Taken together with plans, already announced, to immediately dispense with officers upon reaching 30 years' pensionable service (which inevitably will include many of its most experienced detectives), I wonder how in the longer term the Met will find sufficient competent investigative staff to resource the high profile and complex investigations that it routinely undertakes. I am also concerned about the consequences for other British forces if the Met continues to cream off their specialists.

In researching the PIP (James and Mills, 2012), I was struck by the nostalgia for the 'old school' detective. One ACPO member said that he wanted his force to employ 'hard steely-eyed detectives to relentlessly pursue criminals'. Yet, paradoxically, there was little evidence that he or his peers were doing anything to develop that in his force. Instead, the CID was considerably under-strength and commanders seemed to give little thought to making up the shortfall. No doubt like many others, I am unsure what to make of Assistant Commissioner Simon Byrne's views that the word detective 'is bandied about but the distinction [between the CID and the uniformed branch] does not really exist' and that 'detectives have great skills, but these are labels of the past. We [the Met] want to make sure that uniformed officers are better trained to carry out investigations' (cited in Laville, 2013, p.1).

Given that I have been critical of the detective force throughout this book, I recognize that the reader may feel there is an inherent ambiguity in my position. I see none myself; I do not believe that a desire to see the equitable and, above all, intelligent allocation of resources to policing problems *and* a capable, effective and resilient specialist detective force are incompatible. For the reasons I set out earlier, I believe change is necessary but it needs to be achieved through a coherent plan that harnesses and develops the policing milieu in a holistic manner. I see little evidence of it in those pronouncements.

Byrne's comments certainly are worthy of further scholarly examination. Whilst I commend any effort to raise the status of the patrol constable, that should not be at the expense of the standing of the CID or individual detectives; both of which have been hard-earned over the last 160 years. It seems to me that for any number of reasons, the force should be doing everything that it can to capitalize on the internationally recognized, renowned and admired Scotland Yard brand, and should not be devaluing it in such an apparently casual manner. Particularly, when recent events have demonstrated the continuing value of that brand.[2]

Intelligence work

Intelligence work is important for its predictive value, its capacity to inform strategic decision-making and problem solving approaches, and in managing risk. An intelligence architecture supporting Britain's higher policing function is well established. However, as the failure of the UBP experiment and the NIM narrative attest, the police consistently have found it difficult to develop intelligence work in the mainstream.

The notion that intelligence should drive activity in the mainstream has never gained sufficient traction amongst either service commanders or frontline patrol officers. Self-evidently, intelligence should be at the heart of ILP, just as it should be at the heart of policing. However, as the reader has seen throughout, the problems in local intelligence work run deep. The ability of Britain's intelligence system, as it is currently configured, to lead either operational policing or investigative strategy in the mainstream, is highly questionable.

The assertion that the information technology revolution has fundamentally altered the social organization of policing was not borne out by the intelligence work examined here. Largely, that was because few of the problems previously highlighted by other researchers had been resolved. I question if criminal intelligence work in Britain can be considered a profession. Dictionary definitions highlight that entry to a profession requires considerable training and specialized study. In Britain, some training is provided for those engaged in intelligence work (particularly for those in specialist roles) but whether or not that meets the 'considerable' and 'specialized' tests is moot.

On the basis of commonly accepted definitions, it might be argued that amongst police intelligence workers, analysts alone can claim to be professional. Most are educated to degree standard; many have a Master's qualification, they undergo instruction. Once in post, they receive further training in the tools and techniques of intelligence analysis that goes far beyond anything given to intelligence officers. However, it is questionable whether analysts' claims would pass a 'common-sense' test because implicit to our understanding of the term professional is that it connotes a status, which as the reader has seen, few analysts are afforded.

The intelligence world I joined a quarter of a century ago, included people who were skilled and experienced in covert policing; they had some expertise in intelligence work but they had not undergone any special training or programme of study to equip them for their roles (I described earlier the inadequacy of the detective training programme in that regard). Instead, they had learned those largely practical skills 'on the job' just as detectives had done since 1842, when the first detective department was established in London. Following in that tradition, they had learned the secrets of the 'dark arts' from their forebears.

In time, once I had been accepted into the fold (one certainty in the intelligence world is that an individual's 'credibility' in the eyes of other intelligence workers is everything), those secrets were passed on to me and I, in turn, passed them on to others who were in the process of entering that milieu. As an intelligence manager and a trainer in covert policing at NCPE, I continued to do so until I left the service some five years ago. In my view, what I have described is much more characteristic of a craft than a profession. The distinction between the two is not mere semantics it is important because it goes to the heart of the debate about intelligence work and investigative practice.

By their nature, crafts are exclusive; closed shops, whose rites, rituals and secrets are protected from public view. Craft characteristics may well have suited the 'need to know' world of yesterday but they simply are not fit for purpose in today's 'dare to share' environment. If those directing criminal intelligence work want it to gain professional status they must: cast aside the craft-like trappings of the past; reach out to partners and potential partners in much more inclusive ways; proactively seek out, identify, and adopt best-practice wherever it is found; and above all, recruit the best people (whether detectives or those from any other branch of the service – aptitude, ability, and integrity should be everything) into the intelligence world and demonstrate an unswerving commitment to their continuous professional development. As a start, and it would not really represent any more than that, intelligence work needs a programme of training and development analogous to the PIP, which has provided role-specific minimum standards for investigators.

The problem of intelligence may not be that the police do not have enough of it but that they are unwilling or unable to use it intelligently enough to determine strategic priorities and to guide activity in ways that make the most of their resources, human and otherwise. Certainly, the command teams I observed were unwilling to look for long enough, beyond their performance targets and never really put their faith in their intelligence staff or their analyses. Short-termism dominated decision-making forums.

That being said there are grounds for optimism. The fundamental re-evaluation of intelligence work in Britain that I called for (James, 2012), is under way (though I claim no credit for it). In the last 12 months, the review team *inter alia* has: launched a new communications strategy; established in Britain's forces and law enforcement agencies, a network of 'NIM champions' charged with improving knowledge of intelligence in their organizations; updated the NIM's minimum standards (in the process reducing 135 standards to 13); revised the NIM Codes of Practice; and amended the most impenetrable of the NIM's language (cause for a significant number of complaints in my research). I welcome the fact that there does not seem to be any intention to reinvert this particular wheel. The review team's commitment to: the evolution of the existing structures and processes in ways that encourage understanding and greater participation; and to an institutionalizing of the learning from this process, is surely to be preferred to another putative revolution with all its attendant risks.

The National Crime Agency (NCA), which later this year will replace SOCA, has expressed a commitment to the NIM that was lacking in its predecessor agency and is working with the review team to better describe how that commitment may be operationalized in practice. In principle, the NCA's planned powers of direction through the tasking of police forces in England and Wales may well be exercised in consequence of a NIM intelligence assessment. However, given the history of policing discussed in this book, it is difficult to see the service moving very quickly towards intelligence-led practice. Nonetheless, it is possible to see in the review team's plans, meaningful efforts to simplify and clarify the NIM, with the aim of encouraging intelligence workers and decision-makers to use the model in much more effective ways. The team should be commended for that, even if the evidence suggests that the best it can hope for is that the NIM is incorporated incrementally into the mainstream.

Britain's ILP models

In this book, I have assessed the Aberdeen Policing Scheme, UBP, the KMP, the NIM and other informal attempts to implement ILP. The Kent scheme differed from earlier efforts because its commanders forced through their plans with a consistency and determination that previously was lacking in British policing. Armed with evidence of ILP's 'success' and the endorsement of its policy network partners, the Kent elite secured ACPO's support for its plan. Authorized by ACPO's Council, Kent's chief David Phillips exploited the network's influence (today much diminished) on the wider police service, to commission a 'new-improved' KPM, and on Government, to have that new model – the NIM – written into police reform policy.

The NIM owed its genesis to the belief that the strategies pursued in Kent, that have come to be accepted as the standard for ILP in Britain and across the developed world, were qualitatively better than traditional, reactive, investigative practices pursued in Britain and elsewhere. However, there is cause to question that assumption. Certainly, there is scant meaningful evidence to support such a claim and the obvious difficulties experienced in mainstreaming ILP in Britain and elsewhere, testify to the extent of the challenge law enforcement faces in shifting the investigative paradigm substantially. *A priori*, it is questionable whether even in Kent, the force's plans had full public support. A senior police officer recently told me that the Force's assistant chief constables attended over 300 community meetings to preach the message and keep the plan on track. Even then Kent was forced to return officers to its town centres to calm public fears of lawlessness.

ILP has achieved far less than the rhetoric suggests. Evidence for the success of the KPM, the pathfinder for ILP strategies across the developed world, was at best equivocal. In Britain, evidence that ILP's most recent iteration, the NIM, could revolutionize policing practice is no less ambiguous. Of course ILP strategies are used in mainstream policing in Britain and around the world. However, they usually are employed in addition to, rather than as a replacement for, traditional reactive approaches and then only at the margins of policing activity. They have not allowed commanders to deliver single service solutions and they certainly do not represent the paradigm shift in practice that some would have us believe.

ILP rarely is a significant factor in those situations that involve the need for immediate action which of course make up such a large proportion of policing activity. As a consequence, by far the greater proportion of the policing effort has continued to be directed in the traditional reactive mode, variously described in this research as: the 'ordinary day-to-day work of detection'; 'the background policing'; or the '85 to 90 percent of police business that had to be carried on' to meet government and community expectations of the police as the primary agency of social control.

Ultimately, ILP's failure to revolutionize either investigation or intelligence practice should come as no surprise. Few revolutions are 'glorious' and few organizations welcome changes that may threaten their stability, continuity, and power. It was fear of the contagion of revolution elsewhere that shaped Britain's new police. It was only to be expected that an organization, which is conservative to the core, would revert to type and reject the invitation to throw over the better part of 200 years of tradition, in favour of the *status quo*.

Dimensions of modern ILP

ILP in Britain has at least two dimensions. Firstly, there is a kind of elevated administrative function, which relies on intelligence analysts and techniques such as crime mapping and hotspotting. Home Office officials and the police elite value that function highly because it does not threaten traditional practice and provides data on police performance which is always top of any list of their concerns. That kind of

ILP activity dominated the policing forums I observed during this research. It can be aligned with the kind of preventative mainstream policing activity encouraged by Scarman (1981). In that context, it pays homage to the policing philosophies of Met Commissioner Kenneth Newman and his successors, Peter Imbert and Paul Condon.

In principle, that approach has value. Being reflexive, it has a legitimacy that a wholly police-imposed vision of the social world lacks. The best that may be claimed for administrative ILP is that it performs a valuable management function that, used properly, may promote greater inclusion and partnership, and deliver real accountability. Perhaps the worst is that it in practice it often performs no useful function beyond providing a form of comfort blanket for commanders and administrators, and/or a blunt tool with which to intimidate and threaten middle managers.

The second dimension is what I term operationalized ILP, which is much more explicitly about crime control. It may also rely on the work of analysts but in this case the emphasis is on techniques such as social network analysis and the targeting of groups or individuals using covert methods with their arrest (or some other intervention to prevent offending) the intended outcome. That is to say, there is a more direct link between the analysis, the investigative action and the outcomes. Though there has been some 'cross-pollination', most mainstream ILP activity observed in this study served the administrative function. In practice, the specialist detective force held a near-monopoly on operationalized ILP and few resources to support covert methods were available to those in the mainstream, even when the pressing need for them arose.

What does the ILP narrative reveal?

Sir David Phillips championed ILP in Kent and inspired the creation of the NIM for British policing. He had a 'grand plan' for intelligence and operational policing in the mainstream. He was a proactive and committed policy entrepreneur who sought to initiate change within the service. His credibility as an operational leader, his advocacy and his professional status made a compelling case for the NIM, which ACPO was happy to support. That perhaps tells us something about effective police leadership; it is not enough to have a plan, one must have the executive authority and the political influence to carry it through.

When Phillips' plans were backed by the Association's political masters in the Home Office, the die was cast. Soon that support was translated into a statutory code of practice, which bound police leaders to commit to implementation. However, serious failings in it were identified almost from the outset. Despite those concerns, the Home Office allowed an essentially unreconstructed version of the model to be rolled out across Britain. Largely that was because officials believed they were endorsing a policy that was uncontroversial and relatively cheap. Above all, they believed they were delivering something that the police themselves wanted. Therefore, it was unlikely to get politicians or officials associated with it, into trouble which is always a major concern in bureaucratic hierarchies.

For the Home Office, the NIM's attraction was that it allowed the department to demonstrate a continuing commitment to efficiency and best value in policing. Those considerations outweighed some pretty substantial concerns and the paucity of evidence that it actually could deliver on its advocates' promises. Moreover, concerns that the model conflicted with the other significant change programme of that period, neighbourhood policing, were never properly explored. Ultimately, ACPO and Home Office took the same leap into the unknown. However, beyond the rarefied atmosphere of ACPO, NCIS and the Home Office, the inconsistencies and ambiguities of the NIM quickly became obvious to many of Phillips' peers. That suggests that an extensive, and properly evaluated, pilot should be an essential precursor to change programmes like the NIM.

It is never easy to determine if a public policy has been successfully implemented. Certainly, to be considered to have delivered on its supporters' promises, the NIM would have needed to have made a more meaningful impact on mainstream operational practice than it has hitherto. Implemented according to that plan, the model would encourage partnership working, stimulate the development of high quality, credible, intelligence products, and inspire command teams to embrace intelligence-led practice. By that standard the NIM must be judged a failure.

Yet, that is not the whole story. Public policies rarely achieve their aims without revision and a revised model that incorporated the changes recommended by researchers might just have gained wider acceptance. However, those tasked with implementing the NIM, needed to take proper account of: the conflicting ideologies, interests and values in policing; underlying factors such as performance targets; police budgets; potential conflict with other policing initiatives; and the kinds of compromises that managers always need to make in these situations. My research suggests that none of that happened in sufficiently meaningful or reflexive ways.

That there was so little coordination of the NIM and the neighbourhood policing programmes is, by any objective criterion, inexplicable. The problems created by such an uncoordinated and deficient approach, were not confined to the day-to-day business of reconciling competing demands for resources. They extended to the very top of the police service where competition between the two provided a focus for a continuing rivalry between those committed to a public reassurance agenda and others wedded to the idea of policing as crime control.

The two cases studied, provide good examples of the NIM's impact on operational practice. In the Urban case, senior commanders failed to implement the model at the executive level of the force because they saw it both as an imposition and as something that failed to meet their needs. Ultimately, it was simply ignored at the elite level of the force. Paradoxically, in pursuit of NIM compliance that same elite vigorously forced through NIM arrangements in their BCUs where the attention of HMIC inspectors primarily was focused. In County, there was a greater will to implement the model but at the elite level that just was not carried through with sufficient vigour or expertise. There was an investigative 'orthodoxy' and an inability to comprehend what it really meant to be intelligence-led that mitigated meaningful outcomes.

Beyond the individual cases studied it is difficult, case by case, to unpick the reasons for the elite's rejection of the NIM and I do not seek to generalize my findings in those cases to the whole service. However, my analysis suggests that the following (either singly or in combination) were significant factors in the ultimate rejection of the model as *the* template for operational policing in the mainstream: skepticism about its real value, some felt the model to be demonstrably underdeveloped, inefficient and (in the management speak of the era) 'not fit for purpose'; failings in the pre-existing intelligence architecture; a reluctance to see the cost benefits of undertaking significant structural and organizational change; rejection of the NIM on ideological grounds; and the lack of a popular mandate for ILP.

Commentators have highlighted that the history of policing has been characterized by a steady accretion of power over the police to central government at the expense of chief officers and police authorities. Perhaps that is simply the political reality. The *realpolitik*, of that relationship may not wholly explain the rejection of the original plan for the NIM but it is relevant because it may explain why resistance to it largely was covert. Home Office control over the other parties to the tripartite agreement was so complete that, even though the NIM was an explicitly police-led initiative, neither chief officers nor police authorities were willing to openly challenge what they interpreted as that department's will.

Another perspective on covert resistance to rules has been provided by Reiner (2010). He advanced two competing views on the relationship between the rule of law and working practice. The structuralist view is that police break the rules with the tacit encouragement of senior officers, the judiciary and the state elite. The alternative, interactionist, view is that formal rules like the NIM's statutory code are merely presentational; they justify conduct but they do not affect practice. In that context, interpreting police subcultures is the key to understanding practice. Given the foregoing analysis, the reader can see that for senior commanders the NIM rules did not affect practice in any meaningful way. Even though HMIC inspections of the NIM left much to be desired, it is difficult to see that as 'tacit encouragement' to break the rules. Particularly when Home Office enthusiasm for the NIM was so clear.

That unwillingness to openly challenge formal rules for which senior commanders demonstrated little appetite, was the driver of a compliance agenda. Either through habit or by design, chief officers' interactionist, some might say default, response was NIM compliance. This meant that they avoided official sanction for failing to effect the structural changes in their forces that the original plan had demanded. However, compliance brought a significant cost. Even a half-hearted response (sufficient to provide that thin veneer of compliance) required the commitment of some staff and some resources, which of course was a world away from the single service response that the police seem to venerate.

In practice, orders were passed down the line. The NIM was publicized and marketed across the service even though the implementation strategy, freely chosen by ACPO, meant that few of those tasked with promulgating it understood it any better than their audiences. The absence of a coherent and credible intelligence architecture undermined even the best of frontline staff's intentions. The result was that the service did what it has done so often, it muddled through, it got the job done, without stopping to ask whether 'the job' could be done in a more effective way or to question whether it needed to be done at all.

That pragmatism is the product of a tradition and culture that has its roots in the history of policing and which continues to underpin the rational-legal, bureaucratic, police organization in England and Wales. Despite efforts in the modern era to reform the service along business lines, elements of the militaristic hierarchical 'force' remain. That is to say, that it is common for individuals or teams to carry out an act or perform a function simply because they are told to do so. Establishing those orders as part of the rational-legal bureaucracy, as in the case of the NIM, served only to reinforce compliance.

At one level, it is clear that the police service should not be equated with the armed services nor are police staff unthinking and unquestioning automatons. Police professionalism is under the daily scrutiny of the Home Office, PCCs, the judiciary and the public who are, variously, customers, adversaries and paymasters (and sometimes are all three contemporaneously). All expect the police to perform their duties in efficient, effective, economic, procedurally fair, and accountable ways. However it is also true that within the service the tradition of respectful deference to senior officers remains a factor in the working lives of police officers. That should be unsurprising. It is just one generation since new recruits at the Hendon Police College were taught how to salute and to march before they were taught anything about policing practice.

The persistence of an authoritarian command structure in which instructions and directives flow one-way, from the top down, represents a kind of operant conditioning that can explain much of what may otherwise be inexplicable in this research. It explains the inflexibility and unwillingness to reach compromises of those tasked with rolling out the NIM. Deference to those above them in the hierarchy, which has those same roots of orthodoxy, explains why no one seems ever to have been tempted to tell the emperor that he had no clothes. It explains, for example, why the Urban intelligence manager did not tell his SMT that they were usurping his position and undermining his relationship with his intelligence staff. It explains why neither of the senior analysts could tell their respective commanders that they should be addressing the priorities identified by their intelligence assessments rather than relying wholly on performance data. It also explains why it took the County DOI almost two years to gain control of the intelligence assets that should have been hers from the day that she took up her post.

The NIM narrative also highlighted that a differential value was placed on individuals (at least if judged against the police's working rules). Accordingly, staff had their particular place in the hierarchy so that a specialist detective was perceived to have more organizational value and personal power than a detective constable who in turn was more highly valued than a constable who could use an analyst's desk as a repository for discarded, partly-consumed, foodstuffs, without fear of sanction.

There was little overt resistance to the NIM. However, I have argued at many points that compliance with the rules of the model, rather than a focus on outcomes, has been one of the central features of this narrative. That compliance concealed a covert resistance to the significant structural change that proper implementation of the NIM required. If only incidentally, it also enabled the ACPO membership to escape official sanction, to get on with the day-to-day business of policing and to await the next 'big idea' that surely was not very far over the horizon.

Assessing whether a policy has been properly implemented is always difficult because of the normative assumptions of public policymaking, the variations possible in the implementation process and the complexity of (in this case) the policing institution. However, here, the NIM codes and guidance manuals provided a clear benchmark against which the process could be judged. Ultimately, my research suggested that though a great deal of organizational energy has been expended on plans for ILP, British policing still looks very much the way it did before the NIM narrative began.

A final reflection

Why has ILP failed to deliver what its advocates expected? A hypothesis that considers the immediate organizational and cultural factors highlighted in this book but also looks beyond them to the social world can make a useful contribution to what has become a well-rehearsed but largely unresolved ILP debate.

Perhaps, reactive policing remains the dominant paradigm because communities in Britain and elsewhere in the developed world are culturally conditioned to accept the limits of policing according to Bittner's famous dictum and, at least intuitively, are content to be policed in the manner elucidated by Peel. Conceivably, in modern times, the constant presence of the police in people's daily lives can be misinterpreted as evidence that the social order is under threat. A visible police presence, reassuring to some equally may be disturbing to others. That depends upon a host of factors which may *inter alia* be geographically, socially, culturally, and economically contingent.

Explaining the relative failure of ILP to revolutionize policing, even when most of the pre-conditions necessary for its success appear to have been present (as for example in the case of the KPM), has proved extremely challenging for scholars and police officers alike. As I argued earlier, revolutions threaten the stability, continuity and traditional power of state institutions. It is rare for those who may experience the consequences of revolution to possess the same zeal for its aims as those who are actively seeking to drive change, that applies to organizational actors and 'non-combatants' alike. The events I have explored in this book conclusively demonstrate that in the context of the delivery of policing services, police organizations across the developed world have managed to avoid revolution at almost every turn. As the reader has seen, many putative policing revolutions in Britain have been labelled as failures but perhaps a more grounded reappraisal of those developments is timely. A review that recognizes the realities of the social and political worlds but also acknowledges the intrinsic value of policing's traditions; above all, its tradition of 'policing by consent', to the institution, to its members, to the communities it serves, and to those committed to transparent, accountable and truly democratic policing around the globe.

Notes

Chapter 1 Setting the Contemporary Policing Scene

1 Arguably, because the reader may feel that the Aberdeen Policing Scheme (1948) was the first such scheme
2 Different approaches to interpreting the ways in which means are oriented to the achievement of ends (Weber, 1947).
3 Training in practical skills (such as interviewing, surveillance or searching techniques) was not routinely provided until the end of the twentieth century.
4 Except in London where separate arrangements were made for the Met and City forces.

Chapter 2 A Brief History of Investigative and Intelligence Practice in Britain

1 The 1839 Act also accorded the leaders of the Met the title 'Commissioner'; a designation in use to the present day.
2 First published in 1772.
3 An interesting analysis is provided by Reiter (2008).
4 Wensley later became head of the CID. He was involved in almost every major case dealt with by the department.
5 The 'Big Four' were Albert Hawkins, Arthur Neil, Francis Carlin and Wensley himself.
6 The use of radios was really ground-breaking. In this period, other much larger and seemingly better resourced forces were operating 'wireless' cars but messages usually were transmitted by Morse code.
7 As an indicator of the post-war situation, the Met was as much as 6,000 officers under-strength (Col.93-HL Deb 03 May 1951 vol. 167 c93).
8 I have in mind the classic 'Frost Report' sketch on social class featuring John Cleese, Ronnie Barker and Ronnie Corbett. My version has the specialist units (the upper class) looking down on the divisional CID. The divisional CID in turn, looks up to the specialist CID but down on the (working class) uniform branch etc.
9 The project was so secret that Howe makes no mention of it in his memoirs (1961) or in his *Story of Scotland Yard* (1965).
10 Thomson (1936) claims that a small number of detective officers performed intelligence duties as far back as 1878. Certainly at the end of the nineteenth century, a team of detectives was responsible for logging descriptions of felons (Aylmer, 1897).
11 This pre-dates the modern offender management programmes by at least 50 years.

Chapter 3   Intelligence-Led Investigation

1 The course was part of the development programme for officers on an accelerated promotion scheme.
2 Specialist CID units are not referred to at all in the 1967 Home Office report on the police workforce or by informed commentators such as Gregory (1967).
3 The research was carried out between October 1993 and December 1994 in the Met; Northamptonshire, Thames Valley, West Mercia and West Yorkshire.
4 These were: the Metropolitan Police, Ayrshire Constabulary, Glasgow City Police, Leicestershire Constabulary, West Mercia Constabulary, Merseyside Police, Thames Valley Police, South Wales Police, Hampshire Constabulary and No. 4 Regional Crime Squad (ACPO, 1975).
5 The Met, by far the largest force in the UK, did not establish a computerized intelligence system for mainstream policing until 1998.

Chapter 4   ILP in the Contemporary Era

1 Described by the Ministry of Defence as a 'pragmatic basis for action, decision and reflection' that recognized and delineated the contributions of 'individual initiative, enterprise and imagination' (2008, p.1).
2 The Joint Intelligence Committee (JIC) emerged during the Second World War for the purpose of bringing 'greater rationality into bitter strategic debate' (Omand, 2005). The committee meets to this day.
3 Nor was this common currency in any other force in England and Wales. Police informant handling in this period had come in for particular criticism (see Dunninghan and Norris (1996) and Cooper and Murphy (1997).
4 Announced in the 1999 White Paper, *Modernising Government*.
5 The identity of the forces concerned and the amounts that they were allocated have hitherto been hidden from public view but I believe the list to include the Lancashire, Surrey and Hertfordshire.
6 This was later codified in the *NIM Code of Practice* (NCPE, 2005, p.2).

Chapter 5   ILP as a Catalyst for Policy/Knowledge Transfer

1 The police response usually is to attempt to Remove, Accept, Reduce or Avoid the risk (known by the acronym RARA).
2 Which, in yet another example of police history repeating itself, was exactly the role that Police Community Support Officers were expected to perform in the contemporary era.
3 Though it represented the continuation of an earlier reform of intelligence under the banner of the Force Intelligence Development Steering Committee (FIDSC) a mid-1980s action-oriented project that had introduced Tasking and Coordinating Committees and Collection Plans, which formed part of Sir Kenneth Newman's reforms for the Met (J. Grieve, personal communication 27 April 2013).

4 Arguably, a similar process is now underway in the Met. Certainly, there has been both a very noticeable shift in strategy and a 'freshening up' of the top tier of the force since Commissioner Hogan-Howe took control in 2011.

5 In Britain, index crime is best understood as priority crime (burglar, robbery, etc.). Those same pressures in Britain have led to the corrupt practice known as 'cuffing'. Cuffing is best understood as the practice used by some forces to 'fiddle the books' to claim undeserved credit for crime reduction.

6 The 'Five Eyes' Agreement (formally known as the United Kingdom–United States of America Agreement) was signed in 1946. It established an alliance of five English-speaking countries for the purpose of sharing intelligence, especially signals intelligence.

7 The SPI is a collaborative effort involving the US Bureau of Justice Assistance, CAN Corporation, and 33 local law enforcement agencies across the US.

Chapter 6   Evaluating the NIM: Challenges to the Model

1 The fact that the same official holds an elite position with the Serious Organised Crime Agency may explain (at least in part) that agency's rejection of the model.

2 The reader will have seen that the Met established a criminal intelligence branch in 1960. The senior executive's words suggest that the NCIS senior executive was sceptical about the ability of that department to manage the intelligence from all of the force's headquarters units and BCUs.

3 As Baumber and Ratcliffe also had found a generation before (see ACPO, 1975 and 1986 respectively).

4 The code of practice was issued by the Secretary of State 'in relation to the discharge of the functions of chief officers of police'. A chief officer of police shall have regard to this code, as will the members of the police force for whom the chief officer of police is responsible'.

5 Demonstrating once again the fallibility of the police organizational memory, Stanford (2007) argued that the challenge of combating 'professional' criminals has been recognized since the Victorian.

Chapter 7   Evaluating ILP and the NIM: Urban Case Study

1 In the context of the NIM's 'invisibility' it should be noted that in Flanagan's *Review of Policing* there is not one reference to the model (see Flanagan, 2008).

2 Focus desks – small groups of staff that concentrate on particular crime types.

3 Proposals to merge the NIM and CDA assessments were announced in the CDA review (Home Office, 2006).

Chapter 8   Evaluating the NIM: County Case Study

1 Reiner (1991, p.306) characterized chief constables as *'Barons, Bobbies, Bosses* or *Bureaucrats'*. The Baron *inter alia* likes to lead from the front and to be obeyed.
2 This was the only forum in which specialist detectives were observed, during the fieldwork for this research.

Chapter 9   The Prospects for ILP

1 I recognize that in the history of public policing there have been variations upon these styles from time to time. However, I believe that this 'broad brush' approach describes the major part of police endeavour in that period.
2 I have in mind; the London bombings, the 'Cash for Honours' and phone hacking scandals, and Operation Yewtree – the investigation into the criminal activities of Jimmy Savile, to name but four.

References

ACPO (1975) *The Baumber Report: The Report of the ACPO Sub-Committee on Criminal Intelligence* (London: ACPO).

ACPO (1986) *The Ratcliffe Report: The Report of the ACPO Sub-Committee on Criminal Intelligence* (London: ACPO).

ACPO (2004) *Reform – A Real Opportunity to Reshape Policing* (London: ACPO).

ACPO (2008) *Submission on the Police Reform Green Paper 'The Future of Policing'* (London: ACPO).

ACPO (2011) *National Decision Model* (London: ACPO).

Amey, Peter; Hale, Chris and Uglow, Steve (1996) *Development and Evaluation of a Crime Management Model* (London: Home Office Police Research Group), pp.1–47.

Anderson, Richard (1997) 'Intelligence Led Policing: A British Perspective. International Perspectives on Policing in the 21st Century', *International Association of Law Enforcement Analysts Inc. Journal*, 1, 5–7.

Audit Commission (1993) *Helping with Enquiries: Tackling Crime Effectively* (London: Audit Commission).

Audit Commission (2000) *Hot Property: Getting the Best from Local Authority Assets* (London: Audit Commission).

Aylmer, Alfred (1897) 'Detective Day at Holloway', *The Windsor Magazine*, July.

Baldino, Daniel (2010) *Democratic Oversight of Intelligence Services* (Annandale, NSW: Federation Press).

BBC News (2002, 12 September) *Fighting Crime the US Way*. Retrieved on 14 April 2013 from the BBC News website at news.bbc.co.uk/2/hi/in_depth/uk/2002/cracking.../2251112.stm

BBC News (2009, 10 November) *ACPO Chief Backs Police Mergers*. Retrieved on 11 November 2009 from the BBC News website at http://news.bbc.co.uk/1/hi/uk/8351376.stm

Bennison; Flanders and Hoddinott (1968) *UBP: Visit to the Midlands Region*, Unpublished Special Course report, Bramshill Police College.

Bichard, Michael (2004) *The Bichard Inquiry Report* (London: Home Office).

Bittner, Egon (1974) 'Florence Nightingale in pursuit of Willie Sutton: A Theory of the Police' in H. Jacobs (ed.) *The Potential for Reform of Criminal Justice* (Beverly Hills, CA: Sage).

Brady, Hugo (2007) *Europol and the European Criminal Intelligence Model: A Non-state Response to Organised Crime*. Retrieved 14 April 2013 from the website of Real Instituto Elcano at http //www.realinstitutoelcano.org/analisis/ARI2007/ARI126-2007_Brady_EUROPOL.pdf

Bratton, William (1998) *Turnaround: How America's Top Cop Reversed the Crime Epidemic* (New York: Random House).

Brodeur, Jean-Paul (1983) 'High and Low Policing: Remarks about the Policing of Political Activities', *Social Problems*, 30(5), 507–21.

Brook, Frank (1948) *Report of the Working Group on the Aberdeen Policing Scheme* (London: Home Office).

Brooks, Stephen (2010) *What Gets Measured Gets Done*. Retrieved on 11 July 2010 from the website of *The Guardian* newspaper at http://www. guardianpublic.co.uk/polic-targets-crime-brookes-comment

Browne, Douglas (1956) *The Rise of Scotland Yard* (London: George Harrap).

Burrows, John and Lewis, Helen (with Stobart, Gordon and Tyrer, Rod) (1988) *Directing Patrol Work: A Study of Uniformed Policing*. Home Office Research Study 99 (London: Home Office, HMSO).

Byrne, Simon and Pease, Ken (2003) 'Crime Reduction and Community Safety' in Tim Newburn (ed.) *Handbook of Policing* (Cullompton: Willan), pp.286–310.

Cabinet Office (1999) *Professional Policy Making for the Twenty-First Century* (London: Cabinet Office Strategic Policy Making Team).

Caless, Bryn (2011) *Policing at the Top: The Roles, Values and Attitudes of Chief Police Officers* (Bristol: Policy Press).

Campbell, Elaine (2004) 'Police Narrativity in the Risk Society', *British Journal of Criminology*, 44(5), 695–714.

Chan, Janet (2003) 'Police and New Technologies' in T. Newburn (ed.) *Handbook of Policing* (Cullompton: Willan), pp.655–79.

Chatterton, Mike (2008) *Losing the Detectives: Views from the Frontline* (London: Police Federation).

Clarke, Ronald (1997) *Situational Crime Prevention: Successful Case Studies*, 2nd edn (Albany, New York: Harrow and Heston).

Clutterbuck, Lindsay (2002) *An Accident of History? The Evolution of Counter Terrorism Methodology in the Metropolitan Police from 1829 to 1901, With Particular Reference to the Influence of Extreme Irish Nationalist Activity*. Unpublished PhD thesis. ICJS, University of Portsmouth.

Coe, A.; Crawshaw, A.; Morley, A. and Rodgers, A. (1969) *UBP in the South-West Region*, Unpublished Special Course report, Bramshill Police College.

Cohen, Lawrence and Felson, Marcus (1979) 'Social Change and Crime Rate Trends: A Routine Activity Approach', *American Sociological Review*, 44(4), 588–608.

Cohen, Michael; March, James and Olsen, Johan (1972) 'A Garbage Can Model of Organisational Choice', *Administrative Science Quarterly*, 17, 1–25.

Coldren, James, Jr. Speaker/Project Director (2013, 13 February) *Smart Policing Initiative 101* (webinar). Retrieved from http://www.youtube.com/watch?v=w9NjXAiytK0

Collier, Paul (2006) 'Policing and the Intelligent Application of Knowledge', *Public Money & Management*, 26(2), 109–16.

Cooper, Paul and Murphy, Jon (1997) 'Ethical Approaches for Police Officers When Working with Informants in the Development of Criminal Intelligence in the United Kingdom', *Journal of Social Policy*, 26, 1–20. DOI: 10.1017/S0047279496004886

Cope, Nina (2003) 'Crime Analysis: Principles and Practice' in T. Newburn (ed.) *Handbook of Policing* (Cullompton: Willan), pp.340–62.

Cope, Nina; Fielding, Nigel and Innes, Martin (2003) *Smart Policing? The Theory and Practice of Intelligence-Led Policing*, Unpublished report.

Cox, Barry; Shirley, John and Short, Martin (1977) *The Fall of Scotland Yard* (Norwich: Fletcher and Sons).

Crawford, Adam (2001) 'Joined Up But Fragmented: Ambiguity and Ambivalence at the Heart of New Labour's Third Way' in Roger Matthews and

John Pitts (eds) *Crime, Disorder, and Community Safety: A New Agenda?* (London: Routledge), pp.54–80.

Davenport, Justin (2009, 12 May) *Two-Thirds of CID Detectives in the Met Are Not Trained Detectives.* Retrieved on 1 October 2011 from the website of the *London Evening Standard* newspaper at http://www.thisislondon.co.uk/standard/article-23689474-two-thirds-of-cid-detectives-in-met-are-not-trained-detectives.do

Davies, Caroline (2010, October 8) *Mark Saunders Coroner: Police Firearms Guidelines Should Be Simplified.* Retrieved on 10 June 2011 from the website of *The Guardian* at http://www.guardian.co.uk/uk/2010/oct/08/mark-saunders-coroner-firearms-guidelines

Delanty, Gerard (1999) *Social Theory in a Changing World* (Oxford: Blackwell).

Deukmedjian, John and De Lint, Willem (2007) 'Community into Intelligence: Resolving Information Uptake in the RCMP', *Policing and Society*, 17(4), 239–56.

Dolowitz, David and Marsh, David (1996) 'Who Learns from Whom: A Review of the Policy Transfer Literature', *Political Studies*, 44(2), 343–57.

Doward, Jonathan (2007, 13 May) *Trainees Struggle to Make Up for CID Shortfall.* Retrieved on 21 September 2011 from the website of *The Observer* at www.guardian.co.uk/uk/2007/may/13/ukcrime.jamiedoward

Dunninghan, Colin and Norris, Clive (1996) 'A Risky Business: Exchange, Bargaining and Risk in the Recruitment and Running of Informers by English Police Officers', *Police Studies*, 19(2), 1–25.

Emsley, Clive and Shpayer-Makov, Hannah (2006) *Police Detectives in History 1750–1950* (Farnham: Ashgate).

Emsley, Clive (2011) *Crime and Society in Twentieth-Century England* (Harlow: Longman/Pearson).

Era, The (1878, 14 April) *Topics of the Week* in *The Era* (London, England).

Ericson; Richard and Haggerty, Kevin (1997) *Policing the Risk Society* (Oxford: Clarendon).

Eterno, John and Silverman, Eli (2013) *The Trouble with Compstat: Pressure on NYPD Commanders Endangered the Integrity of Crime Stats.* Retrieved from the website of the *New York Daily News* on 14 April 2013 from http://www.nydailynews.com/opinion/trouble-compstat-pressure-nypd-commanders-endangered-integrity-crime-stats-article-1.197215#ixzz2RadKmMIG

Evans, A.; Ball, A. and Graham, A. (1968) *UBP – The Function of the Collator.* Unpublished Special Course report, Bramshill Police College.

Evans, Peter (1974) *The Police Revolution* (London: George Allen and Unwin).

Ferrier, J. Kenneth (1928) *Crooks and Crime* (London: Seeley, Service).

Fido, Martin and Skinner, Keith (1999) *The Official Encyclopaedia of Scotland Yard* (London: Virgin).

FIRT (1998) *Kent Policing Model* (Kent: Kent Police).

Flanagan, Ronnie Sir (2008) *Review of Policing* (London: Home Office).

Fletcher, Robin and Stenson, Kevin (2009) 'Governance and the London Metropolitan Police Service', *Policing*, 3(1), 12–21.

Flood, Brian (2003) 'Strategic Aspects of the UK National Intelligence Model' in Jerry Ratcliffe (ed.) *Strategic Thinking in Criminal Intelligence* (Annandale, NSW: Federation Press), pp.37–51.

Forcese, Craig (2013) *Cops Without Silos: RCMP and the Future of Federal Policing*. Retrieved 12 March 2013 from http://craigforcese.squarespace.com/national-security-law-blog/

Ford, Richard (2010, 29 January) *Ministers Could Be Blamed for Nottinghamshire Police Failing*. Retrieved on 15 January 2010 from the website of *The Times* at http://www.timesonline.co.uk/tol/news/politics/article7007170.ece

Foster, Janet (2002) 'People Pieces: The Neglected But Essential Elements of Community Crime Prevention' in G. Hughes and A. Edwards (eds) *Crime Control and Community: The New Politics of Public Safety* (Cullompton: Willan), pp.167–96.

Gearon, A.; Morris-Coole, A.; Redding, A. and Sharples, A. (1969) *UBP in the North-East Region*, Unpublished Special Course report, Bramshill Police College.

Gill, Peter (2000) *Rounding Up the Usual Suspects* (Aldershot: Ashgate).

Gilling, Daniel (2005) 'Partnership and Crime Prevention' in N. Tilley (ed.) *Handbook of Crime Prevention and Community Safety* (Cullompton: Willan), pp.734–56.

GMAC (2010) *Greater Manchester Against Crime*. Retrieved on 2 March 2013 from http://www.gmac.org.uk/history.php

GMAC (2011) *About GMAC*. Retrieved on 21 December 2011 from the GMAC website at http://www.gmac.org.uk/about.php

Goldstein, Herman (1979) 'Improving Policing: A Problem-Oriented Approach', *Crime and Delinquency*, 25(2), 236–58.

Gosling, John (1959) *The Ghost Squad* (London: W.H. Allen).

Gospel, S.M.; Howe, D.H. and Metcalf, R.W. (1969) *UBP – An Assessment*, Unpublished Special Course report, Bramshill Police College.

Graphic, The (1880, 4 September) 'Legal', *The Graphic* (London, England).

Gregory, Ernest (1967) *Unit Beat Policing – Implications on the Experiments and Implications of a Widespread Adoption of the System* (London: Home Office).

Gregory, Ernest (1968) 'Unit Beat Policing in England: A New System of Police Patrol', *Police Chief*, July, 42–7.

Grieve, John (2004) 'Developments in UK Criminal Intelligence' in J. Ratcliffe (ed.) *Strategic Thinking in Criminal Intelligence* (Annandale NSW: Federation Press), pp.25–36.

Griffiths, William (1998) 'Zero Tolerance: The View from London' in N. Dennis (ed.) *Zero Tolerance: Policing a Free Society* (London: IEA Health and Welfare Unit).

Gross, Hans (1893) *Handbuch fur Untersuchungsrichter, Polizeibeamte, Gendarmen, u.s.w. (A Handbook for Examining Magistrates, Police Officials, Military Policemen, etc.)* (Graz, Austria: University of Graz).

Hansard HC Deb volume 145 cc1155–60. *Evidence to the Home Affairs Committee* (25 January 1989) (electronic version).

Hayes, Brian (1998) 'Applying Bratton to Britain: The Need for a Sensible Compromise' in M. Weatheritt (ed.) *What Does It Mean and is It Right for Policing in Britain?* (London: Police Foundation).

Heaton, Robert (2011) 'We Could be Criticized! Policing and Risk Aversion', *Policing*, 5(1), 75–86.

Hebenton, Bill and Thomas, Terry (1995) *Policing Europe: Cooperation, Conflict and Control* (Basingstoke: Macmillan Press).

Her Majesty's Inspector of Constabularies (HMIC) (2004) *Modernising the Police Service: A Thematic Inspection of Workforce Modernisation – The Role, Management and Deployment of Police Staff in the Police Service of England and Wales* (London: HMIC).

Herman, Michael (1996) *Intelligence Power in Peace and War* (Cambridge: Cambridge University Press)

Herman, Michael (2001) *Intelligence Services in the Information Age* (Abingdon: Frank Cass).

Hill, Michael (2009) *The Public Policy Process* (Harlow: Pearson Longman).

HL Deb 14 July 1983 vol. 443 written answers, cc969-70WA [electronic version].

HMIC (1995) *Kent County Constabulary Performance Review Inspection – September 1995* (London: Her Majesty's Inspectorate of Constabulary).

HMIC (1997) *Policing with Intelligence: Criminal Intelligence, HMIC Thematic Inspection Report on Good Practice* (London: HMIC).

HO 287/665 *Report from the Home Office Research and Planning Branch, on Plans for Regional Conferences on the Establishment of the Regional Crime Squads.* Held at the National Archives (TNA): Public Record Office (PRO).

HO 287/665a *Letter from HMIC Representative for Wales to Mr J. Haughton Wales to J. Haughton, Head of the Police Research and Planning Branch dated 4 December 1964.* Held at the National Archives (TNA): Public Record Office (PRO).

Hobbs, Dick (1988) *Doing the Business: Entrepreneurship, the Working Class, and Detectives in the East End of London* (Oxford: Oxford University Press).

Hobbs, Dick (1999) *Obituary of Frank Williamson.* Retrieved on 20 April 2008 from the website of *The Independent* at http://www.independent.co.uk/arts-entertainment/obituary-frank-williamson-1076688.html

Home Office (1949) *2nd Report of the Police Post-War Committee* (the Oaksey Inquiry) (London: Home Office).

Home Office (1967) *The Meetings at Blackpool and Bournemouth: Local Intelligence Units and the Police Service* (London: Home Office Police Research and Planning Branch).

Home Office (1967) *Report on Police Manpower, Equipment and Efficiency* (London: Home Office).

Home Office (1991) *Safer Communities: The Local Delivery of Crime Prevention through the Partnership Approach* (The Morgan Report 1991) (London: Home Office).

Home Office (2001) *Policing a New Century: A Blueprint for Reform* (London: Home Office).

Home Office (2002) *National Policing Plan 2002–2005* (London: Home Office).

Home Office (2003) *Crime Reduction Toolkit* (London: Home Office). Retrieved on 2 January 2009 from the Home Office website at http://www.crimereduction.homeoffice.gov.uk/toolkits/

Home Office (2006) *Review of the Crime and Disorder Act 1998* (London: Home Office).

Home Office (2010) *Policing in the 21st Century: Reconnecting Police and the People* (London: Home Office).

Home Office (2013, January 30) *Written Statement to Parliament: Direct Entry to the Police: Consultation.* Retrieved on 12 March 2013 from the UK Government portal at https://www.gov.uk/government/speeches/direct-entry-to-the-police-consultation

Howe, Ronald (1961) *The Pursuit of Crime* (London: Arthur Baker Ltd).

Howe, Ronald (1965) *The Story of Scotland Yard* (London: Arthur Barker).

Ignatieff, Michael (1979) 'Police and People: The Birth of Mr Peel's Blue Locusts', *New Society*, 49, 443–5.

Innes, Martin and Fielding, Nigel (2002) *Intelligence Work: Police Practice in the Information Age*. Paper presented at the British Society of Criminology Annual Conference, Keele University, July.

Innes, Martin (2004) 'Signal Crimes and Signal Disorders Notes on Deviance as Communicative Action', *British Journal of Sociology*, September, 55(3), 335–55.

Jackson, Jonathan and Bradford, Ben (2009) 'Crime, Policing and Social Order: On the Expressive Nature of Public Confidence in Policing', *British Journal of Sociology*, 60(3), 493–521.

James, Adrian (2012) *The Influence of Intelligence-Led Policing Models on Investigative Policy and Practice in Mainstream Policing 1993–2007: Division, Resistance and Investigative Orthodoxy*. PhD thesis submitted to the Department of Social Policy, London School of Economics and Political Science. Available online at etheses.lse.ac.uk/221/

James, Adrian (2013) 'Forward to the Past: Reinventing Intelligence-Led Policing in Britain', *Police Practice and Research: An International Journal*, DOI: 10.1080/15614263.2012.754126 (published online 14 February 2013).

James, Adrian and Mills, Marcus (2012) 'Does ACPO Know Best: To What Extent May the PIP Programme Provide a Template for the Professionalisation of Policing?' *Police Journal*, 85, 133–49.

James, Oliver and Lodge, Martin (2002) 'The Limitations of "Policy Transfer" and "Lesson Drawing" for Public Policy Research', *Political Studies Review*, 1, 179–93.

Jeyes, S.H. concluded by How, F.H. (1912) *The Life of Sir Howard Vincent* (London: George Allen and Company Ltd).

John, Tim and Maguire, Mike (2004) *The National Intelligence Model: Early Implementation Experience in Three Police Force Areas*. Cardiff University, School of Social Sciences, Working Paper 50. Retrieved on 8 June 2011 from the University of Cardiff website at http://www.cardiff.ac.uk/socsi/resources/wrkgpaper-50.pdf

John, Tim; Morgan, Colin and Rogers, Colin (2006) *The Greater Manchester Against Crime Partnership Business Model: An Independent Evaluation*. Treforest: University of Glamorgan (internal document)

Jones, Trevor; Newburn, Tim and Smith, David (1994) *Democracy and Policing* (London: Policy Studies Institute).

Kelland, Gilbert (1986) *Crime in London* (London: Bodley Head).

Kingdon, John (2003) *Agendas, Alternatives and Public Policies* (New York: Addison-Wesley).

King-Taylor, Lynda (1992) *Quality: Total Customer Business* (London: Century).

Kleiven, Maren (2005) *Where's the Intelligence in the National Intelligence Model?* Unpublished MSc dissertation, Institute of Criminal Justice Studies, University of Portsmouth.

Laville, Sandra (2013, 9 January) *Met to Move 800 Detectives from Scotland Yard to Community Policing*. Retrieved on 3 March 2013 from the website of *The Guardian Newspaper* at http://www.guardian.co.uk/uk/2013/jan/09/met-detectives-move-community-policing

Leach, Charles (1930) *On Top of the Underworld* (London: Sampson, Low and Marston).

Lock, Joan (1993) *Scotland Yard Casebook* (London: Robert Hale).

Lombroso, Cesare (2006) *The Criminal Man* (Durham, NC: Duke University Press).

Loveday, Barry (1998) 'Waving Not Drowning: Chief Constables and Accountability in the Provinces', *International Journal of Police Science and Management*, 1(2), 133–47.

Loveday, Barry (2005) *The Police Modernization Programme in England and Wales: A Reform Too Far?* Paper presented at the annual meeting of the American Society of Criminology, Royal York, Toronto. Retrieved on 14 September 2009 from the 'all academic' website at http://www.allacademic.com/meta/p32843_index.html

Lustgarten, Laurence (1986) *The Governance of Police* (London: Sweet & Maxwell).

Maguire, Mike (2008) 'Criminal Investigation and Crime Control' in T. Newburn (ed.) *Handbook of Policing*, 2nd edn (Cullompton: Willan).

Maguire, Mike and Norris, Clive (1992) *The Conduct and Supervision of Criminal Investigation* (London: HMSO).

Manning, Peter (2008) *The Technology of Policing: Crime Mapping, Information Technology, and the Rationality of Crime Control (New Perspectives in Crime, Deviance, and Law)* (New York, NY: NYU).

Manning, Peter and Hawkins, Keith (1989) 'Police Decision-Making' in M. Weatheritt (ed.) *Police Research: Some Future Prospects* (Aldershot: Avebury), pp.139–56.

Maple, Jack (1999) *The Crime Fighter: Putting the Bad Guys Out of Business* (New York: Doubleday).

March, Johan and Olsen, James (1996) 'Institutional Perspectives on Political Institutions', *Governance*, 9(3), 248–64.

Mark, Robert (1978) *In the Office of Constable* (Glasgow: William Collins and Son).

Marshall, Geoffrey (1965) *Police and Government* (London: Butler and Tanner).

Matassa, Mario and Newburn, Tim (2007) 'Social Context of Criminal Investigation' in T. Newburn, T. Williamson and A. Wright (eds) *Handbook of Criminal Investigation* (Cullompton: Willan), pp.41–67.

Matheson, A.J. (1951) *The Aberdeen Policing Scheme.* Lecture delivered at the Port Edgar, Police Training School on 9 March 1951.

Mawby, Rob (2008) 'Unit Beat Policing' in T. Newburn and P. Neyroud (eds) *Dictionary of Policing* (Cullompton: Willan), pp.280–1.

Mayne, Richard (1842) *Memorandum Relative to the Detective Powers of the Police* (London: Metropolitan Police).

McBarnet, Doreen (1981) 'The Royal Commission and the Judges Rules', *British Journal of Law and Society*, 8(1) (Summer, 1981), 109–17.

McElvain, James; Kposowa, Augustine and Gray, Brian (2013) 'Testing a Crime Control Model: Does Strategic and Directed Deployment of Police Officers Lead to Lower Crime', *Journal of Criminology*, 2013. DOI: 10.1155/2013/980128, pp.1–11.

McLaughlin, Eugene (2007) *The New Policing* (London: Sage).

MEPO 2/134a *Report by Detective Superintendent Williamson, Metropolitan Police dated 6 July 1870 regarding plans to reorganise the supervision of detectives.* Held at the National Archives (TNA): Public Record Office (PRO).

MEPO 2/134d *Memorandum dated 26 October 1880 from Charles Vincent to the Commissioner of Police for the Metropolis regarding the capability of the detective force*. Held at the National Archives (TNA): Public Record Office (PRO).

MEPO 2/1880 *Metropolitan Police report dated 10 December 1931, on the vehicles allocated to the force's 'Flying Squad'*. Held at the National Archives (TNA): Public Record Office (PRO).

MEPO 2/4967 *Metropolitan Police record of the work of the Home Office Committee on Detective Work 1933–1936*. Held at the National Archives (TNA): Public Record Office (PRO) MEPO 2/4967.

MEPO 2/8487 *Report of the Working Party on the Aberdeen Policing Scheme*. Held at the National Archives (TNA): Public Record Office (PRO).

MEPO 3/2033 *Metropolitan Police file first dated 18 May 1945, on the formation and subsequent work of the Special Duty Squad (also known as the Ghost Squad)*. Held at the National Archives (TNA): Public Record Office (PRO).

MEPO 10/16 *Draft report of the Working Party on the Aberdeen Policing Scheme*. Held at the National Archives (TNA): Public Record Office (PRO).

Merseyside Police (2009) *Total Policing* (Liverpool: Merseyside Police). Retrieved on 15 December 2011 from the website of Merseyside Police at www.merseyside.police.uk/index.aspx?articleid=2300

Metropolitan Police (1829) *Instruction Book* (London: Metropolitan Police).

Metropolitan Police (1998) *Systems for Investigation and Detection Manual* (unpublished internal document).

Metropolitan Police (2008) *The History of Beat Policing*. Retrieved on 17 May 2009 from Metropolitan Police website at www.met.police.uk/history/beat_patrol.htm

Metropolitan Police (2009) *SID Manual* (London: Metropolitan Police).

Ministry of Defence (2008) *British Defence Doctrine*, 2nd edn. Retrieved on 18 May 2009 from the Ministry of Defence website at http://ids.nic.in/UK%20Doctrine/UK%20%286%29.pdf

Mintrom, Michael (1997) 'Policy Entrepreneurs and the Diffusion of Innovation', *American Journal of Political Science*, 41, 738–70.

Morgan, James; McCulloch, Lucy and Burrows, John (1996) *Central Specialist Squads*, Police Research Series Paper 17 (London: Home Office).

Morris, Bob (2007) 'History of Criminal Investigation' in T. Newburn, T. Williamson and A. Wright (eds) *Handbook of Criminal Investigation* (Cullompton: Willan), pp.15–40.

NCIS (1999) *The National Intelligence Model* (London: NCIS).

NCPE (2004a) *Written Evidence to the Home Affairs Select Committee's Inquiry into Progress Made since the Police Reform Act 2002* (London: NCPE).

NCPE (2005) *Professionalising Investigation Programme* (Bedford: NCPE).

NCPE (2005a) *Practice Advice on Core Investigative Doctrine* (Bedford: NCPE).

NCPE (2005b) *Code of Practice on the NIM* (Wyboston, Bedford: NCPE).

NCPE (2006) *Practice Advice on Professionalising the Business of Neighbourhood Policing* (Bedford: NCPE).

NCPE (2006a) *Guidance on the Management of Police Information* (Bedford: NCPE).

NCPE (2006b) *Practice Advice on Tasking and Coordinating* (Bedford: NCPE).

Newburn, Tim (2003) 'Policing since 1945' in T. Newburn (ed.) *Handbook of Policing* (Cullompton: Willan), pp.84–106.

Neyroud, Peter (2011) *Review of Police Leadership and Training* (London: Home Office).

NZCAG (2001) *Dealing with Dwelling Burglary*. Retrieved on 12 April 2013 from the website of the New Zealand Controller and Auditor General at http://www.oag.govt.nz/2001/burglary

NZCAG (2005) *Dealing with Dwelling Burglary – Follow Up Audit*. Retrieved on 12 April 2013 from the website of the New Zealand Controller and Auditor General at http://www.oag.govt.nz/2006/burglary/part2.htm

O'Connor, Dennis (2005) *Closing the Gap – A Review of the Current 'Fitness for Purpose' of the Current Structure of Policing in England and Wales* (London: HMIC).

O'Neill, Sean (2009) *Secret Pay Deals Give Top Police Thousands Extra*. Retrieved on 8 July 2009 from *The Times* website at http://www.timesonline.co.uk/tol/news/uk/article6653377.ece

Oakensen, Derek; Mockford, Roland and Pascoe, Chris (2002) 'Does There Have to be Blood on the Carpet? Integrating Partnership, Problem-Solving and the NIM in Strategic and Tactical Police Decision-Making Processes', *Police Research and Management*, 5(4), 51–62.

Oliver, Ian (1997) *Police, Government and Accountability* (London: Macmillan).

Omand, David (2005) *Reflections on Secret Intelligence*. Lecture given at Gresham College on 20 October 2005. Retrieved on 14 June, 2011 from the Gresham college website at http://www.gresham.ac.uk/lectures-and-events/reflections-on-secret-intelligence

Osborn, Nick (2012) *To What Degree Have the Non-Police Public Services Adopted the National Intelligence Model? What Benefits Could the National Intelligence Model Deliver?* Professional doctorate thesis submitted to ICJS, University of Portsmouth.

Parliamentary Papers (1833) *Select Committees 62 (1833). Select Committee on the Petition of Frederick Young and Others*, vol. XII: pages 407 el. seq.

Parris, Matthew (Writer and Presenter) (2009) *Parting Shots Episode 3* Parting Shots. London, BBC Radio 4

Peterson, Marilyn (2005) *Intelligence-Led Policing: The New Intelligence Architecture* (Washington: US Department of Justice).

Phillips, David (2006) *Theory of Intelligence*. Unpublished draft.

Pilkington, Diana (2011, 11 November) 'Rioting in London Sparked 'Copycat' Behaviour', *The Independent* newspaper. Retrieved on 15 November 2011 from http://www.independent.co.uk/news/uk/crime/rioting-in-london-sparked-copycat-behaviour-6262030.html

Posen, Ingrid (1995) *Home Office Review of Police Core and Ancillary Tasks* (Posen Inquiry) (London: Home Office).

Rand, Mark (1970) 'Time for a Fresh Approach to Unit Beat Policing?' *UK Police College Magazine* (Spring, 1970), pp.14–18.

Ratcliffe, Jerry (ed.) (2008) *Intelligence-Led Policing* (Cullompton: Willan).

Rawlings, Philip (2002) *Policing: A Short History* (Cullompton: Willan).

Rawlings, Philip (2006) 'A Force Divided', *Criminal Justice Matters*, 22.

Reiner, Robert (1991) *Chief Constables* (Oxford: OUP).

Reiner, Robert (1992) *The Politics of the Police* (Brighton: Harvester).

Reiner, Robert (2000) *The Politics of the Police*, 2nd edn (Oxford: OUP).

Reiner, Robert (2010) *The Politics of the Police*, 4th edn (Oxford: OUP).

Reiner, Robert (2011, October 28th) 'Let's Admit It: Most Police Work Does Not Involve Catching Criminals' *The Guardian* newspaper, 28 October 2011.

Reiter, P.J. (2008) 'Doctors, Detectives and the Professional Ideal: The Trial of Thomas Neil Cream and the Mastery of Sherlock Homes', *College Literature*, 35(3), Law and Literature (Summer, 2008), 57–95.

Reynolds' Newspaper (1880, 15 August) 'Under the Surface; or, Folly and Fashion', *Reynolds's Newspaper* (London, England); Issue 1562.

Roach, Lawrence (2004) *The Origins and Impact of the Function of Crime Investigation and Detection in the British Police Service*. PhD thesis submitted to the Centre for Hazard and Risk Management, Loughborough University.

Rogers, Colin (2004) 'From Dixon to Z Cars – The Introduction of Unit Beat Policing in England and Wales', *Police History Journal*, No. 19, 10–14.

Ryan, Michael; Savage, Stephen and Wall, David (eds) (2001) *Policy Networks in Criminal Justice* (Basingstoke: Palgrave).

Sabatier, Paul (1986) 'Top-down and Bottom-up Approaches to Implementation Research: A Critical Analysis and Suggested Synthesis', *Journal of Public Policy*, 6(1) (Jan–Mar 1986), 21–48.

Savage, Stephen (2007) *Police Reform: Forces for Change* (Oxford: Oxford University Press).

Savage, Stephen; Charman, Sarah and Cope, Stephen (2000) *Policing and the Power of Persuasion* (London: Blackstone Press).

Scarman, Lord Justice (1981) *The Brixton Disorders 10–12 April 1981*, Cmnd 8427 (London: Home Office).

Shapland, Joanna (1988) 'Fiefs and Peasants: Accomplishing Change for Victims in the Criminal Justice System' in Mike Maguire and John Pointing (eds) *Victims of Crime: A New Deal?* (Milton Keynes: Open University), pp.187–94.

Shapland, Joanna (2000) 'Victims and Criminal Justice: Creating Responsible Criminal Justice Agencies' in A. Crawford and J. Goodey (eds) *Integrating a Victim Perspective Within Criminal Justice* (Aldershot: Dartmouth), pp.147–64.

Sheehy, Patrick (1993) *Inquiry into Police Responsibilities and Rewards* (Sheehy Inquiry) (London: Home Office).

Shpayer-Makov, Haia (2004) 'Becoming a Police Detective in Victorian and Edwardian London', *Policing and Society*, 14(3), 250–68.

Sklansky, David (2007) 'Seeing Blue: Police Reform, Occupational Culture and Cognitive Burn-In' in M. O'Neill, M. Marks and A-M. Singh (eds) (2007) *Police Occupational Culture: New Debates and Directions* (Amsterdam: JAI Press).

Skogan, Wesley (2008) 'Why Reforms Fail?' *Policing and Society*, 18(1), 13–34.

Smith, Angus (1997) *Towards Intelligence-Led Policing: the RCMP Experience*. Retrieved on 2 January 2013 from the website of the IALEIA at http://members.ialeia.org/files/other/ILP%20intl%20perspectives.pdf

Stanford, Terence (2007) *The Metropolitan Police 1850–1914: Targeting, Harassment and the Creation of a Criminal Class*. Doctoral thesis, University of Huddersfield.

Stead, William (1888) *The Police and the Criminals of London*. Retrieved on 15 April 2008 from the W.T. Stead Resource website at http://www.attackingthedevil.co.uk/pmg/crim1.php

Stevens, John (2001) *Intelligence-Led Policing*. Paper presented at 2nd World Conference on Modern Criminal Investigation, Organized Crime & Human Rights Durban, South Africa.

Stewart, James (1996) 'Intelligence Analysis of Transnational Crime: Assessing Canadian Preparedness', *Journal of Conflict Studies*, North America, 16 January 1996.

Stone, Diane (2001) *Learning Lessons, Policy Transfer and the International Diffusion of Policy Ideas*, CSGR Working Paper No. 69/01, April 2001.

Taylor, Robert and Russell, Amanda (2012) 'The Failure of Police Fusion Centers and the Concept of a National Intelligence Sharing Plan', *Police Practice and Research*, 13, 184–200.

Thomson, Basil (1921) *Queer People* (Edinburgh: T and A Constable).

Thomson, Basil (1936) *The Story of Scotland Yard* (Garden City NY, USA: Country Life Press).

Tilley, Nick (2003) 'Community Policing, Problem-Oriented Policing and Intelligence-Led Policing' in T. Newburn (ed.) *Handbook of Policing* (Cullompton: Willan), pp.311–39.

Tilley, Nick (2008) 'Modern Approaches to Policing: Community, Problem-Oriented and Intelligence-Led' in T. Newburn (ed.) *Handbook of Policing*, 2nd edn (Cullompton: Willan), pp.373–403.

Tomes, Jason (2004) 'Kelland, Gilbert James (1924–1997)', *Oxford Dictionary of National Biography* (Oxford: Oxford University Press).

USDoJ (2011) *Census of State and Local Law Enforcement Agencies, 2008* (Washington DC: US Department of Justice).

Van der Vijver, Kees and Zoomer, Olga (2004) 'Evaluating Community Policing in the Netherlands', *European Journal of Crime, Criminal Law and Criminal Justice*, 12, 251–67.

Vincent, C.E.H. (1886[1882]) *A Police Code and Manual of the Criminal Law*, 5th edn (London: Cassell and Company).

Waddington, P.A.J. (1993) *Calling the Police: The Interpretation of, and Response to, Calls for Assistance from the Public* (Aldershot: Avebury).

Waddington, P.A.J. (1999) 'Police (Canteen) Sub-culture: An Appreciation', *British Journal of Criminology*, 39(2), 286–308.

Wall, David (1998) *The Chief Constables of England and Wales: The Socio-Legal History of a Criminal Justice Elite* (Aldershot: Dartmouth Press).

Walsh, Patrick (2011) *Intelligence and Intelligence Analysis* (Cullompton: Willan).

Watson, A.; Norris, A.; Crew, A. and Melvin, A. (1969) *UBP in the North-West Region*, Special Course assessment, Bramshill Police College, unpublished.

Weber, Max (1947) *The Theory of Social and Economic Organization* (translated by A.M. Henderson & Talcott Parsons) (New York, NY: The Free Press).

Weisburd, David; Mastrofski, Stephen; Greenspan, Rosann and Willis, James (2003) 'Reforming to Preserve: Compstat and Strategic Problem Solving in American Policing', *Criminology and Public Policy*, 2(3), 421–56.

Weisburd, David; Mastrofski, Stephen; Willis, James and Greenspan, Rosann (2006) 'Changing Everything so that Everything Can Remain the Same: Compstat and American Policing' in D. Weisburd and A.A. Braga (eds) *Police Innovation: Contrasting Perspectives* (New York: Cambridge University Press), pp.284–301.

Wensley, Frederick (1968) *Forty Years of Scotland Yard* (New York: Greenwood Press).

Wholey, Neil and Compton, Jennifer (2010) *How Westminster Became Safer*, Westminster City Council Insight Report, October 2010.

Williamson, W. (1971) *Organisational Change in a Police Force with Specific Reference to Unit Beat Policing* (Bristol: University of Bristol).

Willis, James and Mastrofski, Stephen (2012) 'Compstat and the New Penology: A Paradigm Shift in Policing?' *British Journal of Criminology*, 52(1), 73–92.

Willis, James; Mastrofski, Stephen and Weisburd, David (2003) *Compstat in Practice: An In-Depth Analysis of Three Cities* (New York: Police Foundation).

Willis, James; Mastrofski, Stephen; Weisburd, David and Greenspan, Rosann (2003a) *Compstat and Organisational Change: Intensive Site Visits Reports* (New York: Police Foundation).

Winsor, Tom (2011) *Independent Review of Police Officer and Staff Remuneration and Conditions* (London: Home Office).

Wolff, Sarah (2009) *From The Hague to Stockholm: The Future of EU's Internal Security Architecture and Police Cooperation*. Overview Paper for the Clingendael, Netherlands, European Studies Group.

Wright, Alan (2007) 'Ethics and Corruption' in Tim Newburn, Tom Williamson and Alan Wright (eds) *Handbook of Criminal Investigation* (Cullompton: Willan), pp.586–609.

Young, Malcolm (1991) *An Inside Job: Policing and Police Culture in Britain* (Oxford: Clarendon Press).

Zarkadoulas, Nikos (2010) *Europol's Intelligence-Led Policing Efforts Against Transnational Organised Crime: An Evaluation of the Intelligence Model and Its Implementation*, MSc dissertation, University of Portsmouth.

Index